MORE LIKE US

Books by James Fallows

NATIONAL DEFENSE

MORE LIKE US

James Fallows

MORE LIKE US

Making America
Great Again

BOSTON 1989

HOUGHTON MIFFLIN COMPANY

For information about permission to reproduce selections from
this book, write to Permissions, Houghton Mifflin Company,
2 Park Street, Boston, Massachusetts 02108.

Library of Congress Cataloging-in-Publication Data

Fallows, James M.
More like us.

Bibliography: p.
Includes index.
1. United States — Economic policy — 1981–
2. United States — Social conditions — 1980–
3. Political culture — United States.   4. Asia — Social
conditions.   5. Political culture — Asia.   I. Title.
HC106.8.F355   1989   306'.0973   88-32877
ISBN 0-395-49857-0

Printed in the United States of America

P 10 9 8 7 6 5 4 3 2 1

For my parents

CONTENTS

MORE LIKE US

The Importance of Being Abnormal

THE PURPOSE of this book is to remind Americans of how unusual our national culture is, and of why it is important that we not become a "normal" society.

Growing up, Americans hear that theirs is the strongest country, the freest and most fortunate, the most open to new ideas and change. We also hear that it is the world's most violent society, the most spoiled and pampered, the least sensitive to other cultures and their values. The real significance of such messages, whether complimentary or belittling, rarely sinks in. America is a large country, and most of its people never leave. Its popular culture has spilled over into nearly every part of the world. Americans can buy blue jeans in Thailand, watch *The CBS Evening News* in Korea, find *USA Today* almost anywhere they go. At first glance Tokyo, Singapore, and Frankfurt may look like cities in the United States. It is not surprising, then, that many Americans should half consciously assume that America represents a universal culture, that other countries are steadily becoming more like it, that its peculiarities cannot matter very much. The world is full of potential Americans, since people can come from any other society and be accepted here. Therefore the world may seem to be full of potential Americas too.

The assumption is erroneous: the United States is not an ordinary society. The differences between America and other cultures run deep and matter profoundly. They are differences of kind, not just of degree. Of course people are essentially the same anywhere on earth, but cultures are not. America is unusual because of its fundamental idea of how a society holds itself together. American society is not made of people who all happened to be living in a certain region or who have some mystic tribal tie. It's made of people who came or were brought here from somewhere else. This is perfectly obvious, but some of the consequences of the fact are not, and they affect our dealings with the rest of the world every day.

In the spring of 1988, after the right-wing candidate Jean Le Pen, running on an anti-immigrant platform, did surprisingly well in the French presidential election, a column in the *New York Times* was headlined RACISM STILL RUNS THROUGH EUROPE — LE PEN SHOWS IT. The truth is that racism runs through nearly all of the world, usually much more strongly than in the United States. We often give it some other name — tribalism or ethnic tension or, for Marxists, "the national question" — when Tamils and Sinhalese attack one another or when Indonesians slaughter Chinese, but the essence is the same. One of the things that make America most unusual is its assumption that race should not matter, that a society can be built of individuals with no particular historic or racial bond to link them together. This is a noble belief: it makes America better than most other societies. But it also means that America's strengths and weaknesses are highly unusual. Canada and Australia are the only countries that are remotely comparable.

Depending on their founding principles, different societies can use different incentives to make themselves go — to hold people together and make them rise to their best. Japan and, to a lesser degree, Korea seem to rely on an embattled sense of the national family standing united against the world. China, too large and varied to be a single family, seems driven mainly by the effort and honor of its hundreds of millions of component families. Germany, France, and England each has its national spirit. And America has a peculiar national genius of its own. The force that motivates the country is a vision of people always in motion, able to make something different of themselves, ready for second chances until the day they die.

This vision starts with the act of immigration — choosing to become an American — and continues through the choices and changes that make American life so different from Japanese or Italian life. People go away to college; they come back home; they go west to California to get a new start; they move east to Manhattan to try to make the big time; they move to Vermont or to a farm town to get close to the soil. They break away from their parents' religions or values or class; they rediscover their ethnicity three or four generations after their immigrant ancestors arrived. They go to night school; they have nose jobs; they change their names.

Other people don't do these things, not as much or as often or as gleefully. In most Asian societies, an unmarried woman will live with her parents until she is well into her thirties, unless she wants to give the wrong impression about her family and herself. It is hard to imagine a Belgian exclaiming, "Today is the first day of the rest of my life!" America's peculiar genius is responsible for some of the bad in America but also for most of the good. This country is the world's demonstration of how people behave when the usual limits are removed.

Any country will have trouble if its guiding idea is damaged or changed. Japan would lose its way if people across the nation did not feel a family connection to each other. China has suffered in the twenty years since the cultural revolution tried to uproot its old family values. And America will be in serious trouble if it becomes an ordinary country, with people stuck in customary, class-bound roles in life. Other countries have tools — tradition, ethnic solidarity — to help them get by in those circumstances. We do not. Therefore it's no small matter if America's belief in possibility and starting over is endangered.

This book explores the forces that are changing America's principle of possibility, and the ways in which it can be renewed. As an American, I am an optimist. The country's resilience is immense. But America is temperamentally slow to acknowledge dangers. We are the ones who waited until Pearl Harbor to join a war that had been under way for two years; we needed the surprise of Sputnik to focus our attention on public schools. It is time to acknowledge a cultural danger now.

What follows is not a seamless or relentlessly linear argument. It is an attempt to explore one subject from a variety of angles. For a dozen years I've been absorbed by the idea of possibility in America, and the book reflects the evolving ways in which I have pursued it during that time.

My starting point for the book, in the mid 1970s, was an effort to wrestle with the aftereffects of the Vietnam War, America's most blatant class war since the Civil War itself, when Union men could hire substitutes to take their places in the ranks. The question of why people had such different choices in the Vietnam years — the college-educated class mainly staying at home, the less educated and less privileged class mainly going to fight — led to other questions about the government policies and the family values that steered different people to different fates. My attempt to answer those questions shows up in the book's discussions of the history of American higher education, the nature of measurable "intelligence," and the evolution of America's professional class.

There are regional differences in the American sense of possibility. In California, where I grew up, "class" and "mobility" mean something different from what they imply on the East Coast or in the old cities of the Midwest. During the mid 1980s, I tried to learn more about these variations. I lived in Texas, first during a time when people were driving U-Hauls in from Ohio and Michigan in search of work, and then again when Texans themselves were heading north after the oil business collapsed. I traveled to parts of the Midwest where "deindustrialization" had suddenly left whole communities without work. My question was not simply why the mills had failed but also why some people were better able to adapt — to see possibilities — than others, who felt trapped. There are ethnic and racial differences as well, and for most of a year I followed immigrants arriving in California, Florida, and Texas, learning why they had found possibilities in the same economy that left many underclass blacks feeling hopeless.

For more than two years, I approached the same question from outside the country. With my family, I moved to Asia early in 1986. We lived first in Tokyo, then in Kuala Lumpur, Malaysia, then in Japan again. It was in many ways a traumatic shift. We'd only briefly been to Asia before, had never studied any Asian language, had no idea what the effect would be on our children, who were five and eight when we left the United States. Our motive for going was to understand how the values of the Pacific Rim countries, whose bright future we'd heard so much about, compared with those of America.

The results of the experience show up in the first two chapters of this book, which explain American uniqueness largely through contrasts with Asian societies, especially that of Japan. The rest of the book includes a variety of approaches to the nature of American culture; it emphasizes what has been most liberating and useful about our society's values. It concludes with an examination of the three forces that now most significantly affect the sense of possibility — of upward mobility — in America: immigration, changes in our education system, and a shift in our democratic character toward a more divided, class-bound ethos.

The purpose of the comparisons of America and Japan is not the one that has become so familiar in the past eight or ten years. When Americans measure themselves against the Japanese, they are likely to think only of sheer economic efficiency. For instance, many Japanese employees stay with their companies for a lifetime; we've come to think of that as a competitive advantage for Japan, though it would probably seem stifling and confining to many Americans.

Economic performance can be a useful (though incomplete) gauge of a society's overall health. A society that is true to its own culture will usually have a healthy economy. It will have found the right way to elicit its people's best efforts. The economic progress it makes will, in turn, allow many people to have more satisfying lives. Economic growth, then, is valuable not only in its own right but also because it indicates something about the society in which it occurs.

But debts and deficits and lagging "competitiveness" are not in themselves the reasons to care about changes in American culture. Even if America were the only country in the world, its sense of possibility and openness would be crucial to the decency and stability of American life. Those are, finally, the stakes in the issue I am discussing: whether American society can remain robust and satisfying for Americans.

Since there are other countries in the world, the contrasts between them and America can help us understand our own values. Selling more cars or machine tools than Japan does is not America's highest purpose, but the trends of trade and debt may indicate some deep, important problems. In particular, the rapid changes in the outside world's view of America can be useful in getting our attention, like a nonviolent Pearl Harbor.

The change in the outside view would, I think, shock most Americans. Certainly it has startled me. One day late in 1987 I walked into a coffee shop in Tokyo where I was to meet a group of Japanese friends. One of them said as he saw me, "Well, I still think America might come back." His conclusion was not so startling — I think America can come back, too. What impressed me in such encounters was the nonchalance with which people who grew up when G.I.s ran their country now gave thumbs-up or thumbs-down opinions on America's prospects. It didn't help my spirits when, shortly afterward, I was in the Ginza and ran across one of Tokyo's few panhandlers — an American.

Any foreigner who has stayed in Japan long enough to break through the initial politeness must have noticed, in the late 1980s, the condescension of many Japanese businessmen, bankers, and government planners as they discuss the roots of America's difficulties. "You've been very slow in recognizing your decline," said Masahiko Ishizuka, editor of the English-language *Japan Economic Journal*. "Now Japan and the United States are in a unique situation. America's decline is the other side of the coin of Japan's rise." America's problems derive, in the Japanese view, from too many vacations, too much greed, too little discipline — and, as only a few actually say but many seem to believe, too few Asians and too many blacks. Americans got one glimpse of this attitude from Prime Minister Nakasone's notorious "low IQ" remarks in the fall of 1986. The right conclusion to draw from the incident was not so much that the Japanese are "racist" — their fixation on the factors that make them unique in the world goes miles beyond what we normally think of as prejudice — but that they had reached the stage where they could sit back and analyze why we had slipped.

This assumption was even clearer in a crack made by Nakasone's successor, Noboru Takeshita. Early in 1987, about six months before Nakasone anointed him as prime minister, Takeshita told a joke to warm up the crowd at a school reunion dinner in the north of Japan. It seemed that the rising yen had made things hard for American sailors stationed at Yokosuka, south of Tokyo. James Michener had celebrated this same Yokosuka in his Korean War novel, *The Bridges at Toko-Ri,* as the place where American sailors were kings, a precursor of the Vietnam War R and R paradises. Now, according to Takeshita, the dollar was so weak that the Americans couldn't afford Japanese bar girls anymore. Their only consolation was to stay on base and give each other AIDS.

Before he took office, Takeshita was renowned for an understated, inoffensive, consensus-building approach. He certainly meant no harm and would never have risked the joke if he thought outsiders might overhear. But the intimate nature of the remark is what gave it its bite: this is how Americans have come to look. In 1987, the newspaper *Asahi Shimbun* reported the results of a poll conducted in Tokyo. Eighty percent of the respondents agreed that the Japanese were the smartest and hardest-working people in the world. At about the same time, the Japanese Foreign Ministry launched a campaign ("Be Humble, Japanese!") to prevent businessmen and diplomats from saying what many of their countrymen believed to be true, that Americans just couldn't keep up.

During Japan's big push to increase imports in 1987 and 1988, purchases from Europe boomed — BMWs, Vuitton bags — but American exports barely budged. Virtually the only people who bought American cars were *yakuza,* Japan's gangsters, who like to drive the big, flashy Cadillac land yachts through Tokyo's tiny streets for the same campy reasons that they cover their bodies with garish tattoos. Japanese officials threw up their hands in exasperation when asked to explain America's export failures. *We're* doing our best, they said; we have nothing against imports. But what do the Americans make that we would possibly want? We're already eating as many hamburgers and seeing as many movies as we can stand. In 1986, a company selling Levi's blue jeans launched a new advertising campaign in Tokyo. Its theme was, What else *is* there left to admire about America but rock music and blue jeans?

It is not only the Japanese who have concluded that something has gone seriously wrong with America. Koreans tend to accuse even the Japanese of shiftlessness; their idea of American diligence can be extrapolated from that. After two years of listening to Japanese and Koreans, I've grown accustomed to hearing "lazy" used before "Americans" as if the two words formed a natural compound, like "brazen hussy" or "fellow traveler." Much more than Japan's, Korea's business is dominated by huge industrial conglomerates such as Daewoo and Hyundai, many of which have set up joint ventures with American firms. General Motors hires Daewoo to make "Pontiac" Le Mans cars for sale in America; Caterpillar hires Daewoo to make forklifts. Americans may not like the looks of these arrangements, Daewoo officials told me, but what choice do they have? The only way Americans can think about competing with the Japanese, they said, was to have Koreans do the actual work. In Beijing and Shanghai, Communist Party officials have practically begged me, as the nearest available American, to rush back home and start making factories more productive so as to hold off the Japanese. The Chinese of course have industrial ambitions of their own, but they hate to see a far-off and therefore relatively unthreatening power lose ground to a nearby historic enemy. The cars and forklifts are not themselves the problem, but they are taken in Asia as symptoms of a deeper cultural decay.

The spectacle of four American congressmen smashing a Toshiba radio with sledgehammers in front of the U.S. Capitol was publicized throughout Asia and was a public relations catastrophe for the United States. Not only did it instantly eliminate whatever guilt the Japanese public may have felt about Toshiba's sales of sensitive machinery to the Soviet Union; it aroused contempt for America everywhere. It made Americans look like brutes who destroy what they are not clever enough to create. You big brawny Americans may be able to pulverize delicate Japanese goods, Prime Minister Lee Kuan Yew of Singapore said a few months later. But "the skills, the knowledge, the capacity to dream up the next product — that cannot be broken up with a sledgehammer." Rather than simply destroying, he said, Americans should try to come to terms with the unpalatable fact that Japan's rise represented "a permanent change in competitive position."

Many of the fast-rising Asian countries feel that they too are in constant peril of decline. The Japanese have no extra space, no natural resources, and no inner confidence that the rest of the world will keep selling them food and fuel. I have interviewed urbane government officials about Japan's farm subsidy programs, asking why Japanese families should pay $8.00 for a sack of Japanese-grown rice when they could buy a sack of equally good rice from Thailand or the United States for a dollar or two. The seemingly sincere response is usually "What? And risk being starved out?" Downtown Seoul, showpiece of South Korea's economic miracle, is about one minute away by fighter plane from the heavily armed forces of North Korea's lunatic regime. Hong Kong knows that it is about to be digested by communist China. Taiwan still has a definite émigré feel. The Chinese in Singapore, numbering three million, are sandwiched between about 150 million traditionally anti-Chinese Malays in Indonesia to the south and Malaysia to the north.

But all these vulnerabilities seem, to the Asians, different from America's. They are accidents of history and geography, austere conditions imposed by nature. The Japanese ended up on small rocky islands; Korea was sawed in half; the British couldn't hold Hong Kong forever; the Kuomintang lost to Mao Tsetung's communists and had to flee to Taiwan. America's difficulties, however, look to the Asians like failures of character, evidence that we no longer deserve our place — in traditional Chinese terms, the "mandate of heaven" that confers legitimacy on rulers seems to have passed from the United States. The Americans had their huge, rich continent, they ran the world after the war, they had every advantage, and look what's become of them! Many Asians have concluded that American society no longer functions in such a way as to make America strong.

During the economic summit in Tokyo in the spring of 1986, I had a beer in the Hotel New Otani with an English friend. The beers were 1000 yen apiece — about $6.00 then, by 1988 about $8.00. My friend, newly arrived, seemed cowed by the hustle and bustle of the city's ten million people, five million of whom seemed to be walking down whatever street or crammed into whatever subway passage he happened to be in. We talked about England's competitive troubles, and America's. My friend took a long drink from his glass, put it down on the table, and said, "Why don't you just face the fact that you're second-raters, like us?" This is the other side of England's — and Europe's — typically dismissive view of the Japanese. "Well, they're a lot of little swots, aren't they?" was the way Ronald Dore, an English sociologist who has written extensively about Japan, described the standard Tory attitude.

America could respond to rumblings of decline in a similar way. We could conclude that our economic problems are unavoidable, arising exclusively from Japan's or Korea's determination to build up trade surpluses and therefore indicating no change or failing in ourselves. We could assume that the consumption and debt boom of the 1980s was strictly the result of one administration's policies, which can be turned around. We could take comfort in classic economic analysis, which holds that debt and trade deficits are actually an advantage: we are getting more from other countries than we have to give to them. The same can be said of foreign ownership. When foreigners buy a steel mill or tire plant, they keep jobs in America and may even transfer technology to us, the way American companies have transferred it to Singapore and Mexico. We could, finally, tell ourselves that if what it takes to keep up with the Japanese is to live like them — in tiny houses, with endless working days, under an ethic of lockstep loyalty to the firm — then it may be better to step aside and get out of Japan's way.

There is, of course, another choice. We can use the objective shifts in our position — trade, deficit, appearance of decline — as warnings that something has changed inside. We can tap the resilience that has always distinguished this country: after a peaceful Pearl Harbor, we could rebuild to a peaceful Midway. People have to age and weaken, but societies may not need to. China has been powerful, despite considerable ups and downs, for thousands of years. The Japanese didn't "decline" after they built their Asian empire in the 1930s; rather, they were crushed after they imprudently picked a fight with the United States. Less than fifty years later, after a relatively brief recovery, they've come back stronger than before. When Americans talk about imperial decline, they usually have two models in mind: England dismantling its empire, and the Romans sinking from republican virtue into a soft, corrupt debauch. England's diminished estate meant narrower, meaner lives for Englishmen, and Rome of course was overrun. America is not likely to fall to barbarians, as Rome did, but maybe we'll repeat the pattern of England's decline. We probably will if we think we're destined to. But cultural decline *isn't* inevitable. Talking about that possibility can be useful if it serves as another Sputnik or another Pearl Harbor — the shock that Americans need to start fixing what they know is wrong. It would be disastrous if such talk convinced Americans that they may as well not try.

"It takes a long time to become aware of decline," Henry Rosovsky, then the dean of the Harvard College faculty, said in 1980:

> Most economic historians agree that Britain's climacteric occurred about one hundred years ago, but this fact did not really become a matter of public concern until World War I . . . In my opinion, the principal factors were internal and human, and therefore avoidable: British entrepreneurship had become flabby; growth industries and new technology were not pursued with sufficient vigor; technical education and science were lagging; the government-business relationship was not one of mutual support. When we look at our own country today in the perspective of history, the danger signals seem obvious.

Our problems now are also internal and human and therefore correctable. But we have to take the problems seriously and understand what correction may entail. In his book *Shadows of the Rising Sun,* a young American named Jared Taylor described the factors that, for better and worse, make Japan different from the United States. He had good standing to offer such judgments, having grown up in Japan as a missionary's son, fluent in Japanese. At the end of his book he recounted a conversation with another American Japan-hand, who marveled at how much Japan had wrought in so short a time. "Do you think we need to learn how to be more like the Japanese?" Taylor asked. "Hell, no," his friend replied. *"We need to be more like us."*

What does it mean to be "more like us," better able to do the things America does best? That is the subject of this book.

CHAPTER ONE

Why Culture Matters

IN THE LONG RUN, a society's strength depends on the way that ordinary people voluntarily behave. Ordinary people matter because there are so many of them. Voluntary behavior matters because it's too hard to supervise everyone all the time. The Pyramids of Egypt, the Great Wall of China, the giant Siberian dams — these all show that certain brute-force accomplishments are possible under centrally controlled, involuntary systems. But societies are more likely to be successful over the years, more likely to satisfy their people's physical and spiritual needs, if they can entice rather than force people to act in useful ways. Anyone who has compared daily life in Japan or England with that in Colombia or Nigeria understands the point. Things are easier for everyone when people voluntarily obey the traffic laws, pay their taxes, wait their turn, behave more or less honestly even when there's no immediate risk of being caught. In warfare, commanders like Captain Queeg, who rule by intimidation and monitor every maneuver from the top, have sometimes won battles and even wars. But from the German blitzkrieg to Asian guerrilla struggles, the most adaptable forces, and the most effective, man for man, have been those in which soldiers and subcommanders understood the objective and could be trusted to work toward it on their own.

This voluntary behavior is what I mean by "culture." We

might say that Japan's culture has been part of the basis of its economic success or that Latin American culture seems more hostile to two-party parliamentary democracy than British culture does. Sir W. Arthur Lewis, a prominent development-economics specialist from the West Indies, was referring to culture in this sense when he wrote that social progress and economic growth depend "on attitudes to work, to wealth, to thrift, to having children, to invention, to strangers, to adventure, and so on, and all these attitudes flow from deep springs in the human mind."

In the long run the habits, values, and behavior of ordinary people determine national strength. Mussolini's Italy had essentially the same economic structure as postwar Korea and Japan, with extremely close coordination between industries and the state. The system worked much better, both politically and economically, after the war in Asia than before the war in Europe. Part of the difference was the war itself: Japan could rebuild in more tranquillity under MacArthur than Italy could in "partnership" with Hitler. But the greater difference was probably social. Japanese and Korean social values lent themselves more readily to cooperative, disciplined, hierarchical projects than Italian culture did.

Successful societies — those which progress economically and politically and can control the terms on which they deal with the outside world — succeed because they have found ways to match individual self-interest to the collective good. The behavior that helps each person will, as a cumulative ethos, help the society as a whole. Individual Singaporeans know that they and their families will be richer and better regarded if they study and work hard. The whole country profits from the efforts that millions of people voluntarily make. When societies fail — when they lose ground economically and come under the control of other societies — it is because this useful match ceases to exist. People no longer voluntarily do what helps the larger society. The Philippines as a nation suffers because so many powerful Filipinos are corrupt. Yet Philippine culture has so far found no tool, not even the example of an incorruptible new president, to persuade people tempted by corruption to resist. The anticorruption campaign therefore has to rely on police efforts, which means that it is doomed. The same is true of the attempted control of narcotics in the United States. As long as people are willing to buy, the police don't have a chance. Japan, Korea, and Singapore have only minor drug problems, not because their police are more vigilant but because family disapproval and other cultural forces reduce the willingness to buy. Drug addiction was widespread in China in its decadent days before World War II. Many of the addicts were executed, and the idea that drugs were shameful took hold.

Different societies find different ways to make individual behavior serve the collective good. The call to holy war against Iraq, backed by a draft law, drew hundreds of thousands of Iranians to their deaths. By the Iranian government's definition, at least, these young victims served the public good. The same call would fail in the United States; in the late twentieth century, religion is not a strong enough reason to persuade most Americans to go to their slaughter in human-wave assaults. Under American pressure since the mid 1980s, South Korea has grudgingly begun to let American cigarettes, beef, and other imports into the country. But when the products began to come in, posters went up in Seoul telling Koreans that they should resist the temptation to buy these higher-quality, lower-cost goods from overseas. The posters showed a harmonious, traditional, ethnically pure Korean village besieged by swarthy foreign merchants. They played to a sentiment that is powerful in Korea but feeble (although present) in the United States: the desire to preserve traditional society from changes brought by commerce.

Except in emergencies, Americans will not voluntarily spend more money for an inferior product just because it's made at home. If GM wants to take business back from Toyota, Americans think, it has to make better cars. Korea could tell its people to buy less "competitive" products just because they were Korean and expect that many people would cooperate. The different cultures lead to different behavior. Most Americans believe that buying made-in-U.S.A. goods that are of poor quality is not only stupid but in the long run harmful to the country, since it artificially shields producers from the competition that would force them to improve. Americans are so used to seeing editorials make this point about the necessity of competition that they may not realize how odd the argument would sound in Seoul or Taipei. There, proposals to remove protectionist barriers are usually described as threats to the home industry, not as spurs to greater efficiency. Western economic theory, like the American Constitution, is based on the principle that people need incentives to overcome their natural tendency to slack off or to abuse power. The standard Japanese and Korean assumption is "Our producers will in any case try their hardest, so why penalize them or push them below their break-even price?"

THE LIMITS OF A CULTURAL THEORY

There are of course many forces beyond culture that account for a society's health. Think, for instance, of the three ways in which the countries of the world can be categorized. One division is between communist-bloc countries and all the rest. A second is between the rich Western countries plus the rapidly rising "newly industrializing countries" of Asia and the countries of Africa, Latin America, and South Asia that are not industrializing and are growing poorer. A third division, within the industrialized countries, is between the Asian powers — Japan, Korea, Taiwan — and those of Europe and North America. Culture explains nothing about the first division (North and South Korea had identical cultures forty years ago), part of the second division (many of the former were once colonial powers; many of the latter were once colonies), and most of the third, as will be seen.

To emphasize what culture can explain, it is important to acknowledge the things it cannot. The other factors that affect a society's development include:

Politics and Policy. Government policies make a difference in how any society develops — in the short run, the greatest difference. Culture didn't cause the Great Depression; governments unintentionally did. And culture wasn't enough to end the Depression in America. There simply weren't enough jobs until the war-production boom began. The voluntary decisions that make up culture are the result of rational choices, not blind instinct. Therefore, laws and government policies can heavily affect how people "choose" to behave. If the price of wheat is subsidized, farmers will choose to grow more of it and consumers will choose to buy less. If segregation is outlawed, people will eventually "choose" more tolerant racial outlooks than they would under a system of apartheid. After World War II, when the United States occupation authorities broke up Japan's landed estates and redistributed the land to many more people, Japan "chose" a more egalitarian economic structure than it had had before. As Daniel Patrick Moynihan put it, "The central conservative truth is that it is culture, not politics, that determines the success of a society. The central liberal truth is that politics can change a culture and save it from itself." David McClelland, a psychologist, gave this advice to politicians and national planners in developing countries:

> Pay attention to the effects that your plans will have on the values, motives, and attitudes of people because *in the long run* it is these factors that will determine whether the plans are successful in speeding economic growth.

Religion, Education, and Trends. Religious doctrine also affects "voluntary" choices: under Islam there is less drinking; under Catholicism there are more babies; under Thailand's form of Buddhism most men spend a portion of their lives as monks. Parental example, straightforward moral teachings, and even fads have an effect. During the early 1960s, the Peace Corps made overseas service seem glamorous. By the early 1980s, frittering away two years as a do-gooder seemed an unwise career move. Sometimes people choose "useful" behavior because they believe they don't have any choice. For centuries the feudal doctrines of Europe and Asia convinced peasants that there was no alternative to serving their lords. One reason Japanese employees tend to stay in the same firm is that other companies are suspicious of those who transfer in midcareer.

Forces of Nature. Climate, natural resources, sheer size, and other noncultural factors also affect how societies develop. Japan is always nervous because it has no oil. South Africa might bow more quickly to outside pressure if it didn't have so much gold. Until the 1970s, the United States had abundant energy reserves and low oil prices. These enabled Americans to "choose" a society of big cars and sprawling suburbs. The country would probably have developed in a different way if it didn't have its own oil supplies — which it wouldn't if it hadn't taken Texas and California from Mexico in the Mexican-American War and bought Alaska from the Russians twenty years later. The continental United States enjoys the good fortune of having an enormous river flow through its heartland. Australia, which is about the same size, has no river in the middle and practically no water anywhere except along its coasts. Because of this accident it will never support as many people, farms, or industries as North America can. One of Japan's advantages over South Korea is that Japan has three times as many people; Japan can try out future exports in its large domestic market, which is much harder for Korea to do. When Asians say that China is certain to be a major power again, their reasoning usually boils down to its being "so big" in people, resources, and territory.

*Twists of Fate.*The accidents of history, like those of geography, affect culture and development. America "helped" bombed-out Japan rebuild largely by its occupation policies and then by fighting the Korean War. Contracts to supply the United Nations forces (which were overwhelmingly American) in South Korea gave many Japanese manufacturers their first opportunity to produce in volume, allowing them to reinvest and rebuild.

Two countries in Southeast Asia, the Philippines and Indonesia, are in many ways very similar. Each has a large and mainly Malay population, distributed across a vast and fragmented archipelago. But because of the machinations of European colonial competitors, Indonesia ended up being colonized by Holland, and the Philippines was a colony first of Spain and then of the United States. The Dutch were thoroughly unenlightened colonialists. They left behind fewer than a thousand Indonesian high school graduates when the Japanese drove them out in 1942. But through their obstinance they may unintentionally have aided Indonesia. Bitterness against the Dutch was so intense and widespread that it helped unify diverse tribes and religious groups that otherwise might have flown apart. On the other hand, the Spanish left the Philippines with the same *hacienda* agricultural system and the same extremes of wealth and poverty that have bedeviled Spain's other former colonies in Latin America. The United States, in its turn, was a far more benign colonial power; it built schools, hospitals, and courts and in good time agreed to give the Philippines its independence. But the very kindness of U.S. rule is now part of the Philippine pathology, since it leaves most Filipinos torn between wanting to break free from American influence and wanting to move to L.A. In 1982, in a survey, 207 grade school students in the Philippines were asked what nationality they would prefer to be. Most said American; exactly ten replied Filipino. Most of the political conversations I have had there, with Filipinos of the right, left, and center, have ended on the same note of Philippine dependence. "Of course, it's not really up to us," a soldier or politician or communist would tell me. "We have to wait and see what the Americans have in mind." In 1987 I met a group of economics students at the University of the Philippines. One young woman berated me about the presence of U.S. military bases in the Philippines, saying they totally warped the Philippine-American relationship. I agreed and said maybe it would be better to move the bases somewhere else. "You mean you'd abandon us?" she asked with a gasp. "We thought we could count on you."

Meanwhile, the remaining Malay population of Southeast Asia, those living on the Malay peninsula, came under British rule, rather than Dutch, Spanish, or American. When the British pulled out, peacefully, in the 1950s, they left some mild anticolonial resentfulness: in the 1980s, Malaysia was gleefully pushing a "Buy British Last!" campaign. But they also left good schools, a fairly honest and competent civil service, a respect for courts and parliamentary democracy, and near universal fluency in English, all of which helped Malaysia. Britain's other bequest to Malaya was an unhappy racial mix. Through the nineteenth century Britain had sponsored the immigration of Indians and Chinese to Malaya to do jobs on the rubber plantations and in the colonial bureaucracy that Englishmen thought Malays could not or would not do. Each of the three groups — Malays, Chinese, and Indians — resents the presence of the other two, and the racial balance that the British worked out is now the country's major problem.

The point is not that one of these colonial systems was better than the other but that they were different. The accident of who colonized whom hundreds of years ago now gives these three otherwise similar countries very different economic and political prospects, in part because the accidents changed the culture.

Misjudgments of Culture. Sometimes "cultural" explanations are misperceived, or reflect only the bias of the observer. The Britons and Americans who poured into China in the nineteenth century were sure that Confucianism was an insuperable obstacle to economic development. So much hidebound tradition and mindless obedience! So little room for individual initiative! By the late twentieth century, of course, the conventional wisdom has reversed. Now Confucianism is supposed to be the Asians' secret weapon against the West.

The prime minister of Malaysia, Mahatir bin Mohamad, first came to prominence in his country with a broadside arguing that the Chinese Malaysians were better businessmen than the ethnic Malays because they were racially superior. Mahatir said that centuries of famine and flood in China had produced a race of hardy survivors, whereas the Malays had been weakened by a life that was too abundant. Mahatir, it should be stressed, was speaking as the *Malays'* champion; he said all this to justify a sweeping program of pro-Malay affirmative action, which has been in effect since the end of the 1960s. But in fact, no such racial theorizing is necessary, since there are more obvious and straightforward explanations of why the Chinese do as well as they do. Chinese parents raise their children to compete and excel; Malay parents emphasize such values as gentleness, restraint, obedience to Islam. Malays place great emphasis on not hurting other people's feelings; it is easy to believe, after watching the Chinese argue and yell, that this concept cannot be translated into Chinese. Conspicuous display of prosperity is much more important to Chinese than to Malays. Chinese small-businessmen demonstrate the famous self-exploitation of the entrepreneur. (In my own dealings with them, I have often felt too weary to counter the efforts they are willing to put out to make a sale. "You can't come to store to see the camera? I come to your house now! You eating dinner now? How late you stay up? I come tonight!") All these factors make for Chinese business success, and they have nothing to do with the racial analysis on which the recent Malaysian politics have turned.

The original version of *The Bridge Over the River Kwai,* published about a decade after the end of World War II, was superficially a war-adventure novel but actually an essay on the cultural inferiority of the Japanese. They couldn't plan ahead; they couldn't organize a work force; they couldn't in a million years make something that was up to Western quality standards. The British colonel whose troops have been captured by the Japanese and forced to build a railway bridge declaims, "They're what I've always said they were: primitive people, as undeveloped as children, who've acquired a veneer of civilization too soon. Underneath it all they're absolutely ignorant. They can't do a thing by themselves . . . As far as I can make out, they're only just capable of making a footbridge out of jungle creepers." In the same farsighted spirit, as Robert Klitgaard has pointed out, an Australian expert visiting Japan just before World War I reported to the Japanese government:

> My impression as to your cheap labor was soon disillusioned when I saw your people at work. No doubt they are lowly paid, but the return is equally so; to see your men at work made me feel that you are a very satisfied easy-going race who reckon time is no object. When I spoke to some managers they informed me it was impossible to change the habits of national heritage.

Judgments such as these were shortsighted even when they were made. In many other cases, cultural explanations may be true at one time but then change to become untrue, because the underlying culture has changed. In the eighteenth century, England was the workshop of the world, and most descriptions of it at that time emphasize that its society was fluid, untraditional, full of rich and poor people but not "classbound," since people could move quickly from one status to another. "More than any

other society in Europe, probably, British society was open,"
the historian David Landes has written of that age. "Not only
was income more evenly distributed than [elsewhere], but the
barriers to mobility were lower, the definitions of status looser."
Another historian, Bernard Bailyn, has demonstrated that the
migration that first populated New England was merely an extension of rapid migrant flows within England itself. By the mid
twentieth century, of course, even Britons were speaking of the
"British disease" — essentially, a stagnant class system — as
the cause of their ills.

WHAT CULTURE CAN EXPLAIN

Still, culture matters. Because culture can't explain everything
about national development, for all the reasons just discussed,
some people are tempted to conclude that it can't explain anything. This temptation is especially strong for members of three
groups. The first are the Marxists, who assume that the same
laws of class analysis can be applied to any society, regardless of
its culture. The second are the classical free-market thinkers,
who believe that "economic man" responds consistently to incentives, wherever he may live. The third are Americans in general, whose own culture is so malleable and open to outside
influence as to foster the belief that "culture" itself may not
matter at all.

Some American academics, for instance, contend that wise
government policies and industrial strategies are the only reasons
that Japan has grown more quickly than the United States. Why
does Japan have such high quality standards in its plants? Because it followed the advice of the legendary American production expert, W. Edwards Deming, immediately after the war. If
American companies had been humble enough to listen to him,
they could have done just as well — and some of course have,
by adopting Japanese-style management and production techniques. Economists have pointed out that if America had promoted savings as much as the Japanese government has,

encouraged industrial cartels with the same zeal, arranged the same labor-management understandings, and so forth, then American cars and radios would now be as successful as Japan's.

This is probably true. The question is *why* American policy has been so different from Japan's. Is it just that American politicians and industrialists made bad choices, or is there something about the two societies that made different policies more appropriate to each one? In Japan, Korea, Singapore, and Taiwan, the government offers only meager retirement benefits. People save a much larger proportion of their income than in America, principally for the retirement years. If a Korean wants a comfortable retirement, he starts saving for it the day he gets a job, and he supports his parents in their old age, knowing that his children will help support him. If you believe that policy determines behavior, the moral is obvious: cut back heavily on Social Security, and then Americans will save more. But if you believe that culture also determines behavior, then you will doubt that the transplanted Asian approach would work quite so well in a country that doesn't have the Asian tradition of strong families to build upon.

What, in specific, does it mean to talk about "culture"? What traits do productive cultures have in common?

Gunnar Myrdal, the Swedish economist, tried to answer these questions in his monumental book of the late 1960s, *Asian Drama*. His purpose was to explain the roots of poverty in all of "South Asia," from India and Pakistan through Indochina to the Philippines. He ended up concentrating on India. India's predicament is compelling because there are many reasons that it should succeed. If ever there was a country, apart from China, with the potential to prosper simply by giving ordinary people a chance, it would seem to be India. It has so many people, and they are so noted as merchants, scientists, and professionals when they emigrate. Britain shipped them to Africa and Southeast Asia to help administer the empire. Emergency rooms in many U.S. hospitals ran on Indian and Pakistani manpower during the 1960s and early 1970s, when a "doctor shortage" loophole in the American immigration code drew them in. Yet India itself, despite improvements in the 1980s, has been slower to take off than the East Asian economies, and if China keeps relaxing controls on its economy, it seems certain to surpass India.

Myrdal considered all the political and geographical and historical constraints on India's progress, but finally concentrated on culture. He attempted to distill those cultural traits which were useful for development. There were thirteen items on his list:

1. Efficiency
2. Diligence
3. Orderliness
4. Punctuality
5. Frugality
6. Scrupulous honesty (which pays in the long run and is a condition for raising efficiency in all social and economic relations)
7. Rationality in decisions on actions (liberation from reliance on static customs, from group allegiances and favoritism, from superstitious beliefs and prejudices, approaching the rationally calculating ''economic man'' of Western liberal ideology)
8. Preparedness for change (for experimentation along new lines, and for moving around spatially, economically, socially)
9. Alertness to opportunities as they arise in a changing world
10. Energetic enterprise
11. Integrity and self-reliance
12. Cooperativeness (not limiting but redirecting egoistic striving in a socially beneficial channel; acceptance of responsibility for the welfare of the community and the nation)
13. Willingness to take the long view (and to forgo short-term profiteering; subordination of speculation to investment and of commerce and finance to production; and so on).

Myrdal then argued, through thirteen hundred pages, that Indian culture, rather than promoting these traits, encouraged unproductive behavior by ordinary Indians. Because the caste system froze most people in position, those in the higher castes didn't have to work and those in the lower castes had no chance to rise. Religion became a ''tremendous force for social inertia.'' (''The writer knows of no instance in present-day South Asia where religion has induced social change . . . It is remarkable

that today practically no one in South Asia is attacking religion.'') Corruption bled off such surpluses as the country managed to produce and made people distrust the government —
indeed, they distrusted anyone outside their own caste or tribe.
The patterns of behavior he described were not racial; Indian
emigrants behaved in many of the ways Myrdal endorsed — unlike their cousins and countrymen at home. Instead, something
in the home culture pushed Indians in a destructive direction.

Lawrence Harrison, who spent twenty years in Latin America
as an official of the Agency for International Development
(America's main foreign-aid organ), undertook a similar analysis
of the ingredients of a ''useful'' culture. He reduced them to a
list of seven ''conditions that encourage the expression of human
creative capacity'':

1. The expectation of fair play
2. Availability of educational opportunities
3. Availability of health services
4. Encouragement of experimentation and criticism
5. Matching of skills and jobs
6. Rewards for merit and achievement
7. Stability and continuity

For an understanding of American culture, the list can be reduced even further, to two crucial items. People are naturally
energetic and creative. A society should be able to harness the
voluntary efforts of ordinary people just by getting out of their
way. Whether it is in fact able to do so — whether America can
do so — depends on two things: whether the radius of trust is
large enough and whether people feel they can control their destiny.

1. Radius of trust. Except for psychopaths, everyone treats
someone else decently. The question is how many people are
classified as ''us,'' deserving decent treatment, and how many
are ''them,'' who can be abused. When the radius of trust is
small, the society is carved into tribes, castes, clans. People are
loyal to the handful of brothers inside the circle and may as well
be at war with everyone else. The obligation to behave decently
— and the expectation of decency in return — ends with family
or friends. This is what Hobbes had in mind when he talked about

the war of Every Man against Every Man. It is Lebanon, Haiti, the Philippines — and the New York of *The Bonfire of the Vanities,* by Tom Wolfe. Samuel Huntington wrote:

> The absence of trust in the culture of the society provides formidable obstacles to the creation of public institutions. Those societies deficient in stable and effective government are also deficient in mutual trust among their citizens, in national and public loyalties, and in organization skills and capacity. Their political cultures are often said to be marked by suspicion, jealousy, and latent or actual hostility toward everyone who is not a member of the family, the village, or, perhaps, the tribe.

Successful societies have devised some version of a "most favored nation" code among their people so that the majority of members qualify for decent treatment from most others they meet and deal with during the day. America has done this by stressing the ideas that anyone can be assimilated, that everyone should have a chance, that mass culture can give all people something in common, and that citizenship imposes similar obligations on everyone. When these ideas are strongest, so is the bond of trust in American society.

2. Control over destiny. Most people work in the hope of reward. The tighter the connection between effort and reward, the harder ordinary people will try. Superstitious religions, which assert that fate cannot be understood and is beyond earthly control, break the connection between effort and reward. So do exploitative class systems that freeze people in place, no matter what their merit, or systems of punishment and reward that seem whimsical or unconstrained by natural justice. People won't care as much about traffic laws if they know they can bribe the police; they won't trust the laws if they think the courts are crooked; children won't absorb a sense of right and wrong if parents and teachers discipline them according to passing mood. Edward Banfield wrote that child rearing in an impoverished village in southern Italy was harmful because, in part, of "the reliance upon blows to direct behavior and the capricious manner in which punishment is given."

When these two conditions are satisfied — when the radius of

trust is broad; when people think they can affect their destiny —
then ordinary people will behave in a way that makes the society
rich, strong, and fair.

Different societies have different ways of creating these cultural conditions for economic growth and political stability.
America is perfectly capable of doing so; after all, it is still one
of the world's great success stories. But it can't do it the way in
which Japanese or Korean or Chinese or German or Swedish
culture does. Other societies, most of all Japan, can match individual self-interest with the collective social good by using tools
that America does not and cannot possess. If we have to out-
cooperate and out-sacrifice the Japanese, we may as well quit.
We need, instead, to find our own tools.

CHAPTER TWO

The Japanese Talent for Order

JAPAN has two cultural advantages America can't match: a concept of racial unity and a tradition of effort for its own sake. The first expands the radius of trust to include everybody in the country. The second gives people something more important than money or individual gain to work toward. Both of these advantages make it easy for Japan to marshal nearly everyone's efforts to a productive end. Both have at least blurry reflections in other successful Asian countries but are very different from the cultural assumptions in the United States.

RACIAL UNITY

Japan's powerful emphasis on its racial purity and uniqueness is its most noticeable and exasperating trait. It has a thousand familiar manifestations. One is the constant murmur of *Gaijin da!* (It's an outsider!) or *Harroo!* (Hello!) that washes around a foreigner as he moves through parts of a city even as cosmopolitan as Tokyo. Another is the assertion by seriously regarded Japanese people that they and their countrymen have different brains or intestines from the rest of the world. Yet another indication is the offhanded way that Japanese use the phrase "we Japanese" in English, as if they were one large, undifferentiated group, like a school of fish.

Even the Japanese language illustrates the sense of tribal unity. Americans assume that anyone could (and should) learn English. They act put-upon when foreign tourists show up and can't respond to "So whaddya want?" The traditional Japanese assumption has been the opposite: that non-Japanese were physically, culturally, and mentally incapable of speaking Japanese. As more foreigners have learned the language, this assumption has started to change. Still, the idea that Japanese is different from all other languages remains. The grammatical structures of the Korean and Japanese languages are practically identical. Many people make this point in Korea (in part, because most people over forty-five or fifty were required to learn Japanese during Korea's years as Japan's colony), but Japanese people are more likely to say that their language is "unique."

For years, Japan avoided accepting any Vietnamese refugees whatsoever. It said that, unlike the United States, it had no special moral or political obligation to Vietnam, and that in any case it had never purported to be a haven for immigrants. "We prefer the 'financial solution' to this problem," a Foreign Ministry official told me, meaning they'd rather pay for refugee camps somewhere else. Finally the complaints from America, Thailand, and Australia grew bitter enough that Japan took in a few thousand refugees, whom it housed in a railroad yard south of Tokyo. The most dumfounded expression I have seen on any Japanese person's face was that of a resettlement official after I asked him whether these Vietnamese, or even their children who had been born in Japan, could eventually become Japanese citizens. Many "Koreans" in Japan, known as such even though they were born and raised in Japan, carry Korean, not Japanese, passports.

Before Prime Minister Yasuhiro Nakasone made Japan's bias seem antiblack and not just antiforeign, the outside world hesitated to call this attitude racism. If white people aren't the ones looking down on someone else, can it really be racism? Indeed, Asians in general and Japanese in particular have suffered racial discrimination in the United States, from the Chinese coolies working on the railroads to the Japanese in the wartime internment camps. During World War II the anti-Japanese racial propaganda in the United States was more ferocious and slanderous than the anti-Western propaganda in Japan. For instance, as John Dower, a historian, pointed out in his book *War Without Mercy*, Ernie Pyle explained to the readers of his famous wartime column that the difference between the Germans and the Japanese was that the Germans "were still people," whereas the Japanese were seen as "something subhuman and repulsive, the way some people feel about cockroaches or mice."

Whatever forms American xenophobia took in the 1940s, Japan is today by far the more racially exclusive of the two societies. The results can be a healthy tonic for any visiting white American. My own modest proposal for solving America's racial problems is to make all white Americans live in Japan for a year or two. It's a quick way to learn how it feels to have your race be the most important — and on the whole unfavorable — thing about you. The first time I took my sons to the public bath in the neighborhood where we were staying in Tokyo, we spent half an hour in the requisite scrubbing and cleansing rituals before entering the bath itself. Even so, all the Japanese men stepped out the instant our skin touched the water. We were not really that dirty.

Edward Seidensticker, one of America's great authorities on Japanese literature and culture, lived in Japan after the war and then, in 1962, announced his intention to depart. "The Japanese are just like other people," he wrote in a *sayonara* newspaper column. "But no. They are not like other people. They are infinitely more clannish, insular, parochial, and one owes it to one's self-respect to preserve a feeling of outrage at the insularity. To have the sense of outrage go dull is to lose the will to communicate; and that, I think, is death. So I am going home." On a sultry summer evening in 1986, I met Seidensticker in a bar in the Shinjuku district of Tokyo. What was he doing back in Japan after his bitter farewell? He was now spending half of every year in the country. "It's a living," he said. At the table next to ours a Japanese salaryman, or white-collar worker, was turning red-faced and tipsy over his glasses of beer. He reeled over toward Seidensticker, waved his arm in greeting, and, to the man who had won prizes for translating the novels of Kawabata and Mishima and the *Tales of Genji*, yelled out *Harrooo!* Seidensticker looked at me as if he wished that Commodore Perry had never come with his Black Ships to open up Japan.

"In my own case, having been born and educated in Japan and speaking accentless Japanese doesn't make me any less an outsider," a business consultant named George Fields wrote in 1986. "For instance, I gave a paper at an international marketing conference in Tokyo. The paper was in English, the official language of the conference, and was simultaneously interpreted in Japanese . . . It had some jargon, for which my interpreter sought clarification: she expected it in English. I decided that it was more logical to clarify the items in Japanese. But when I finished, she looked at me in a strange way and said, '*Ah, kimochi ga waruii,*' meaning, 'Oh, it gives me the creeps!' In other words, no 'foreigner' should speak exactly like a Japanese."

Fields made the essential point about the differences between the two societies: "It is as hard for a Japanese to understand that somebody would want to be one of them — a sheer contradiction in terms to them — as it is for an American to imagine that every immigrant doesn't want eventually to become an American . . . Americans think everybody is going to be like them one day. Whereas in Japan, foreigners are supposed to go back where they came from."

In the long run, the let's-all-be-the-same ethic is Japan's greatest vulnerability. Already the country is trying to figure out how to cope with the "returnees" — the Japanese children who have grown up in New Jersey or London while their fathers did battle for Matsushita or Nissan. When the children come back, they're no longer quite Japanese. Japan will either open up to them, becoming less like itself, or it won't, in which case there will be a lot of bilingual and bicultural talent drifting around for American and European companies to recruit. Some Japanese and American economists have concluded that the two countries could solve most of the world's (or at least their own) trade problems by merging. In a stroke, most trade and investment imbalances would vanish. This will never happen in the form of an official political merger, of course. But even the de facto integration of the societies would be traumatic for the Japanese because of the new (and different) *people* it would bring in.

Even worse, Japan's idea that it is separate from the world

leaves the rest of the world feeling separate from Japan. The United States is the closest approximation to a friend that Japan has. Whenever waves of anti-Americanism would start breaking over me in Korea, China, or the Philippines, I'd wait until the subject switched to Japan and sit back to hear some real vitriol. But in fact, as the U.S. State Department constantly stresses, everyone would be worse off if Japan began to feel truly isolated and unloved, as it did in the years before World War II.

These are problems for tomorrow. For now, the racial bond is indispensable to Japan, no matter how much it may annoy outsiders. As almost every outsider has pointed out, Japanese culture is far more uniform than that of any other major country. Schools from north to south teach the same subjects during the same weeks every year. Most swimming pools open and close for summer use on the same date across the country, even though the northern island of Hokkaido is subarctic and southern Kyushu is like the tropics. As Jared Taylor wrote, Japan *looks* the same from top to bottom, as if it had taken great care to present people with familiar, uniform surroundings at all times. The country's inside-versus-outside ethic even enables people to overlook the small but real racial variation that exists among "pure" Japanese.*

All this reinforces the idea that the Japanese are One and non-Japanese are something else — and the One-ness, in turn, convinces each Japanese that all other Japanese deserve basically

---

* Kenichi Ohmae, Japan's most prolific and best-selling author in the 1980s, said in his book *Beyond National Borders:*

> While we may not intend to appear so, the world outside is beginning to perceive us as racially arrogant. Again, the problem is in part our language. In order to cheer ourselves over rough times, we developed many phrases and expressions that now cause problems . . . [For example:] "Single race." We are the offshoots of Manchurians and Koreans, and belong to the Mongolian family. We are the product of these bloods mixed with Polynesians and Ainus. We are no more pure than any of our neighboring nations. The idea of a "single race" was a convenient myth to cheer us up and to get the nation united in catching up with the West. [Pp. 67–68]

Beyond National Borders: Reflections on Japan and the World (Homewood, Ill.: Dow Jones–Irwin, 1987) is the English translation of a book that was a best seller when first published in Japanese. This passage, however, was inserted into the English edition after Nakasone's comments. Therefore, it did not reach the Japanese readers, whom Ohmae appears to be addressing.

decent treatment. The radius of trust reaches all the way out to the borders of the society — as America's did during World War II (with the enormous exception of blacks and the Japanese Americans locked up in internment camps) and probably never since then. The standard Japanese slogan during World War II was *ichi-oku isshin* (one hundred million with one heart). Police officials routinely say that "our homogeneous race" is the explanation for Japan's low incidence of crime. When I asked the manager of a semiconductor plant in Kyushu why his chips had fewer defects than those made in California or Texas, he said, "We are all Japanese working here, one race." His company was planning to open a plant in rural Wisconsin. "The people are all Swedish," he said. "They will understand each other without many words. Like us." In fairness, part of the problem is linguistic. The manager and others were speaking in English and may not have understood the weight the word "race" conveys to native speakers. The word they would have used in Japanese, *minzoku*, is closer to "tribe." Still, beyond semantic subtleties the sense of bonding is intense and gives most Japanese an instinctive reason to cooperate with each other.

Most of the Japanese I interviewed have stressed how easy it is to manage a nation when nearly everyone shares the same values. The American group that most resembles the Japanese is the Mormons. Same orthodox family patterns, same virtues of work and thrift, same emphasis on consensus and conventional wisdom, same abundance of steady, high-average performers as opposed to flamboyant superstars. Just as Utah is easier to govern (yet duller) than New York or California, Japan is easier to manage than the United States. And Utah is only 70 percent Mormon; Japan is nearly pure. In 1983, at the annual commemoration for those killed by the atomic bomb in Hiroshima, Nakasone, then the prime minister, made the point as crudely as possible. He said, "The Japanese have been doing well for as long as two thousand years because there are no foreign races." This comment was especially graceless since a large number of Koreans, probably more than ten thousand, were also killed in Hiroshima. They had been brought to Japan from colonized Korea as laborers during the war.

In addition to its more obvious conveniences, Japan's racial unity permits its style of meritocracy to work as well as it does. It is a system both more open and more closed than America's. Everyone is given a more or less equal chance in the beginning. Although schools are becoming stratified along family-income lines, as in America, within each school there is no tracking or grouping during the elementary years. All students move along at the same pace; no one skips or fails a grade, including many who would be classified in the United States as retarded. Then, in junior high and high school, a rigorously "fair" system divides students according to examination scores until, in the end, some make the grade into the right universities and others do not. Everyone knows which university is best (University of Tokyo), which is second best, and so on. The best jobs go to graduates of the best university, second best to second best, and on, quite precisely, down the line. The second chance is not a cherished Japanese ideal.

This kind of merit system, based on one or two big dividing points in the teen years, leaves Japan with many people who are, objectively, losers: the men who drive the miniature dump trucks through Tokyo alleys, collecting trash while wearing white cotton gloves, the day laborers on construction gangs in their medieval-looking cloven-toed work booties, the subway-ticket punchers who stand in little underground cubicles and work like robots for hours on end. A more modern tribe of losers is made up of the *madogiwazoko,* or window-side people, those passed over for promotion at big firms but still guaranteed their jobs as part of the social contract. Every society has its losers, but Japan's seem less scorned — and therefore less resentful and more willing to try hard — than losers anywhere else. The Japanese ethic of doing every job well is part of the explanation, but the idea of racial and cultural unity is also important. Certain people have failed, but they're still brothers and cousins — not the Other, as lower-class blacks often are to whites in the United States. In Japan, failures and successes alike are all part of the family, the tribe.

Japan is nowhere near as "democratic" as America, either politically or socially. Until the beginning of the Second World War, Japan was as thoroughly class-ridden and feudal a society as anything found in Europe. Even now the upper levels of its society are dotted with descendants of prewar barons and counts. Women defer to men, the young defer to the old, everyone fits in above and below someone on the national chain of command. The biggest nuisance in studying Japanese is the system of honorifics — the different titles and entirely different vocabularies from which you select words according to whether the person you are addressing stands above you or below.

Japan, that is, works like a family, in which people are definitely not equal but instinctively recognize shared interests and pull together for the common good. "Everyone knows there's a hierarchy," Wick Smith, an American advertising man long resident in Japan, once told me. "The executives are driven around in black Nissan Cedrics by drivers with white gloves. But you don't see that raw hatred you do in New York, when the thirty-year-old stockbroker roars past in his Porsche."

No other country in Asia has put quite as much emphasis on racial unity as Japan has. China is too vast to be pure. Koreans, although proud and xenophobic, talk about their role as "peninsular people" in bridging the cultures of China and Japan. Taiwan has its own ethnic split between indigenous Taiwanese and mainland Chinese who arrived with Chiang Kai-shek. The Overseas Chinese — émigrés from southern China living in Southeast Asia — come in many mutually suspicious clans and regional groups. But compared with America, all Asian cultures are relatively homogeneous, and all take it for granted that societies are stronger when they are pure. The racial exclusiveness is annoying to Americans, especially since it classifies most of us as impure, but it helps Asian societies, above all Japan's, to buffer individual desires with a sense of what is good for the whole tribe.

EFFORT FOR ITS OWN SAKE

Obviously the United States cannot match the tribal consciousness that provides part of Japan's strength. But Japan and some neighboring cultures get tremendous effort out of ordinary people in a second, less obvious way. People in every culture do their best when they think there is a reward, but in Japan much of the reward is in the effort itself.

This difference is so simple-sounding that Americans may be tempted not to give it the attention it deserves. It is a fundamental difference between Japanese and American culture, because it takes us back to the first principles of what economic life is for.

The starting point of Western economics, especially in America, is that the world is full of "economic men," who go through life making rational cost-benefit decisions. Their appetites and preferences may vary. If wages go up, some people will work more because the payoff is greater, and others will work less because they can earn what they need in a shorter time. But everyone will respond to market signals to get the most satisfying deal for himself. This is the basic force that makes economies run. People choose different specialties; they invent new devices and invest in more productive plants; they buy from lower-cost suppliers in other locations, because every time they do so they have more goods available at a lower cost. This is how two hundred–plus years of capitalism have raised material living standards around the world.

But this picture of economic man rests on an even more basic assumption about the purpose of life — at least the economic part of it. Efficient production and foreign trade are good because they lead to lower prices, and lower prices are good because they let people have more: more food, more clothes, more leisure, more variety, more of everything that money can buy. This is the principal justification for the turmoil of capitalism. Under a competitive, capitalistic system, people suffer indignities as *producers* — companies fail, products don't sell, workers are laid off, competitors force down the price — in order to enjoy benefits as *consumers*. And as long as societies around the world all have the same goal — more — then trade among cities, regions, and nations will steadily increase. Everyone wants a bargain; the best bargains are by definition available from the world's lowest-cost producers; and the constant shift of exchange rates and technical advantages will attract people to bargains in new sites.

For most of its history, the United States has behaved more or less in accordance with the proconsumer capitalist model. Japan has not. The welfare of its consumers has consistently taken second place to a different goal: preserving every person's place in the productive system. The reward of working hard in Japan is to continue to be able to work.

Of course, some people in every part of the world work for the joy of work itself, and some Japanese work only for the pay. Taken one by one, the economic goals of most Japanese are like those of people anywhere else in the world. I've seen housewives in suburban Yokohama poring over prices in the *kutto puraiso* (cut price) corner of the grocery store just as their counterparts in America would. But Japanese society as a whole has goals quite different from America's. American culture and politics usually promote the consumer's interest; Japanese culture and politics are usually biased the other way. Japan has consistently protected its producers — farmers, unions, small shops, big corporations — at the expense of all the Japanese consumers, who must pay exorbitant prices for everything they buy.

Food is the classic illustration of the bias in favor of production and effort. Japan imports about half the calories its people eat each day, but if it were interested mainly in giving its people the best food for the best price, it would import much more. Rice grown on the tiny little plots that, together, take up about half the nonmountainous land in the country costs at least six times as much as American-grown rice and ten times as much as rice from the world's price leader, Thailand. (When my family moved from Malaysia to Japan, we stuffed drawers and crannies in our household-goods shipment with sacks of rice. It cost about twenty-five cents a pound in Malaysia, more than $2.00 in Japan.) Food accounts for about 15 percent of an average American household's expenditures; in Japan, it's 30 percent — and the average Japanese eats eight hundred fewer calories per day than the average American. Since so much of Japan's usable land is tied up by inefficient farms, the Japanese pay exorbitant prices for housing. The average Japanese home is about one-third smaller than the average American home but costs about twice as much. (The land-price problem is further aggravated by tax policies that discourage resale or development of land — the opposite of our mortgage-interest deduction and other incentives to build.) At the market and currency exchange rates prevailing in early 1988, Japan's land was worth much more than America's — even though the United States is more than twenty-five times larger and is endowed with every natural resource that Japan lacks.

Almost every nation protects its farmers to some degree. Farm-support programs are the chronic sore point when the industrialized powers meet for their annual economic summit meetings. Still, no other country's consumers pay as high a price for protecting their farmers as the Japanese do. Moreover, in most Western economies, crop-support programs, though widespread, are controversial. Consumer groups complain that higher food prices hurt them. Japan's rice program, in contrast, did not even begin to be questioned until the mid 1980s, and Japanese consumer groups generally defended the current policy.

Japanese consumers have been more patient because they've had less information; the Japanese press has, until recently, been timid about exploring the consequences of expensive rice. Japan's rice subsidies may be slowly whittled away over the next decade, but not without resistance from both farmers and consumers. Many buyers are willing to pay more to keep the farmers from going out of business; that is, the farmer's right to make an effort matters more than the consumer's right to cheaper food. In a Japanese poll conducted in 1980, 75 percent of the respondents agreed that "in principle, domestic [farm] production should be increased whenever possible." Only 16 percent answered what most Americans, through their actions, endorse every day: "It is better to consume imported products if they are less expensive than domestic ones."

The retail network is another famous example of the Japanese preference for production and effort rather than for consumption. A hundred years ago, the United States had a retail system much like Japan's today: fragmented, diverse, family-owned, and inefficient for the consumer, with enormous markups. America doesn't have mom-and-pop stores anymore, except for those run by the immigrants, because they've been bulldozed under by

Sears, Safeway, K mart, and other big-scale, low-cost opera-tions. The mom-and-pops put up a political fight in the 1920s and 1930s and tried to outlaw the chain stores. But, as Thomas McCraw and Patricia O'Brien pointed out in *America Versus Japan,* they were snubbed by courts, legislatures, and even vot-ers in referenda. Chain stores gave you more for your money; therefore they were good. "In the most significant decisions con-cerning American public policy, low prices have almost always been accorded far greater importance than the preservation of small enterprise," McCraw and O'Brien wrote.

Japan, meanwhile, has been protecting the little stores and thwarting the chains. In the past fifteen years one government directive after another has made it harder to open discount stores, supermarkets, or other low-cost outlets that would im-prove the consumer's standard of living but imperil the tiny greengrocer down the block. Small retail stores, not affiliated with a chain, account for nearly 60 percent of all sales in Japan. In the United States, they account for 3 percent. Here, as in its farm policy, Japan has sacrificed its welfare as a consuming society to protect its producers — if small shopkeepers can be so called.

Right-thinking Americans know that monopolies and cartels are bad. They stifle competition and therefore shortchange the consumer. The United States grudgingly protects only natural monopolies like the electric system — and in the name of con-sumer welfare even broke up the seemingly natural telephone monopoly. Japan likes cartels and some monopolies, because they strengthen Japanese producers against the world. Japanese steelmakers, in the 1960s and 1970s, and semiconductor makers, in the 1970s and 1980s, invested far more heavily in advanced production equipment than any of them would have dared on their own. It would have been cheaper, and therefore economi-cally more rational, to keep using the old machines, which is what many American companies have done. The Japanese com-panies could take this "risk" because of their cartel-based faith that the famous Ministry of International Trade and Industry, MITI, would divide the work fairly whenever the market went slack.

One further illustration of the bias toward production comes from the humble but important soda ash business. Soda ash is a staple chemical used for making glass, other chemicals, and detergents. Because soda ash is produced in big petroleum-fed cookers, Japanese suppliers, with their very high energy costs, are at an inherent disadvantage compared with American suppliers. Nonetheless, Japanese customers buy five sixths of their soda ash at home. An executive of Asahi Glass, a major purchaser, announced in 1986 that he would never leave his high-cost Japanese supplier. After all, they'd been friends in school. "This isn't exactly collusion," an American diplomat told me. "It's just a refusal to act on price."

The reluctance to act on price — to be consumers above all — is what, along with racial unity, predisposes Japan to success in export competition. It's like the behavior any government expects from its soldiers and diplomats. If it has to get into a bidding war with the enemy for the loyalty of its troops, it is doomed. It needs to know that its people will refuse to act on price — won't sell secrets, won't defect just for cash. We can understand this nonconsumer behavior in war and national emergency. Japan promotes it in peacetime business competition too. There was a wonderfully revealing moment, in the summer of 1986, after the United States and Japan negotiated their cartel-type arrangement to hold down Japanese semiconductor production. The deal was unpopular in both countries, but for opposite reasons. The Japanese were unhappy because they could no longer *make* so many cheap chips, and the Americans because they could no longer *buy* them. A typical American reaction was this, from a computer-industry newsletter:

> Protection of a domestic industry invariably comes out of the consumers' pocket. The U.S.–Japan trade agreement, signed July 30, was ostensibly to protect American chipmakers from "predatory dumping practices" from Japan. Instead all it does is illustrate how trade barriers wind up being paid for by consumers . . . The net result of higher chip prices may mean higher PC [personal computer] prices, reversing an uninterrupted trend of ever lower prices since microcomputers first arrived on the scene 10 years ago. That is not likely to be good for our country, short term or long range.

That is, the consumer's welfare is most important. In Japan, the complaint about the agreement was that it reduced Japanese companies' market share. Beyond this economic choice was the cultural preference for effort over consumption.

Obviously this is not an all-versus-nothing contrast. Sometimes the United States also rises above price. Alexander Hamilton's famous "Report on the Subject of Manufactures," issued in 1791, was a classic argument for penalizing the consumer (through higher prices) so as to get infant industries under way. Through much of the nineteenth century, American trading policy tried to protect new American industries and farms. Today's U.S. sugar quotas are as economically indefensible as Japan's rice policy, and they probably do more damage to the rest of the world, since they keep the Philippines and struggling countries in the Caribbean from selling sugar in the United States. Still, America is a "consumer culture" in a more profound way than that cliché indicates. In the spring of 1987, soon after the U.S. Congress passed a mildly protectionist trade bill, the *New York Times*'s "Washington Talk" page ran a story about the many politicians who said "Buy American" but drove imported cars. The story was meant to expose them as hypocrites, but all it really showed was that they had behaved in normal American style. "People think I should only buy an American car, and I've always had one," Representative Douglas Bosco of California was quoted as saying. "But I decided to do what I want to do in my private life, and for that I like a Mercedes better." Deciding to do what they want to do in their private lives is the way most Americans think and behave.

The Anticonsumer Social Compact

By American standards, it is a strange victory indeed that Japan has won through this behavior. It has continually expanded its market share, but only at the price of living more austerely than its customers do. Japan provides slightly more job security for its people, but only as part of an overall package that most Americans would find objectionable. Women are excluded from the package, for instance; they occupy almost none of Japan's influential jobs. Even the men pay a price for their protection. In 1986, the average employee in a Japanese manufacturing company was putting in 254 more hours on the job each year than the average American — the equivalent of more than six additional forty-hour weeks.

American economists warn that if the United States does not become more productive, its standard of living will suffer. Japan's standard of living already suffers. Because the yen's value has soared, Japan's per capita income is now considerably higher than America's, but its real living standard is far below America's and lower than those of Italy and France. Houses are cramped and expensive; the country has worse roads, sewers, and parks than anywhere in Europe or North America; everything costs more than its counterparts in the United States. New York and Washington have 19 square meters of park per resident. Tokyo has 2.2. Ninety-seven percent of Britain's houses have sewer service, as contrasted to 37 percent of Japan's. In 1986 a Japanese TV network planned a documentary comparing the daily lives of a Japanese family earning $25,000 with their counterparts in Italy. The network called off the project. The Italians' standard of living was simply too high for Japanese viewers to comprehend. The per capita income in Malaysia is about one tenth as high as in Japan, but by most of the measures of basic human comfort — housing space, clothing, food, leisure time, recreation, and amusement — the difference between the two societies is not very large. A headline in the *Wall Street Journal* in 1987 said, POOR JAPAN: SO MUCH YEN, SO LITTLE ELSE.

In the late 1980s, an embryonic proconsumer political movement began to develop in Japan, nourished by an increased awareness of how much better people were living in "noncompetitive" countries. One bizarre manifestation was the "reimport" fad of 1988. A number of renegade retailers discovered that they could go to the United States, buy Japanese-made products there, bring them back to Japan, and still sell them for less than the standard Japanese price. Re-imported Japanese-made camera film cost about half as much in Japan as film that never made the 15,000-mile detour through the United States. The most extreme case involved cordless telephones: the re-imported models sold for one eighth the price of those which never left Japan. Customers snapped them up until the original manufacturer, Matsushita Electric, bought the discounter's entire supply of cut-rate phones.

In time, Japan's bias may continue shifting toward consumption. Its companies are slowly moving production overseas and eroding the Fortress Japan mentality. A group of experts known as the Maekawa Commission recommended in 1986 that the Japanese adopt a five-day work week, omitting the half day on Saturday that is standard in most businesses (and schools). By early 1988, Ministry of Labor figures showed that the average Japanese salaryman was cutting out of work a minute and a half earlier each day. Meantime, foreign governments keep exerting their pressure — toward a more open Japanese market, with less protectionism, lower prices, and a generally easier life. For the moment, however, Japan's policy and behavior remain deeply anti-consumer.

The Ultimate Importance of Effort

There are several "normal," noncultural reasons that Japan is not as biased toward consumption as the United States. One explanation, of course, is that the United States has been consuming too much; during the 1980s our standard of living rose much faster than our productivity.

Another obvious explanation is the balance of political power in Japan. Much more than in the United States, the political economy in Japan is run by special-interest groups, whose interests are protected at the consumers' expense. Although this is hard for Americans to believe, it costs more to be a politician in Japan than in the United States. (Campaign and operating expenses are high, and official allowances are very low.) Therefore, big-money contributions are very important in Japan, and there is little involvement by groups representing average citizens or consumers to counter the effect of large donations. Politicians get their biggest cash contributions from the groups that have gotten the most protection, and whose interests are most at odds with the consumers': rice farmers, the small-shopkeepers' lobby, the construction industry.

Yet another noncultural explanation for Japan's bias toward producers is that, until very recently, most Japanese had no idea how much worse off they were than they needed to be. Most Japanese born before or during the war can remember the days of rice shortage and deprivation, when people walked around in paper shoes and foraged in the country to find food. Most Japanese now above the age of forty-five attach great weight to the word *mottai-nai*. This is practically untranslatable; it is related to the idea that it is haughty, selfish, and above one's station to live too well. It has some resemblance to the Puritan saying "Use it up, wear it out, make it do, or do without." According to the concept of *mottai-nai,* it is shameful to complain about material hardship, especially when conditions are improving. Year by year since the late 1940s, life has been easier and goods more plentiful than the year before. Naturally many Japanese feel fortunate, even though their standard of living remains well below the West's.

Still, a basic cultural predisposition lies behind Japan's reluctance to consume. Almost as much as its racial harmony, the hard-life ethic that has helped pull Japan's industry ahead reflects cultural values that are not only deeply rooted but also very difficult for America to duplicate.

"The Japanese have never really caught up with Adam Smith," wrote the sociologist Ronald Dore. "They don't *believe* in the invisible hand. They believe — like all good Confucianists — that you cannot get a decent, moral society, not even an efficient society, simply out of the mechanisms of the market powered by the motivational fuel of self-interest . . . The morality has got to come from the hearts, the wills and motives, of the individuals in it."

In countless ways many East Asian cultures, but most of all Japan, show that they value the effort that goes into an activity about as much as the reward that comes out. For example, by American standards Japanese junior highs and high schools are needlessly onerous. Yes, Japan makes nearly all its people literate; yes, sheer memory work is the only way for students to master the written Japanese language. Nonetheless, the schools often seem to be harassing the students for the sake of building character. In her book about the Japanese school system, Merry White, of the Harvard School of Education, quoted this statement of purpose for Japanese public schools: "It is desirable that, in the lower grades, one should learn to bear hardship, and in the middle grades to persist to the end with patience, and in the upper grades, to be steadfast and accomplish goals undaunted by obstacles or failure." It is hard to imagine an American public school that could issue such a document. When my older son was in sixth grade in a Japanese public school, his teacher would make the class of usually squirming boys and girls sit perfectly still for five or ten minutes during "concentration" exercises every few days. The teacher would prowl between the desks with a cane in his hands, rapping the knuckles or necks of students who let their attention wander.

The standardized tests that are so famous a part of Japanese education also reflect the emphasis on duty for its own sake. The Japanese tests differ from American IQ-style tests in their con-sequences: the major companies hire strictly according to where job applicants went to college, and the colleges admit students mainly on the basis of test scores. But they also differ in their content. Few people in Japan contend that the tests are primarily measures of "ability" or "intelligence." Instead, the tests are straightforward measures of memorized information. No one seems interested in discussing whether the knowledge measured on the tests is related to skills that will later prove valuable on the job. That's not what the tests are about: they are measures of determination and effort, pure and simple, so the pointlessness of their content actually enhances their value as tests of will. The most common encouragement for students in "exam hell," cram-ming for the tests, is *Gambatte!* In context it means, Keep trying! Never give up! It reflects something deep in the Japanese scheme of values.

Even Japanese sports illustrate the importance of effort for its own sake. Japanese baseball, as described in Robert Whiting's comic masterpiece, *The Chrysanthemum and the Bat,* is a run-ning cultural war between the Japanese baseball team and the few *gaijin* (foreign) players each team is allowed to bring from America each year. The *gaijin* stars are, irritatingly, much more talented than most of the Japanese players. Typically, they are aging sluggers or second-tier journeymen who would have had trouble making the team in the American big leagues but can easily win the batting championships in Japan. The talent gap seems to inspire the Japanese to even greater efforts in an attempt to beat the *gaijin* on guts alone. Japanese coaches and sportswriters criticize the American players for being talented but lazy — like the country as a whole.

Of course there are areas in which American culture encourages pure effort. Political campaigns, athletic teams, fledgling businesses, summer theater troupes — in such groups and others, Americans can be team-spirited, self-sacrificing, proud of the effort itself and not just the payoff. But for the foreseeable future, cooperation, self-discipline, and self-denial will come much more naturally to the Japanese than to Americans. Once in Shanghai, I rounded a corner in a cavernous "Friendship Store" and saw a mass of identically dressed people heading toward me. They had the same white beanie caps, the same white I-am-on-vacation slacks, the same white shoes and turquoise socks, the same matching turquoise sweaters thrown across their shoulders. They were Japanese, members of a group sea cruise who had all bought the matching outfits the tour operators offered. It is hard to imagine any other people on earth voluntarily behaving this way.

As the Australian journalist Murray Sayle, a long-time resident of Japan, has pointed out, similar voluntary cooperative behavior lies behind Japan's export successes:

> The Japanese exporter to the United States needs only to offer a better or cheaper product, and he's honorably in. But the would-be exporter to Japan finds the marketplace already seized up solid with a dense network of "friendships," of layer upon layer of middlemen who have been doing business together for years, and who are, of course, all Japanese . . .
>
> Purged of its pejorative overtone, "conspiracy" in its literal meaning of "breathing together" is not a bad way of describing the Japanese system. The school that wants to see an American counterconspiracy has to devise ways of doing so within the American tradition, no easy task.

Since the publication, in 1979, of Ezra Vogel's *Japan as Number One,* the idea that America should be more like Japan has been a constant theme in American political and intellectual life.

American industrial planning should be more like MITI's. American schools should be more rigorous, like Japan's. American labor relations should be more consensual. American companies should treat their employees more like family and take the long, strategic view. Since the American work ethic and American management values have let us down, we should emulate those of the Japanese.

Any attempt to understand another culture is laudable, and some specific Japanese practices might work well in the United States. To respond to Japanese export-promotion or market-shielding policies, the United States may sometimes be forced to resort to similar tactics. But the underlying idea, that America should imitate Japan, is flawed. America is not like Japan and can never be. From the American perspective, some of Japan's most distinctive traits look praiseworthy and others do not. The emphasis on duty is admirable; the anticonsumer bias seems foolish (what's the point of success if it feels like failure?); and the racial-purity fetish is the ugliest thing about Japan. "Let's be like Japan!" an American diplomat who used to serve in Tokyo likes to say. "First we rig politics so that one party is always in power and big-city votes basically don't count. Then we double the cost of everything else but hold incomes the same. Then we close the borders and start celebrating racial purity. Then we reduce the number of jobs for women by 70 or 80 percent. Then we set up a school system that teaches people not to ask questions. After a while we can have a trade surplus too!"

Whether these Japanese traits are "good" or "bad" is not really the point. They are different from those elsewhere in the world, especially America. They give Japan certain advantages America cannot match. For Japan, they are the right traits. They allow the voluntary efforts of ordinary people to serve the whole nation's needs. But for America, they are wrong.

Can the United States ever harness individual efforts as fruitfully as Japan has? Yes, if it understands the traits that make it unique.

CHAPTER THREE

The American Talent for Disorder

AMERICA'S CULTURE is America's greatest potential strength. Something about American values has enabled ordinary people, assembled haphazardly from around the world, to build the largest, richest, and freest economy in history, and to do so mainly through voluntary actions rather than state direction. The essence of our approach, the true American genius, is a talent for *dis*order.

Japan gets the most out of ordinary people by *organizing* them to adapt and succeed. America, by getting out of their way so that they can adjust individually, *allows* them to succeed. It is not that Japan has no individualists and America no organizations, but the thrusts of the two societies are different. Japan has distorted its economy and depressed its living standard in order to keep its job structure and social values as steady as possible. At the government's direction, the entire economy has tried to flex almost as one, in response to the ever-changing world. The country often seems like a family that becomes more tightly bound together when it must withstand war, emigration, or some other upheaval.

America's strength is the opposite: it opens its doors and brings the world's disorder in. It tolerates social change that would tear most other societies apart. This openness encourages Americans to adapt as individuals rather than as a group.

Few other societies could endure the unsettled conditions that have always typified America. Modern Japan would be shattered by the threat of substantial immigration. Few other Western societies have seen women's roles change as dramatically as in the United States. Western European countries generally have trouble finding new jobs for displaced workers or attracting them to new places when the jobs shift. In 1980, one American family out of thirty moved to a different state. Only one of about ninety families in England and one of eighty in West Germany made similar moves.

America not only can tolerate these disruptions, it needs them. Ceaseless internal change is good for America. It causes America to bring out the best voluntary efforts of its ordinary people by offering them the constant prospect of changing their fortunes, their identities, their roles in life. Americans are most likely to try hard, adapt, and succeed when they believe that they can improve their luck, that the rules of competition are more or less fair, and that if they take a risk and fail, they won't be totally destroyed. Although these conditions have never been entirely met — the competition has never been completely fair; some people have been permanently stuck; many have been ruined when they took a chance — they have been closer to realization in the United States than anywhere else. They are America's counterparts to Japan's sense of duty and racial solidarity in that they give ordinary people a reason to make their best efforts voluntarily. America's radius of trust is expanded not by racial unity but by the belief that everyone is playing by the same set of rules. Indeed, in a country cobbled together from so many races and religions, the belief in playing by similar rules is the source of such "community" as we can have.

America's talent for disorder allows it to get surprising results from average people by putting them in situations where old rules and limits don't apply. That's the meaning of immigration, of the frontier, of leaving the farm for the big city, of going to college or night school to make a new start. No other society has managed disorder so well in the past; none of our competitors needs to keep promoting disorder, by endlessly rotating establishments, as much as we do.

To put the point yet another way, Japan is strong because each person knows his place.* America is strong when people do *not* know their proper places and are free to invent new roles for themselves. Therefore, if Americans lose their sense of possibility and instead believe that they belong in predictable, limited roles, the United States will have lost what makes it special. It will have a harder time prevailing in economic and military competition, and it will no longer offer the freedom to start over that people have always come to America to find.

Talk about "adaptability" and "knowing your place" may sound like so much theorizing, especially to Americans who have not lived overseas and therefore cannot *feel* how odd their society is. Coping with our purely economic problems, such as budget and trade deficits, will involve very specific, practical steps — investment incentives, research projects, changes in tax law, and the like. But ideals and abstractions can have as much impact as these technical adjustments. The tens of thousands of airplanes that American factories turned out during World War II helped beat Hitler, but so did the ideals of freedom and democracy. "Nationalism" and "anticolonialism" were potent weapons against the United States during the Vietnam War. If America is to remain a success in the broadest sense, giving its people the greatest opportunity to realize their ambitions and satisfy their needs, it must make the most of its basic cultural strengths — adaptability, mobility, disorder.

* Sticking to your place, which the Japanese endorse, is different from sticking to your narrowly defined duties, which they deplore. Although large Japanese corporations assume that most employees will be with them through their careers, during the career each person may be shuffled around from specialty to specialty. On the assembly line, Japanese workers are supposed to pitch in and handle whatever job most needs doing. Japanese industrialists vigorously denounce the not-my-job attitude of American industries and unions; they say it makes American workers unwilling to deal with anything that is not in their narrow job description.

THE CULTURE OF CONSTANT CHANGE

For better and for worse, this has always been a changeable, self-defining, let's-start-over culture, in which people with talent, energy, or luck believed they could invent their own lives. Not everybody has wanted to start over or invent a new role; the Amish, for example, seem content as they are. Many American blacks, descendants of the country's only involuntary immigrants, for years were not allowed to get a new start. Still, if antitraditionalism is only part of American culture, it is a very important part, which clearly distinguishes America from most other countries and has been responsible for much of our economic and political strength. On the whole, America's history is not the story of Amish-style traditionalism. It is the story'of people who try to bend tradition to suit their immediate needs. The various forms of American mobility — social, occupational, geographic — have been connected with and have reinforced one another.

Geographic Movement

In the early 1970s, Vance Packard wrote a book, called *A Nation of Strangers,* about the many ways in which America injured itself because people moved so often. They didn't get to know their neighbors; they didn't have a stake in their towns; they couldn't sink any roots. Mona Simpson made the same point far more lyrically in her recent novel *Anywhere But Here.* One character in the novel was a hopeless dreamer who could never face reality or see things through to the end. While the rest of the family remained rooted in the Midwest, it was she who moved to California and kept switching houses, jobs, friends, and lives.

No doubt America pays a higher price for constant movement than, say, France or China does. But this has always been the case — Americans have moved, both socially and geographically, much more easily than other people — and it's not all bad.

"Historically, as new lands, new forms of wealth, new opportunities, came into play, clamoring to be seized upon, America developed something of a compulsion to make use of them," the historian David Potter wrote in his study of the American character, *People of Plenty*. "The man best qualified for this role was the completely mobile man, moving freely from one locality to the next, from one economic position to another, or from one social level to levels above."

Another historian, James Oliver Robertson, wrote about America in its brave, big-shouldered nineteenth-century days. "The first requirement of individualism was the 'wish to change your lot.' The American was not fixed in his or her lot by class, location, or inheritance, or by family, education, or even, necessarily, by ability. The pursuit of happiness required a change of lot, and those who did not change theirs were objects of pity or, more commonly, of contempt."

Almost every chapter of American history is a saga of people moving from place to place geographically and from level to level socially. The flow of immigrants from overseas is only the most obvious illustration. The other great theme in this saga is the continuing migration from the American farm. Before the Civil War, three times as many people worked on the farm as in the city. Fifty years later, twice as many people worked in cities as on farms. After World War II there was another huge exodus. At the beginning of the 1940s, farmers made up one fourth of the work force; at the beginning of the 1980s, only about one fortieth. During the 1970s and early 1980s, Texas surged to become the third most populous state, overtaking Pennsylvania and Illinois. But even during those decades of very rapid growth, most counties in the state lost rather than gained population as people moved to cities from farms.

Creative Destruction and Unpredictable Change

In most cases, people moved because business was changing. They could no longer make a living where they were, or they were drawn by the hope of better opportunities somewhere else.

Behind this continual motion lies the hard truth about capitalism that is summed up in Joseph Schumpeter's famous phrase "creative destruction." "Capitalism" usually calls up images of big machines or powerful financiers or perhaps of class war, but what capitalism really means is change. Its essence is that nothing stands still. In the thousand years before the beginnings of

eighteenth-century capitalism, Europe was feudal and its economy relatively static, built around guilds and traditional occupations. Industries remained concentrated in certain regions; jobs
were passed down from father to son. Suddenly, with the coming
of industrial capitalism, predictability vanished. Businesses
started and then failed; products were invented, grew popular,
became obsolete; people trained for one career at the age of
eighteen and ended up doing something else at forty-five.

In the long run, all these shifts, changes, and adjustments bring
more wealth, more jobs, and more leisure to more people. That,
at least, has been the record of industrial capitalism until now,
especially in America. For each blacksmith shed that disappears,
some auto body repair shop opens up. The process is not, of
course, that neat or symmetrical, but over time it works. Max
Geldens, of the management consulting firm McKinsey and Company, has pointed out that in the three centuries since the beginning of the Industrial Revolution, two thirds of the jobs existing
at the beginning of each century have been "destroyed" during
that century — but three times as many people have been at
work by the century's end. Despite all its problems of competitiveness and debt, the United States in the late 1980s employed a
higher proportion of its population than ever before. (The official
unemployment rate is higher than in the mid 1960s, but the work
force itself represents a larger share of the population, mainly
because more women are included.)

These long-term benefits are what Schumpeter meant by "creative," but there is a reason for his saying "destruction" too.
Capitalist change is the enemy of order and tradition not simply
because it never stops but also because its direction is impossible
to predict. Governments and businesses can sometimes make
sensible guesses about the very next round of technical change.
By subsidizing canals, railroads, and eventually highways, the
U.S. government helped expand the country's industrial base.
Federal agricultural experiment stations have been almost as important as the blessings of geography in making the United States
a farming colossus. By steering young people toward "growth"
occupations, schools and government can reduce the numbers
who must change course later on.

But most of the time, the trends we can't predict are more

important than the ones we can. Everyone knows that computers are a huge business, but in the 1950s IBM didn't know; it estimated that the potential worldwide market for computers would be fewer than ten machines. At about the same time, the Xerox Corporation made about the same prediction for copiers. Decades earlier, engineering experts all agreed that radios would mainly be backups for the telegraph system when the wires were down. At the turn of the century, respectable opinion held that the American forests were about to disappear. THE END OF LUMBER SUPPLY, the *New York Times* warned in a headline in 1900. HICKORY DISAPPEARING, SUPPLY OF WOOD NEARS END — MUCH WASTED AND THERE'S NO SUBSTITUTE, another *Times* headline said a few years later. By the 1980s, more of the United States was forested than had been a hundred years earlier. The experts hadn't foreseen that people would heat their homes with natural gas rather than wood fires, that the railroads (which used huge numbers of logs for ties) were about to be replaced by cars and airplanes as the nation's main transportation system, or that plastics would be invented and could substitute for wood. Magazines like *Popular Science* and *Popular Mechanics* predicted in the 1940s and 1950s that by the 1970s Americans would be commuting in their own helicopters and driving automatically piloted cars. They did not predict that computers would be commonplace in American homes, or that people would watch movies and TV shows when they wanted, on their VCRs.*

In the 1960s, many American experts warned that the latest form of capitalist disruption, the "automation crisis," was about to put most Americans out of work. Productivity had gone up so fast that American industries were already making everything

---

* In 1980, Charles Schultze, who was then chairman of President Carter's Council of Economic Advisers, pulled together a list of the products and industries that had grown fastest during the preceding decade. Of the twenty leading items, perhaps five might have seemed "predictable" in retrospect: various forms of plastics, oil- and gas-drilling equipment, semiconductors, small cars. But what about "utility vehicles," number two on the list? Vacuum cleaners, 9? Construction glass, 13? Cheese, and tufted carpet, 18 and 19, respectively? "And where have you had the highest productivity increase in the past generation?" Schultze asked when I spoke with him at the time. "Poultry and turkey rearing. Who was going to pick that as a big 'winner'?"

that people could want, as Karl Marx had predicted long before. Because of automation, industries were turning out more goods with fewer employees. One professor told a congressional committee in 1963 that 99.5 percent of the American homes with electricity already had refrigerators, 93 percent had televisions, and 83 percent had washing machines. There was very little more they could be expected to buy. "The only sharply rising sales curve in the consumer-durables field today is that of the electric-can-opener industry," he said. Another expert told the congressional committee that automation was eliminating forty thousand jobs a week, or a million a year. At this rate, every job in America would disappear by 1999.

Obviously it didn't happen that way. American manufacturing employment is higher in the 1980s than it was in the 1960s, despite all the labor-saving machines that have been installed and all the difficulties U.S. manufacturers have had. Naturally, the industries where employment has fallen fastest are those which automated least, since they lost ground faster to more efficient competitors in Europe and Asia. In its predictably unpredictable way, capitalist innovation created other desires to satisfy, other needs to fill.

In her book *Cities and the Wealth of Nations,* Jane Jacobs explained why unpredictability and disruption were built into capitalist life:

> In its very nature, successful economic development has to be open-ended rather than goal-oriented, and has to make itself up expediently and empirically as it goes along. For one thing, unforeseeable problems arise. The people who developed agriculture couldn't foresee soil depletion. The people who developed the automobile couldn't foresee acid rain. . . . Scientists are used to the fact that discoveries are often the unanticipated by-products of other intentions. It is the same in economic drift. The first oil wells were drilled to get lamp fuel only a few decades before electricity was to begin making oil lamps obsolete . . . Edison, an inventor of the phonograph, thought the chief use of the device would be for business dictation . . .
>
> Economic development [is] a process of continually improvising in a context that makes injecting improvisations into everyday life feasible.

Although Jacobs was not writing a business-strategy book, her point was similar to what the most prominent business books of the 1980s have emphasized: that merely surviving in economic competition means unending, unpredictable adjustments. As soon as any product enters routinized mass production — cars, radios, chips — manufacturers in lower-wage countries can underbid producers in the United States. Jacobs's point is also very similar to the reasoning of classic military strategists. As Count von Moltke put it, a plan is valid only until the opponent makes his first move.

Adaptable People

With its turbulence and unpredictability, capitalist growth represents a frontal assault on some other basic human desires. A society that is developing new businesses, products, and skills cannot be stable. By definition, children end up with different jobs, often in different places, from their parents. Traditional skills and means of livelihood are destroyed — blacksmiths, chandlers, Studebaker automobile workers.

Every society strikes its own balance between these forces: more economic growth and more social chaos (New York, Hong Kong); less rapid growth but less change in values (today's Burma or Nepal). "An increasingly productive economy should be recognized as necessitating simultaneous painful growth and shrinkage, disinvestment and reinvestment," wrote Donald Hicks, an economist at the University of Texas. "Empty plants, shops, mills and factories were as much signs of a healthy process of shedding outmoded physical arrangements as they were signs of economic stagnation." Japan will have found a way out of this dilemma if it can keep developing rapidly while holding many of its old values intact. But for a society to do this, it would have to be like Japan's to begin with.

The crucial fact about America is that it has consistently set the balance in favor of economic adaptability, not tradition and order. Even when America has been most successful — growing rapidly, raising its standards of education and opportunity, becoming fairer and more tolerant — many Americans have failed. In a book about factory shutdowns and America's "deindustrialization" in the 1980s, two scholars quoted a study about the social cost incurred when American manufacturers could no longer compete: "Perhaps the most serious impact of shutdowns, particularly for many of the long-term unemployed, was a loss of confidence . . . The unemployed worker loses his daily association with his fellow workers . . . When he is severed from his job, he discovers that he has lost, in addition to the income and activity, his institutional base in the economic and social system."

This would seem an apt description of the trauma felt throughout the American Midwest in the 1980s. But in fact the study was published in 1963, when American manufacturers dominated world markets and the economy was by any measure a success. That is, even at its best and most creative, capitalism will be destructive. The question is how much disruption a society can absorb — and America's tolerance has been very high.

Long before the Civil War, industrialization was forcing Americans to invent new roles and lives for themselves. Young men and women from the farm flocked to the New England mill towns in the early nineteenth century to take advantage of opportunities there and escape the narrowing prospects on the farm. Clyde Griffen, of Vassar College, has offered a case study of how this nineteenth-century social churning affected one of the moderate-sized industrial cities, Poughkeepsie, New York. Poughkeepsie was a center of cooperage — barrel making — for the brewing industry, a business that boomed in the decade before the Civil War. There were four times as many coopers in 1860 as in 1850. New firms sprang up; coopers felt entrepreneurial urges and went into business for themselves; wage rates soared. Then, after the war, people stopped drinking so much beer and needing so many barrels. Wages fell, and by 1875 the coopers were making only about as much as common day laborers. At that point, according to Griffen, most of the younger coopers moved somewhere else. They were not like European or Asian craftsmen, determined to spend generations perfecting their craft in the same village. They were like Americans, changing their idea of themselves to fit the market. The same was true of the local cabinetmakers, whose market was destroyed by the advent of mass production. Those young enough to leave, left. Likewise, the shoemakers watched shoe factories open up in nearby towns and finally right in Poughkeepsie. Many young shoemakers moved away; the older workers who stayed, Griffen said, preferred the risks they knew to the unknown.

With allowances for regional idiosyncracies, the Poughkeepsie story was the American story in the nineteenth century. Cities rose and fell; people moved off the farm; new technologies bloomed and faded. The whole economy adapted and individual Americans radically altered their lives, and each of these changes seemed to speed the other. "For two centuries, different groups of skilled artisans have faced technological changes that made their skills less valuable than they had been, though the changes were part of the country's overall development," Stephan Thernstrom of Harvard's history department has said. "Their choices were to remain and make half the wages that they used to, or to move to some smaller place away from the mainstream where their skills might be more valuable." Donald Hicks told me, "The movement of people off the farm through the last century had a greater social impact than any industrial dislocation that may be going on in the 1980s. Henry Ford had a tremendous impact. So did the decline of the textile factories."

Even the industrial Midwest rode to greatness on the crest of migration, technical change, sudden regional shifts in competitiveness. Most descriptions of nineteenth-century Chicago make today's Los Angeles or Miami look like tame, polite places. Nearly fifty years ago, the economist Glenn E. McLaughlin wrote a book called *Growth of American Manufacturing Areas,* which focused on the astonishing increase in American manufacturing power between 1899 and 1929, when America was (as we would now think of it) the Japan of the world. The book described the thirty-three most important industrial areas — fast-growing, prosperous, unsettled places where migrants were pouring in and social values were in flux. All but three (Los Angeles, San Francisco, Seattle) were in the Northeast and upper Midwest. Toledo, Scranton, Dayton, St. Louis, Youngstown, and of course Chicago and Detroit — these were the upstart areas of America that offered migrants from Poland and Georgia opportunities they couldn't find at home. Not even Houston in the 1970s grew as fast as Cleveland and Detroit did after the turn of the century. In 1930, Detroit's population was five times larger than it had been in 1900. In 1930, Akron's population was nine times larger than it had been in 1870. It was very hard on people in Youngstown and Detroit in the 1980s when imports surged in and people moved out. But these cities themselves had been built a century earlier by people moving from somewhere else.

American migration actually slowed down during the Great Depression. This is contrary to the familiar image of the Joad family from *The Grapes of Wrath,* but demographers say that people usually move more rapidly toward opportunities, which obviously were scarce, than away from hardships. During the Depression, the federal government offered a little-known but successful program, named the Transient Bureau, to help people move to places where more jobs were available. California seemed to have the most opportunities, so it attracted many of those who did decide to migrate. By 1940 a scholar reported that "a recent study in California indicates that over a period of time the large migration to that state has raised the general standard of living."

After World War II, American migration neared a new peak. During the following twenty years, now seen as the golden age of automatic prosperity and almost boring social order, unprecedented numbers of people moved back and forth across the country. Mostly, they were glad they did. A scholar named George Myers studied the way industrial workers moved into and out of Racine, Wisconsin, during the placid 1950s and compared their attitude with that of English workers who had to move after their plant was relocated:

> An overwhelming view that emerges from these two studies is that migrants, either voluntary, as in the case of the United States migrants, or involuntary, as in the case of the English workers, tend to make reasonable adjustments to their new situations and generally seem to be satisfied with the moves . . . In spite of the many problems produced by large-scale population shifts, labor movement remains, on balance, a dynamic force for human betterment and economic prosperity.

To sum up, America has developed much more rapidly than other societies because it has been willing to endure extreme disruption. It has endured disruption, in turn, because individual Americans have been so quick to adjust.

Social Looseness

When Vance Packard warned that constant movement could warp a society, he was talking about something real. The great postwar migrations — to the suburbs, to California and the rest of what became the Sun Belt, to the northern cities as blacks left the South — had damaging side effects. The old cities were hollowed out. Middle-class people abandoned the urban public schools. "Most new housing was built in suburban areas that nonwhites were barred from, kept out by low incomes, racial prejudice, or — usually — both," William O'Neill wrote in his history of the 1950s, *American High*. "Blacks migrating north by the millions were forced into deteriorated central cities abandoned by the new suburbanites . . . What to do about 'white flight' from the cities, urban decay, and inner city poverty were questions not answered then or later."

Still, people were moving voluntarily, because they saw an advantage in doing so. Both the fact of constant movement and the idea that it is possible have made American society looser, less hierarchical, and less class-bound than others. The ideal of movement has changed the reality of the culture.

American culture has always been famous for its self-made, and continually self-making, quality. Our literature, from the Leatherstocking tales and *Moby-Dick* to *The Gilded Age* and *The Great Gatsby* and *Catch-22*, is full of stories about ad hoc societies in which people feel free to invent new rules, backgrounds, and identities for themselves. The masters of American literature also include Edith Wharton, Henry James, John P. Marquand, John O'Hara, but they are notable because their loving studies of dense social networks are the minor theme. Most of our national myths are about the people who won't listen to others and end up doing what supposedly can't be done. Benjamin Franklin moves to Philadelphia and succeeds; Abraham Lincoln is elected after countless defeats; the American colonies throw off the British. Chuck Yeager bent the army's admission rules to get his chance to fly; Lee Iacocca made Chrysler profitable — for a while. In a *sumo* training camp (so aptly known as a "stable"), I once listened to a former grand champion instruct new wrestlers on the rituals that had been observed for five hundred years. The point was that the new wrestlers should behave just the way their predecessors had. American sporting traditions don't last even a generation: imagine Don Budge giving a similar speech to John McEnroe. The adage "A rolling stone gathers no moss" is taken by the British to be a warning: a British dictionary interprets it, "One who constantly changes his place of employment will not grow rich." To the Japanese its meaning is equally clear: a Japanese specialist in English wrote, "This is obviously a proverb warning against lack of perseverance." But he had to go on to advise his readers that Americans read the proverb differently: " 'If you keep on moving and being active, you will not get rusty' . . . Social mobility has a positive value there. Americans even say that mobility proves ability." It is easy to imagine Japanese puzzlement over the American neologism "tree hugger," meant to disparage someone who stays with one company too long.

Outside observers from more settled societies — most European visitors except Tocqueville; domestic travelers from Boston or Philadelphia who've been touring the frontier — have usually been alarmed by the self-made and mobile aspect of American society. The two most famous English visitors of the nineteenth century, Charles Dickens and Fanny Trollope, both regarded frontier America with distaste. It had no refinement, no manners, no sense of style. Until the arrival of Aleksandr Solzhenitsyn, Mrs. Trollope was the foreign visitor most annoyed by American indiscipline. She observed in the late 1820s that "the 'simple' manner of living in Western America [Ohio] was more distasteful to me from its levelling effects on the manners of the people, than from the personal privations that it rendered necessary . . . I very seldom, during my whole stay in the country, heard a sentence elegantly turned and correctly pronounced from the lips of an American . . . Captain Hall, when asked what appeared to him to constitute the greatest difference between England and

America, replied, like a gallant sailor: 'The want of loyalty.' Were the same question put to me, I should answer: 'The want of refinement.' "

That is, she hated America for what was best in it, the instability of people's social roles. For a culture to be "refined," as she and others would have preferred, its members must have settled ideas of who they are and where they belong. Societies that give people the greatest chance to start over and change their luck cannot, by definition, be as mannered as London or Imperial Peking. (" 'Now you take Washington,' he said. 'It's old. People in old places get picky. They run out of energy so they make do with taste, which is not as good a thing.' " This is Larry Mc-Murtry in *Cadillac Jack*.) The fastest-growing parts of America — which is to say, the ones that offer the greatest number of people a new chance — have always been the most vulgar and unrefined. The "good" old families of New York sneered at upstart immigrants like John Jacob Astor, who had made piles of money but lacked breeding and taste. Now the Astors are New York's First Family, but New York is still a mecca for unrefined newcomers (Donald Trump) looking for the big score. So are Los Angeles, Miami, Denver, and a score of other fast-growing, fast-changing cities.

Houston, America's forlorn victim during the oil bust, kept itself going for a while in the early 1980s on sheer adaptability. After 100,000 jobs disappeared in 1983, the city's unemployment rate quickly recovered; a sudden surge in self-employment took up the slack. "Houston was always the kind of place where you could walk in with a good business plan and walk out with $50,000," Lance Tarrance, a Republican pollster, once told me. "In Dallas, where I grew up, they wanted to know about your mother and father and probably your blood type. In Dallas there are five country clubs and you sign up when you're born. In Houston they just create new ones."

During Houston's boom, Gregory Curtis, of *Texas Monthly*, recounted a one-sided conversation he'd held with the English poet Stephen Spender, who was spending a term teaching at Rice, in Houston. Spender was taken aback by the rawness and incivility of Houston, as well as by its total lack of tradition. As

Curtis recalled the encounter, it perfectly illustrated the contrast between American and European cultures:

> I launched into a fairly standard [that is, classically American] defense of Houston. It was a city of constant change. A building that held a filling station one day could hold a flower shop the following day and restaurant the next. Thus Houston was being created and re-created before your eyes. Houston had hustle and vigor and grit. Houston welcomed everyone into its great chaos . . . It was exciting to see what happens when people live in a place where few of the old rules apply, the bonds are let loose, and life is lived with the accelerator to the floor.
>
> I let myself get carried away, so it wasn't until I neared the end of my speech that I looked up at his face, only to see quite clearly that there was no hope of carrying the day. Everything that I said was good about Houston was exactly what he thought was bad.

By Stephen Spender's standards, apparently, a disorderly, mobile society was a failure, not a success. Many other cultures are built on the same view: that the social costs of complete fluidity outweigh the economic benefits. Even though the expatriate Overseas Chinese are pure agents of "creative destruction," China itself has usually been tightly controlled. Before the communists came, one dynasty after another tried to freeze China as an agricultural aristocracy or oligarchy, with a scholarly, nonmercantile upper class and millions of serfs. (China's rulers have been similar in this way to the upper class of the antebellum American South, which knew that capitalism would destroy its aristocratic pretensions and its plantation system.) Even the quasi-capitalist reforms of the last decade are subject to constant reappraisal, since the Chinese understand that as people become freer to start businesses and choose jobs, it becomes harder for the ruling group to maintain central control. Western Europe and Japan also resist, in different ways, real, unbridled capitalist change.

America has fought the same inner battle, because even here creative destruction is an ordeal. In 1932, many of the most prominent Southern writers and intellectuals issued their manifesto, "I'll Take My Stand," warning that the traditions and culture of the old South were being sacrificed to the counting-house mentality. Many Americans have dreamed of making the country more like Florence or Vienna, or some other haven of good taste, and less like Albuquerque or Anchorage. (Indeed, the rise of the "foodies" in the 1980s reflects a lamentable desire to make America into Europe; sun-dried tomatoes are available at every corner grocery, and there is a general preoccupation with food.) Americans acquire the patina of old money by pretending that they are Englishmen. William F. Buckley, Jr., has basically the same lineage as, say, Lyndon Johnson. Johnson was descended from rural Texas politicians, and so is Buckley, whose grandfather was a sheriff in South Texas. But instead of wearing a cowboy hat and leisure suit, like Johnson, Buckley made himself sound as if he were a tenth-generation Old Etonian. In a sense, he is the classic American, since he has completely invented a new identity for himself. "Americans typically want nothing so much as to make themselves *new,* an appropriate yearning in this New World," Nelson Aldrich, Jr., wrote in his book *Old Money.* "Old Money Americans want to make themselves new in the most radical way a New World can imagine, by making themselves Old."

But in America, unlike Europe and China and Japan, the forces of disorder have usually won. When I was at graduate school in England, my English classmates talked about the jobs they would "get" with banks and firms and the civil service. Soon afterward, when I was living in Texas, my friends talked about the jobs they would make for themselves. That difference — creating slots rather than merely filling them — is the mark of America at its most adaptable ideal.

Not Knowing Our Place

The historian John Baskin wrote about New Burlington, one of Ohio's fast-growing nineteenth-century industrial towns. As with so many of these towns, the boom ended and people moved away. Baskin said that the young people who stayed in town when others were leaving were viewed by the town's old-timers as upstanding young men. "Fine boys," one old woman said about them. "But *dull* boys. They were frightened to go out." As long as they stayed in their home town, she said, they knew

exactly where they fit in society, since "everyone had a place."
But "outside, there was no place."

Baskin was talking about the peculiarly American virtue of not
knowing your place. David McClelland, the psychologist from
Harvard, argued that precisely this trait was a key to American
vitality. In his famous book *The Achieving Society,* published in
1961, McClelland said that cultures became more successful
when they had a lot of the factor to which he gave the jargonlike
name "*n* Achievement." The *n* Achievement amounted to a refusal to know your place. People who had this quality believed
that they were in control of their lives — rather than being controlled by their parents, society, or fate. McClelland analyzed
children's stories, popular myths, and other ingredients of folk-
lore to see what values and goals different cultures passed to
their children. He concluded that when cultures did transmit the
appropriate message — that anyone could succeed — on the
whole people did find new possibilities, certainly more than they
found in cultures where religions and popular lore taught people
that their lives were controlled by fate. If a man born a peasant
believes that, no matter what, he will die a peasant, he may be
shrewd and crafty in his peasant ways but he probably won't be
truly inventive. He will not imagine that his work or his familiar
equipment, if used differently or applied to different products,
might propel him out of the peasantry. A society with a large
amount of *n* Achievement, McClelland said, was one whose people routinely overestimated their chances for success. They
launched ventures that by rational standards were likely to fail.

Overoptimism is in fact the common theme in many of the most
purely American phenomena: the myth that anybody can grow
up to be president, that immigrants' children can be doctors and
lawyers, that you can turn your franchise into a fortune, that
salesmen can make it on a smile and handshake. McClelland said
that the "famous self-confidence" of businessmen — really,
their refusal to face discouraging facts — was an important tool
for economic development. One of the best examples was the
completion of America's transcontinental railroads in the nineteenth century. "When they were built they could hardly be justified in economic terms," McClelland said. "They would never

have been economically justified if the country had not been 'swarming' . . . with thousands of small entrepreneurs who repeatedly overestimated their chances of success, but who collectively managed to settle and develop the West while many of them individually were failing."

People could feel this useful overconfidence, McClelland said, only if they thought that society was open and their lives were changeable. He wrote, "What a modern society needs for successful development is flexibility in a man's role relationships. His entire network of relations to others should not be traditionally determined by his caste or even by his occupational status." That is, he should not know his place.

Societies are healthiest when their radius of trust is broad and when people feel they can influence their own fate. America meets these conditions when it encourages and allows Americans to start over and invent new lives. I know, because this is my family's story.

CHAPTER FOUR

The Golden Dream

IN THE SUMMER of 1955, my father took the Greyhound bus from the East Coast to Michigan to buy a new car. He went to the main Ford factory, in Dearborn, and put down $1800 in cash. He chose a cream-colored Mercury station wagon, with wood-look side panels and a streamlined modern shape. Then he drove nonstop back to Philadelphia, where we were waiting for him.

I was five years old that summer, impatient to turn six. There were reports that a polio vaccine was almost ready, about to be released, available any week now. But it hadn't come out, and my mother was always sticking my arms into sweaters on summer evenings, bundling me and my sister and brother in towels the instant we stepped out of our wading pool, waiting and praying for the polio season to be over.

I remember waiting too, wishing that my baby brother would grow up, hoping that my three-year-old sister would stop tagging after me all day. I was sitting on the porch steps of my grandmother's house, kicking my feet back and forth, listening to my mother and grandmother reassure each other about the fever I'd just had — "I'm sure it's nothing" — when my father appeared, in the car, at the end of the street. The new car was barely visible through the thick summer foliage of the trees, but as it came into view it looked impossibly glamorous. When he drove to the curb I ran out to greet him, he lifted me into the air and swung me back down again, and my sister and I hung on to his hands as we walked into the house. My father had just turned thirty, my mother was twenty-seven, and they were about to take their three small children off to start a new life.

By now I recognize that the essentials of our story look like clichés. Upward mobility, a family that had suffered reverses during the Depression, the postwar trek west. That they are clichés is the point: my family's story directly fits the classic pattern of American mobility.

After we'd settled in California, my mother always acted as if she'd come from some sort of dignified eastern background, but she'd had a very hard life as a child. Her father, Joseph Mackenzie, owned and managed a small ceramics work in New Jersey, not far from the sign that still says TRENTON MAKES, THE WORLD TAKES. One of her uncles ran a small steel plant producing its exclusive Mackenite Metal. One of her maiden aunts was a schoolteacher who had been to France in the 1920s, had a grand piano in her apartment, became a naïve fellow traveler of the Communist Party, and always tried to set an example of the high-toned life. My mother's father had graduated from Brown and was a dashing, handsome figure. But he was killed in a car crash in 1930, when he was twenty-nine and my mother was three. The family business suffered, and my mother was farmed out to relatives and shuffled from house to house while she grew up. Her mother went through two unhappy marriages and fed the family during the Depression by selling the *Volume Library* encyclopedia door to door. It took a hard-nosed character to talk families into laying out money for encyclopedias during the 1930s. My grandmother thrived in the work and retained her toughness long after the Depression ended. All the children in the family eventually went to college. My mother did well on a competitive examination and won a scholarship to Jackson College, the women's affiliate of Tufts. Both of her brothers finished graduate school; one became a veterinarian and the other a successful businessman.

My father's relatives had fewer pretensions but weathered the Depression better. The English branch of the family had come from Lancashire to Pennsylvania some time in the nineteenth century, and the German branch — my father's mother and her family — had come over just before World War I. All the relatives lived in the staid suburbs north and west of Philadelphia: Jenkintown, Wyncote, Abington, Willow Grove. My father's paternal grandfather, Josiah Fallows, was a railroad engineer; he stayed aboard a locomotive that had been mistracked onto a collision course with a passenger train. He directed the locomotive off the tracks and saved the passengers' lives, but he was killed. Josiah Fallows was the family hero. I grew up seeing his picture, which looked like a twin of my father's with a nineteenth-century handlebar mustache added on, in a big, old-fashioned oval frame hanging in my father's study at home. "My grandmother could ride free on the trains after that, but she still didn't think it was worth it," my father would tell us — waiting a minute before tousling our hair to show it was a joke. His other grandfather, whose last name was Hoerr, had opened a restaurant after arriving from Germany. During the First World War, his daughter — my father's mother — was heckled about her German name and her father's presumed Hun loyalties. That bothered her deeply; through the rest of her life she tried hard to set an example of upright, community-minded behavior. In the last conversations I had with her, when she was nearly ninety, I had to lie and reassure her that, yes, my wife and I were now raising our children according to all the rock-ribbed, fundamentalist values she believed in. She had absorbed many blows by then — I'd married a lapsed Catholic and neglected to baptize my children; both my sisters had divorced — but she let herself be consoled at the end.

She married my grandfather when he returned from tank corps service in France. He went to work for the Atlantic Refining Company, the predecessor of today's ARCO, where he became a sales representative, and they and their two grade school sons made it through the Depression more or less undisturbed.

Most of my parents' friends from childhood seemed happy with life in Pennsylvania, or at least didn't plan to abandon it. On a visit to my grandmother in the 1970s, I saw an item in the paper saying that Pennsylvania led all other states in the percentage of its current population who'd been born in the state. That is, not many people left, and even fewer moved in. That was certainly the way my parents' home town looked to me. Most of their school friends seemed to be still in the vicinity; so were the children, and so were nearly all of my relatives.

My parents were sprung loose by the aftereffects of World War II. My father's older brother left college to serve in the army engineers during the Battle of the Bulge and then came home to graduate. My father was in high school until 1943 and then went into the navy's V-12 program. Through V-12, the navy offered him a two-year crash course in college-level sciences in return for years of service afterward as a military doctor. He went to Ursinus College in Pennsylvania, usually noticed by the outside world only during the college football season, when the Ursinus–Slippery Rock score was a dependable joke item. The navy sent him to Harvard Medical School when the war ended, after which his father supported him for three and a half years. He rejoined the V-12 when the Korean War started and was sent on six-month or one-year postings to Maryland, Mississippi, California, and finally back to Pennsylvania, where he was mustered out of the service. He and my mother had been married while he was in medical school, with half a dozen years of navy duty still ahead of him. I was born a year later, one month before my mother turned twenty-two. By the time my mother was twenty-five, she had three children.

Because my father doesn't like speculative conversation I've never asked him about it directly, but I have always believed that the trip we made in 1955, across the country to our new home in California, was the crucial event in his life. Becoming a doctor, which the war made possible, eventually gave him more financial freedom than anyone else in his family had. But the simple change of scene, which took him away from his roots, seemed to provide a more important, more sweeping kind of freedom.

Southern Californians spend a lot of time congratulating themselves on the good weather. From September through May each year the local TV news usually shows film clips of blizzards in Chicago or floods in Tennessee to remind the viewers how lucky they are to look forward to another sunny day, high in the 80s. During the two-week buildup to each year's Rose Bowl game,

California's weather *Schadenfreude* gets entirely out of control. The visiting Big Ten team is always from some ice-bound Siberia of the Midwest, so the *Los Angeles Times* runs feature after feature about the Ohio farm boys or Detroit urban toughs who are amazed by being able to sit outside in shorts on Christmas Day. My wife grew up in Minneapolis and outside Cleveland. The first time she came to visit my parents, I just had to take her to the beach on New Year's Day.

I'm sure this attitude seems childish to outsiders, and it is; but it also reflects something deep in the culture that is not so absurd. When you live without a winter, you give up the timeless rhythm of the seasons and similar qualities that Easterners think they value, but you gain freedom. You don't have to put up the storm windows, or get out the heavy clothes, or dig out from the fall leaves, or put away your basketball and tennis racquet — or stop doing what you want — just because the seasons have changed. You are freer simply because decisions that were previously nature's to make are now yours. Because I could barely remember what a winter with snow was like, I never felt the difference as passionately as my father did, at least not before I went east to college myself. But I remember how cheerful he was when he headed out to ride his bicycle or play tennis or drive his showy white Ford convertible, with the top down, in January. He would chuckle about how much he enjoyed it, how lucky he was, how sorry he felt that he'd had to spend so many winters in the cold. It was a fantasy life, an evasion of reality, but in a healthy, invigorating way. My father, like many other people who'd come to California, felt that he had more months of each year, and therefore more years in his life, to use as he chose.

New arrivals like my father paid such attention to the weather because it stood for many other kinds of freedom they felt they'd found in California. People who were born and raised there didn't go on and on about the climate; they took it for granted. My youngest sister, who was born in California five years after the rest of us moved there, would give me a bored *Of course!* look when I'd come on Christmas visits from Boston and say it was nice to be in a climate you didn't have to defend yourself against. I felt like a Hungarian refugee, raving about the joys of liberty to a bunch of jaded Americans who took it as entirely normal that they were free. I know that hard-boiled New Yorkers often take the balmy California weather, and the Californians' obsession with the weather, as signs that West Coast life is soft at the core. Maybe they're right about some of the natives, but I think that people like my father, who'd deliberately come to California, never felt for a moment that the gentle climate was an excuse to slack off. It let him do more, not less, and in that way it represented the general license he'd earned, by moving west, to invent a new life for himself.

I keep saying "my father" because he was responsible for the move, back in those days of one-career families, and because my mother always had more complicated feelings about leaving the East. On the last leg of our five-day cross-country drive in the station wagon, the three children constantly squabbling and everyone red-faced from the 100 degree heat of the Mojave Desert, we roared along Route 66 to the town of Redlands, which was henceforth to be our home. The town, which then had about twenty thousand people and now has grown to more than fifty thousand (because stories like ours keep being repeated), lies on the edge of the desert, at the foot of imposing mountains that keep rain clouds, such as they are, from moving farther inland. Redlands considered itself elegant, in comparison to nearby towns like Fontana and San Bernardino, because wealthy eastern asthmatics and tuberculars had moved there at the turn of the century and built a few grand houses and planted stately trees. In those days the city's principal business was orange growing, and as we drove in we passed row after row of lovely, glossily dark-leaved trees. But the elegance was only relative, and the greenery was strictly confined to irrigated areas. This was still the edge of the desert, where six months can pass without any rain, where if ground isn't irrigated nothing but thorns and cactus will grow. On the outskirts of Redlands, the car rolled across a wash, a sandy riverbed a hundred yards wide that for two or three weeks each decade holds a river. My mother looked at the blasted gray hillsides and the tumbleweed growth; she thought of Philadelphia's lush Wissahickon Drive; and she broke into tears. That was more than thirty years ago, but when people ask where she is from, she still says Philadelphia. She found the most East Coast–like house in town and made it look like something that could have been in Chestnut Hill. She kept the shutters closed, filled the house with antique furniture, and always dressed in tweeds and scarves once she and my father could afford to have the house air-conditioned, which was after I had moved away.

That is, my mother did not value the "freedom" of California as highly as my father did, at least not consciously. I have always been close to my mother, but on the freedom-versus-tradition issue my heart was with my father. To her, moving to California from Philadelphia meant saying goodbye to the old houses and the leafy parks and the established social gradations whose complexities made life so interesting. To him, it meant escaping claustrophobic settings and their offer of a predictable life: the regular canasta games, the neighborhood church, the long Sunday afternoons in some aged aunt's parlor, the summer trips to the Poconos or the Jersey shore. When he was about to leave the navy, my father asked doctors in Jenkintown and on the Main Line about setting up practice there. Fine, but not right here, was the regular reply. The doctors in California hadn't discouraged him. They planned to grow; there was room.

As it happened, my father re-created many rituals similar to those he left behind — the regular poker game, the Redlands Rotary Club, the summer trips to Newport Beach. But they were rituals he'd chosen himself, not ones he'd just fallen into, which made them seem (at least to me, interpreting his feelings) less confining. And they didn't take up much of his life, whereas the church and the Rotary Club had been the twin pillars of his father's life in Jenkintown. Before and after work, in the early morning and late into the night, my father acted as if there were no niche into which he was supposed to fit, no limit imposed by his background. Because of his rushed wartime education, he had never taken a college course in liberal arts. He decided to remedy that for himself: for a year or two he studied Greek early in the morning, then Hebrew, then a systematic empire-by-empire course in ancient history, then Shakespeare. When I was in the fourth and fifth grades, he made me get up with him at 6:00 A.M. to watch *Sunrise Semester* lessons in calculus and Greek.

Before my sister and brother and I went to bed, he'd line us up on the couch and take us through the latest set of plates in the Metropolitan Museum's *Introduction to Art* series. To people in New York, who had actually seen paintings in the Met, this might have seemed hopelessly mass cult. To my father, it was what books were for. He and my mother made their first trip overseas in the early 1970s and visited my sister on her junior-year-abroad in France. My mother, who had studied French, had the educated American's proper diffidence about her flawed accent. My father plunged right ahead, phrase book in hand, putting sentences together mechanically and making huffy Frenchmen tell him what he wanted to know. When I was thirteen, he took me and my brother sailing, without informing us he didn't know how to handle a boat. He rented a sixteen-foot sloop, put us in the bow, and sat at the tiller, *Beginner's Guide to Sailing* open on his lap. "Ready to come about," he'd read from page 39. Then he'd flip to page 40, push the tiller, and read, "Hard alee!" He wanted to become a sculptor, took lessons, and eventually displayed his work in a show. He was the original autodidact. He had never been on a horse before he was forty but became captain of a horseback search-and-rescue team by the time he was fifty. He couldn't be abashed by anyone who was supposed to be intellectual or upper class, because he thought he could learn to do anything if he tried.

When I was growing up in Redlands, I used to hear people talk quite sincerely about the "good life" in California. Since the time I went away to college, I've heard the phrase used only facetiously. I'm aware of all the reasons for skepticism about California's or America's good life. But I don't use the expression mockingly, because I know what the sense of wide-open possibility meant to my father.

In talking about possibility, I'm mainly trying to describe an idea, not a place. True, there are some objective differences between California and Pennsylvania, between the West Coast and the East, that affect their openness to new people with new plans. It's been a long time since anyone thought of Pennsylvania as part of the American frontier or talked about the "Pennsylvania dream." The weather is different; the ethnic balance is different (white ethnic groups don't really count in Southern California, where ethnic politics means the relationship among Asians, Mexicans, blacks, and whites in general); the public-private balance is different. Many of the prettiest places in California and the rest of the West are public, open to anyone — beaches, mountains, lakes, redwood forests, houses designed to be seen from the street. None or next to none of the coastline is carved up into the private beach clubs that are more common in the East.

Still, what I want to emphasize is the change in my father's heart, not the physical surroundings. He *felt* much freer after our family moved west, and he lived a fuller life than he thought would be open to him if he'd stayed at home. Other people might have sought the same opening-up through a move in the opposite direction. The successful and "sensitive" one in *American Graffiti,* after all, was the one who forsook the California good life not merely for the East Coast but for frigid Canada; the big loser was the one who stayed home. The big city, east or west, has always been the promised land of opportunity for people stifled in small towns. My parents took three children with them to a small town in California; in time my sister settled in Boston, I in Washington, my brother in New York. For what each of us wanted to do, the old, crowded, East Coast cities offered more opportunity and freedom than California did. My youngest sister, the native Californian, ended up near San Francisco, the most eastern western city.

In moving to California, then, my parents revealed a little about the West Coast and something more about themselves. But they also illustrated the American characteristic that has applied in all regions of the country and throughout our history. That is the belief that people can learn to do things they haven't done before, can take on identities they hadn't had, can will themselves into stations in life different from those in which they were born.

When this side of our national character is discussed in university courses or literary essays, the representative self-defined man is usually someone like Jay Gatsby. I am not trying to praise Gatsby or Ivan Boesky (who bragged that he slept only four

hours a night and used the extra time to become a Shakespeare
expert) or John DeLorean or Sammy Glick or anyone else who
pretends to be something he is not. Driving to a new state or
learning a new activity is not, by itself, a solution to any problem.
But I know that my parents' life was transformed when they put
themselves in a different setting and learned that they had new
choices. Even my mother now concedes that she is glad they
went west.

I lived for only eleven years in California. I left for college in
1966 and have never been back except to visit my parents. But I
still say I am from Southern California, and I believe it, because
moving there was the decisive experience in my family's life and
in my sense of how people can change their luck.

And there *was* something different about the place itself that
made it more "American," in the sense of encouraging opportunity.

Ten years after my family migrated, Joan Didion, whose family
had been in the Central Valley of California for several generations, described the same landscape my parents had found. In
one of the famous magazine pieces she wrote in the 1960s, she
had this to say about Redlands and the similar, nearby towns of
the San Bernardino Valley, which the Chamber of Commerce
preferred to call the "Inland Empire":

> The San Bernardino Valley lies only an hour east of Los Angeles
> by the San Bernardino Freeway but is in certain ways an alien
> place: not the coastal California of the subtropical twilights and
> the soft westerlies off the Pacific but a harsher California, haunted
> by the Mojave just beyond the mountains, devastated by the hot
> dry Santa Ana wind that comes down through the passes at 100
> miles an hour and whines through the eucalyptus windbreaks and
> works on the nerves. October is the bad month for the wind, the
> month when breathing is difficult and the hills blaze up sponta-
> neously. There has been no rain since April. Every voice seems a
> scream.

That was the lead paragraph in her article in *The Saturday
Evening Post*. When I first read it, as an active Boy Scout and
civic-minded student at Redlands High School, I told myself,
"She's just criticizing the scenery. I can stand this." She did

have a point about the winds. When they were bad they would reach beyond the parched San Bernardino Valley toward the coastline, and there they would destroy like a blast from Hell. They roared out of the desert, humidity zero percent. When they got to Costa Mesa or Newport or some other coast-zone town that was usually coddled by "soft westerlies off the Pacific," they would suck the moisture out of pianos and big mahogany tables in fifteen seconds and rupture them with a loud, long *keee-rrrraaacckkkk*. The Santa Ana winds made everyone edgy; still, I thought, this Miss Didion sounded unnecessarily high-strung.

Then I read further and found the parts that hurt. She described the people who'd moved to the valley and what they found when they got there:

> This is the California where it is easy to Dial-a-Devotion, but hard to buy a book. This is the country . . . of the teased hair and the Capris and the girls for whom all life's promise comes down to a waltz-length white wedding dress and the birth of a Kimberly or Sherri or a Debbi and a Tijuana divorce and a return to hairdress-ers' school . . . The future always looks good in the golden land, because no one remembers the past. Here is where the hot wind blows and the old ways do not seem relevant, where the divorce rate is double the national average and where one person in every thirty-eight lives in a trailer. Here is the last stop for all those who came from somewhere else, for all those who drifted away from the cold and the past and the old ways.

I knew how attractive this part of Southern California seemed to people like us, who had come precisely in the hope of drifting away from the cold and the past and the old ways. Reading this article, so much more caustic than anything else I'd remembered seeing in *The Saturday Evening Post,* was the first step toward understanding how our life might look from the outside.

Years later, I was ready to concede that Joan Didion may have been right about some of the things she mocked. But I was also ready to make a larger defense of the starting-over life that people like my parents had made for themselves. There was a side to the no-tradition, no-taste Southern California culture that was not contemptible, that was even magnificent, because it went a long way toward freeing people of the constraints of class.

I had many occasions to wonder about the effects of my Southern California background in the months after Joan Didion's article came out, because soon afterward I headed off to college, at Harvard. I had gotten to Harvard the same way my mother got to Tufts and my father got into the navy's doctor-training program: by scoring well on standardized tests that let me measure up against people from more impressive-seeming schools. I also had the "advantage" of coming from a small, out-of-the-way town on the West Coast, which added to the freshman class's geographical mix. It's easy to overestimate how much of an advantage the small-town background really is. It is a milder version of being black in the era of affirmative action: other things being equal, it gives you an edge on the competition, but usually you never reach the point where other things are equal.

At college I soon discovered that things really weren't equal. Despite my father's contagious, self-directed scholarship, I was more ignorant of more things than the hotshots I met from Groton and Dalton and Great Neck South. My high school had had no advanced-placement courses; I'd never been out of the country, except to Tijuana; my parents got *Scientific American* and *The Atlantic*, but I'd never heard of *Partisan Review* or *The New York Review* or even once read the *New York Times*.

In time I recovered. Like every other small-town public high school boy at Harvard, I latched on to a piece of "scientific" evidence designed to shore up my self-esteem. The prep school kids, who'd had those AP courses and could identify I. F. Stone, might start out stronger, but by the end of the four years the wholesome youth from the hinterland were supposed to pull ahead. That was the reassurance the counselors gave me and my roommate, who had had an even more backwater upbringing in Brownsville, Texas, on the Rio Grande. I always imagined that in the next room they were telling the kids from Cranbrook and Exeter, "Look, here's the deal. You start out with a big advantage — and you get to keep it!" But mainly because of the contrast between Redlands and Cambridge, I found myself trying to figure out what class I belonged to — and wondering why questions of class seemed so much more powerful in Massachusetts than in California. The explanation for this preoccupation, I think, involved something more than the typical eagerness to theorize during the college years.

The class-placement question might not seem all that challenging. My father was a medical doctor; therefore, I was from the professional or upper middle class. Moreover, my mother had always pumped her children full of a sense of noblesse oblige that had no obvious basis in reality. "With privilege comes responsibility," she would say when my brother or I acted like the common folk by sneaking beer into a high school dance. Perhaps she was carried away by the near coincidence of my birth and that of Prince Charles. Maybe she had dreamed up a fancier-seeming heritage for the Mackenzie family to compensate for the real hardship in which she was raised. In any case it was an act of will, more than an effort based on accurate social observation, to make us think we were among the privileged few. Since I was born while my father still had internship and residency ahead of him, I had absorbed the atmosphere of the scrimping early stage of medical training, which leaves many doctors, though not my father, feeling that they are entitled to rake in everything they can later on. When we made the cross-country drive, we ate sandwiches out of a big cardboard box. When my father went to medical meetings in San Francisco, he took a room in the YMCA; this was in a more innocent day. It was a cause for celebration, which all the children cheered with heartless mockery, when we finally started buying milk from the milkman. Until that point, when I was in fourth or fifth grade, my mother had mixed a vile, bluish, weak-flavored mixture from powdered milk in a carton, trying to convince us that if it was icy cold it tasted fine.

More important, before I went to college I really hadn't worried about whether I was supposed to fit in at any particular point on the social pyramid; I was a teenager and had other things to worry about. But another reason was that the social environment in Redlands did not encourage such speculation.

I remember feeling as if I had crossed some permanent divide the afternoon I first showed up in Harvard Yard. It was not the change in my life that impressed me; it was the change in the surroundings. The narrow road that ran through the Yard was jammed with the station wagons and big sedans of families who had driven their sons to college. Like most students from the West Coast, I'd flown out by myself. The looks of the cars, the parents, even the gear being lugged into the dorms, suddenly hinted at a vastly greater range of social stations than I'd even guessed existed. Lacrosse sticks, skis, and squash racquets came out of the trunks. Car windows, even then, bore decals from prep schools. Fathers wearing sweaters and horn-rimmed glasses showed their sons where they'd stayed as freshmen in the Yard before the war. Mothers greeted friends they'd known for years, from private schools and summer clubs, speaking in accents I'd never heard before.

It wasn't that I resented this whole, dense world in which I had no place. On the contrary, I had a perverse pride in what I started to think of as a log-cabin upbringing. The surprise was how settled and permanent it all looked, how comfortable these families were in their social station. Arrival at Harvard, which left me abashed, seemed part of their entitlement.

This takes us back to Joan Didion. Much as it initially galled me to admit it, she had seen something important about the civilization of the Inland Empire. Her characters were pathetic, out of control, because they were carried away by fantasies of becoming something more glamorous than what they really were. They had thought that everything would be better when they drove out to California from their midwestern farm town or dreary East Coast home. The central figure in the article was a woman who was caught up in a lurid love triangle, came to think that her husband would never be sufficiently successful, and got rid of him by planting a firebomb in his Volkswagen. Didion introduced her this way: "Of course she came from somewhere else, came off the prairie in search of something she had seen in a movie or heard on the radio, for this is a Southern California story." (The murder trial was by far the most exciting public event of my childhood. The jury found her guilty.)

If the California dream always came true, the typical California story would be like Ronald Reagan's: midwestern boy comes west, escapes troubled childhood, finds happiness and success. But many times the dream didn't come true, Didion said. She was not exactly the first person to make this point; in fact, the California-migration school of literature is generally depressing. Consider *The Grapes of Wrath, The Day of the Locust, The*

Postman Always Rings Twice, The Loved One. But Didion showed how hard it was for people to stop pretending, stop dreaming, face the reality of cramped, inelegant, lower-middle-class lives.

I found myself resisting her portrayal, but not because it was inaccurate. The flight from reality by first-generation Southern Californians could be even wider than her article showed. The grocery stores were full of old ladies wearing rouge and pink jumpsuits and batting their eyes at the checkout boys, pretending they were still comely and twenty-five. An elderly patient of my father's had made his house into a shrine to his accordion-playing career; the walls were covered with kinescope photos of his one appearance on the old Jack Paar show, and he kept talking about his big comeback, which would happen any day now. One of my high school classmates became a blackjack dealer in Las Vegas and tried to wow everybody at the class's tenth reunion by saying that he knew Wayne Newton *really well*. In junior high school, I'd had a brief career as a 4-H'er, raising a black Angus steer on a lot behind our house. To my friends, the most impressive thing about the project was that the calf was born on a ranch that Danny Thomas owned. The desire to slip the bonds of reality was so strong that several of my friends started a club whose members promised one another to emigrate to Australia when they were old enough. If things were going wrong even in California, where everything was supposed to be great but where race riots and crime waves kept breaking out, perhaps Australia was the last unspoiled place left.

But this escapist view had another side. Southern California might have been expected to have a higher proportion of dashed hopes than anywhere else in the country, since so many people were yearning for so much. But it has never been described as a depressed or downcast society, precisely because of the fantasies and impermanence that Joan Didion described. You haven't lived Ronald Reagan's life so far, but your life isn't over yet — who knows what will happen tomorrow? There is always a chance of becoming someone different, finally getting the big break. Reagan himself seemed washed-up when he was in his late forties, when his movie career had peaked and he hadn't switched to politics yet. This, I think, was a part of Reagan's appeal rarely discussed but deeply felt. Even more than Jimmy Carter or Jesse Jackson, he embodied the American promise of a second chance. His example was more impressive because he managed to start over so much later in life.

For people not raised in the culture, this may be the hardest point to accept, but I always thought there was a useful, even noble side to the fluid, dreamer's spirit in Southern California. Precisely because everything and every role was so impermanent, people could avoid being discouraged by circumstances that would depress normal people. Things could always change. A friend of mine from Boston said, after a trip to Los Angeles, "The difference is the car wash. The people can work there without feeling like they'll always work there, so they aren't angry." Put just that way, it may sound as if he were reporting on oppressed but cheerful peasants, but I knew that he meant something more. A kinder term for self-delusion is hope, and there was a hopefulness to the dreary small-town California life that taught many people to expect second and third chances — even if that meant going to Australia as, for our parents, it had once meant going to California.

The idea of an impermanent social structure, in which people could keep trying out new identities, affected the way people carried themselves and dealt with one another. Life was fairer there, more democratic, than it would have been in a setting that taught people not to expect anything different. There were assorted status games and bouts of one-upmanship just as there were anywhere else. But most people could not display or use permanent marks of class, since nothing seemed to be permanent. Apart from the speech of those Mexican Americans who had not learned standard English and a few very recent arrivals from Pennsylvania or the South, people's accents did not vary. You usually couldn't tell, just by listening or looking, who was going to college and who was going to work at the orange-packing plant.

Starting that first afternoon in Harvard Yard, I realized that in other places you *could* tell. You could see a stranger on the bus or in a coffeeshop, and the instant he opened his mouth you knew a lot about his life story. In England, where I went to graduate school, the mouth itself was a giveaway, since even as teenagers working-class people had lost many of their teeth. In Boston you could hear townie accents and "lockjaw" accents and tell someone's fortune without even seeing his face. The connection between class and accent sounds commonplace to an Easterner, but it was different in California. Like TV broadcasters, everybody sounded the same. People make fun of broadcasters for that reason, but the lack of identifiable class accents was a sign of a healthy, hopeful society.

The leveling of manners, I still believe, made it easier for people to imagine that many possibilities were open to them. You could imagine that no one was so different from anyone else. People dressed the same and had approximately the same manners and went to the same public schools. In reality, people were different and had different chances, based mainly on family circumstance. It was always in the cards for the children in my family to go to college and for some of my friends not to. But even the fiction of equality was useful. By encouraging people to behave as if everyone had a chance, this transient society gave more people more hope. Because it seemed more fair, it *was* more fair — not entirely open to talent and energy, but more than it would have been if people continually had their noses rubbed into the inborn differences that come from social standing.

I am not ignoring the ugly sides of this transient culture or defending them in themselves. It is no accident that Southern California is the home of so many wacko religious cults and political movements. "Once they arrive hardly anyone 'settles' — no familiar or community traditions bind them," *Time* magazine wrote in a report on California at about the time of the Manson family killings. " 'That's why we have so many nuts out here,' says Los Angeles pollster Don Muchmore. 'People come and do things here they wouldn't normally do back home because such behavior is unacceptable.' " Cookie-cutter tract houses, endless shopping malls, lives centered on cars and suntans and MTV — these are not necessarily the ideal expressions of the human spirit. Southern California culture was and is more nouveau and lowbrow than that of Boston or New York, to say nothing of

Europe. The high-culture boosters of Los Angeles spend all their time claiming that L.A. is the new cultural capital, but like their counterparts in Dallas and Atlanta these people are mainly counting orchestra performances and judging art acquisitions by the pound. Real culture depends on permanence, tradition, and accepted social gradations, precisely the things people have come to Southern California to escape.

What I do claim about these blemishes on my homeland's complexion is that they were closely connected to its most admirable trait — the sense of possibility — and that they are America's story in miniature.

Outside descriptions of our society have usually stressed a mixture of good and bad similar to what I have tried to describe about Southern California. America has always been vulgar, untraditional, naïve, short on refined culture and behavior (these parts to the bad); and (to the good) democratic in its manners, relatively unhampered by class distinctions like those in Europe, more optimistic, readier to change. The two sides, good and bad, were connected: the society was open to new people *because* it was relatively unaffected by tradition and the culture that was nursed by tradition. Or maybe the "because" worked the other way; in either case, openness and unculturedness bore a relation to each other. "America has a high standard of living of low average quality," the critic Paul Goodman wrote in *Growing Up Absurd*. In that one line of Goodman's is the story of our industrial decline: the Japanese and Germans and Koreans, with higher average quality, overtook us. But America has always offered so much to so many because the cultural threshold has been low. Anyone could cross it and join in.

"Among democratic peoples new families continually rise from nothing while others fall, and nobody's position is quite stable," Alexis de Tocqueville wrote in *Democracy in America*. "The woof of time is broken and the track of past generations lost. Those who have gone before are easily forgotten, and no one gives a thought to those who will follow . . . There is nothing of tradition, family feeling, or example to restrain them. Laws have little sway over them, and mores still less."

Not everyone has to like California or want to move there. My mother never would have moved if she'd married someone else. But the open, changing spirit of its society was similar to what Tocqueville described. It is a large part of what makes America "more like us."

CHAPTER FIVE

Reinvented Lives

IS THE FREEDOM my parents found in California part of America's lost past, like the family structure of *The Donna Reed Show* or America's easy postwar superiority over the world? Many Americans speak now as if the age of mobility had ended. The freedom to start over, it may seem, was something America offered during the 1840s, when there was almost boundless land for pioneers to settle; or in the 1890s, when immigrants could quickly find jobs in America's booming industries; or during the wartime exodus from Nazi Germany or the later waves of departures from Hungary and Cuba; or during the late 1940s and the 1950s, when California seemed so promising to so many people like my parents. But not anymore.

Such a sense of resignation is premature. As a political unit, the United States has become old and somewhat tired. But American culture can still be young, flexible, full of possibility. It still derives its energy from people who think they can change and control their fate. The United States may be "deindustrializing"; its relative power in the world may be in decline. But for people determined to reinvent their lives and create new roles for themselves, even the America of the 1980s can be a malleable, forgiving culture. The more America allows people to make new choices and changes, the healthier and more productive the whole society will be.

As a reporter, I have seen three powerful instances of what people can do, even now, when they want to remake their lives. The first involves two migrants from the Midwest who left home in order to get a new chance. The second is about a man who stayed where he was but insisted on changing the rules of the society around him. The third is of a group of people who started life over in the most fundamental way. Incidents like these can and do occur in other countries. But in Germany or Japan they would be novelties, whereas in America they illustrate the fundamental culture of American success.

BUDDY AND JUDY GINN

In the fall of 1982, I went to Alvin, Texas, a tiny town south of Houston, to the headquarters of a family-owned well-service company. Well-service companies perform maintenance work on oil wells — replacing pipe when it gets worn, redrilling holes, coping with blowouts and other emergencies. The high price of oil had taken the U.S. "rig count" of producing wells to its all-time peak of 4531 late in 1981. It was already heading down in 1982 and would be in the 2000s by the year's end (on its way to a low in the 800s in 1986), but well-service companies were still in tremendous demand at the time I made my visit.

I went to the company to ask about one of the major social changes then under way in Texas: the coming of the black-platers. These were the thousands of migrants from the Midwest, usually arriving in cars with black Michigan license plates, who flocked to Houston looking for oilfield work. They were generally sneered at by the local Houstonians, who conveniently forgot that the city had been built by migrants from rural Texas and who couldn't, of course, foresee that a few years later, when the oil business crashed, Houstonians themselves would be hitting the road to look for jobs.

I wanted to meet some black-platers and find out how they felt about their change of scene; because there was such rapid turnover in the oilfield business, with new jobs opening up all the time, I thought it would be easy to find them. When I went into the corrugated-metal warehouse that served as the company's office, I found the personnel director and told him what I was looking for. "You got your man," he said.

Buddy Ginn was then forty-three years old. (This is a pseud-onym, but his real name has a very similar down-to-earth ring.) He was a short but rough-looking man with long matted hair, USMC tattoos on his arms, oily blue jeans, and bad teeth. He seemed to enjoy playing the tough guy: when we started talking, he told me, "If you walked in here looking to sign on, I'd have a hard time placing you on a rig. I'm just judging by appearances, now." But in that meeting and subsequent ones over the next two years, he explained that he saw himself as a classic American success story, and that taking part in the black-plate migration had totally changed his life.

Ginn was born and raised in New Castle, Indiana, a town of twenty thousand people in the eastern part of the state, between Indianapolis and Dayton. As I later learned, this part of Indiana manages to seem strangely rural and industrial at the same time. Most of the landscape consists of cornfields interspersed with stands of sycamore and buckeye. Every few miles, however, a big, black, pre–World War II factory looms up out of the fields. Most of them were built early in the century to provide parts for the auto industry in Detroit. In the middle of New Castle was a big Perfect Circle piston-ring plant.

Ginn had grown up within sight of Perfect Circle, in a little white frame house. His father was killed on Okinawa when Ginn was two, and he was raised by his mother and his stepfather, who worked at the plant. Ginn quit school at sixteen, worked on con-struction crews, and joined the marines. After four years as a military policeman he came back home and in 1966, aged twenty-three, was hired by the local police.

By the early 1980s, people started leaving eastern Indiana be-cause the factories were laying off workers or shutting down altogether. But Ginn left earlier and for messier personal reasons. He'd gotten married in New Castle and had children, but he began fighting with his wife in such a way that he became an embarrassment to the police force and was fired. He tended bar for a time and while doing so met Judy O'Leary, a young, twice-married mother of two, who had been married for the first time when she was fifteen. She became pregnant by Ginn, and they decided to leave town. On the Fourth of July, 1976, when he was thirty-three and she was twenty-one, they piled their belongings into the back of a Pontiac and drove to Texas, carrying $500 in cash.

The most striking thing about Ginn's story from that point on might seem to be its instability. He had been in Texas for six years when I met him, and he'd averaged a job per year. He and Judy O'Leary, who had divorced their spouses and gotten married in Texas, had moved several times and wound up in a mobile home park off a freeway interchange in Alvin. They were involved in constant quarrels with their former families in Indiana over the care of the children they had left behind. Considered objectively, their lives were still difficult. But to Ginn, the clear moral of his story was that the move to Texas had been a success.

As he saw it, a new, more open environment gave him a chance to work his way steadily up. He started out as an Astroworld security guard for $4.50 an hour, got promotions within the firm, but argued with his boss and lost the job. Then he started looking for oilfield work. In that time of rising prices, when jobs were easy to get, crews frequently quit out of pique or boredom. Through a friend, Ginn got on the waiting list at the small well-service company where I later met him; he was first called to work one Sunday when the regular crew stalked off.

Oilfield work is about as close as modern America comes to a free-swinging frontier culture. The men who owned the rigs were typically small-town Texans who struck it rich during the oil boom of the 1970s. During the boom, many flaunted their success by buying gaudy Cadillacs or going to conventions in tailored jumpsuits. (Larry McMurtry's *Texasville* depicts a nouveau riche owner on his way up and down.) The man who owned Ginn's company lived in a small house and dressed modestly, but he drove the very short distance home for lunch each day in a Cadillac with its air conditioner roaring. The roughnecks who drifted from place to place and job to job were as uninterested in fine social gradations as anyone Fanny Trollope had met on the frontier.

Even in this extremely open environment, however, the odds

seemed stacked against Ginn. The problem was his age. Work on the rigs is both dangerous and physically demanding; it means wrestling 200-pound lengths of grease-covered pipe into and out of the drill hole while dodging an enormous swinging pulley block that itself weighs four tons. Ginn was now thirty-six, about fifteen years above average for starting out as a "worm," the lowest and dirtiest job on the rig. For him to begin was like a man's entering the army as a private in middle age, or starting in a supermarket as a stock boy. But, he told me later, it was a gamble he felt he had to take. "Whenever the dirtiest jobs come up, that's the worm," he said. "You can stay there all your life unless you drive yourself. I knew I could push myself to become lead floor hand. You might clean the hand tools, when there's slack time, instead of laying down. If you're willing to do your own work, and 10 percent more, then there's no doubt you can get ahead."

The floor hand's job was both safer and better paid than the worm's, and in a few weeks Ginn had made it that far. A few months later, one rig's driller didn't show up for work, and Ginn volunteered for that job, which involved controlling the huge draw works that lift and lower the pipe. His strategy was to keep learning about the next highest job so that he would be ready to move up when the inevitable vacancies occurred. The only rig job superior to driller was tool pusher. This is an independent, delicate responsibility; the tool pusher operates on the boundary between two layers of society. He's the foreman of the worms, floor hands, and drillers on his rig, but he also serves as a glad-hander and salesman for the company men from the major oil producers that own the wells. Within a year of Ginn's joining the company, a job as tool pusher opened up, and Ginn was selected. The business kept booming. One year after he first became a tool pusher, Ginn moved into management as the company's person-nel director, handling the dozens of new men being signed on for the rigs. "I did not hesitate one minute when the offer came," he said. "I moved in and took over."

Ginn was in this job when I first met him. He seemed to spend all his time thinking about how he could do more than the normal duties. He had a two-way radio installed in his mobile home so that night or day he could track the movements of every crew. He complained that the office would never leave him alone, in the way that people do when they're actually pleased to seem indispensable. "It's not like a union shop, where if you're not there nobody misses you," he said. "If you're not on the job here, you're *missed*." He stood to make about $40,000 per year, in salary and bonuses. He bought a second mobile home and planned to move farther up in management, starting with a job in sales.

But only a few months after he became personnel director, Ginn suffered another complete reverse. Through 1983 the price of oil kept plummeting. The major oil companies started shutting down their high-cost wells in the United States, and suddenly there was almost no well-service work to be done in Texas. As the price and the rig count chased each other down, Ginn was moved back out of the office to a rig as a tool pusher, then back to being a floor hand, then to part-time roughneck work. The company had borrowed heavily to buy new rigs during the boom, and when the market changed it could not service the debts. The company had survived ups and downs since the Depression, but in 1983 it went into bankruptcy court.

Ginn was out of work and the Houston job market seemed hopeless; 100,000 jobs disappeared about the same time his did. But when I talked to him at the time, he said he wasn't discouraged or thinking about going home. His wife took on part-time work, for piece rates, at a local ceramics plant. She had to leave by 6:30 in the morning, and she bundled their small daughter off to stay with a mother in another mobile home before she left. The company briefly came back to life in 1984 and Ginn worked on rigs for a while. But he was injured when a length of pipe smashed into his hand, and by the time he recovered the business was completely bust.

At that point, early in 1985, Ginn decided he had to start a new career yet again. Because he'd had a good reputation at the well-service company, he got into a training program at Phillips Petroleum, one that again was designed for younger men. Eventually the program would train him in mechanics, but it began with a period of unskilled labor. At the age of forty-two Ginn was dig-

ging ditches and fixing leaks for $7.00 an hour. But while he was
doing so, he got hold of the manuals for the mechanics course
and started studying on his own. He'd been told that once he
passed the Phillips Class A Mechanic test, he'd be qualified to
earn $13.13 an hour, rising to $14.60 after a year. When the
course began, Ginn was the star. The instructor, whom I met
when Ginn was halfway through the course, said that Ginn was
the quickest student he'd had in twenty-two years. Ginn passed
on his first try and doubled his income. When I saw him soon
afterward, at the Phillips yard, he said that his goal was to surpass the $51,000 the instructor had earned the previous year.
"I've never lost my confidence," he said then. "I'm going to
make it."

There is a danger of sounding patronizing in talking about
Ginn's successes. From an economic point of view, what he'd
mainly accomplished was to survive catastrophes — first his
problems in New Castle and then the collapse of the oil business.
But surviving changes while continuing to earn more money and
take on more responsibility, as he'd done, is what most of economic life is about. More important, Ginn stressed each time I
saw him that even when he was out of work he still felt personally
freer and more satisfied, because he'd come to Texas. "If we
were back home, everybody would have an idea of what kind of
people we were supposed to be. Here, they take you for what
you can do. Nobody has a set idea about me."

I went back to New Castle to see the kind of life Ginn had left
behind. The contrast between his old and new setting could
hardly be more extreme. The mobile home park in Alvin is what
people have in mind when they talk disparagingly about the root-
lessness of American life. The families in New Castle, on the
other hand, were nothing if not rooted. Ginn's stepfather, Horace
Potter, had grown up with eighteen brothers and sisters. Sixteen
still lived in the area. Judy O'Leary's mother and father lived
next to a cemetery where the mother's parents and grandparents
were buried. Neighbors all knew each other and had watched
children grow into adults. The good side of life in the town was
the tradition and social network that would probably never develop in Alvin. The bad side was that its opportunities had with-

ered away. The town had a shrunken look. As Potter drove me around town he said, "See those big buildings over there, the brick ones? They used to belong to Sears, back before it pulled out. That used to be the railroad station. That was a lumberyard. That used to be the dairy." Ginn's mother said, "If we were young, I don't think we'd stay. But I just don't feel like moving now."

Ginn's life is not necessarily better or worse than his family's life in Indiana. They preferred the stability; he preferred the chance to change. But he clearly thought that his life was richer, both materially and socially, than it would have been if he stayed home. By letting him start over, American society got more of his energy than would have been available if he'd been stuck in place.

WYMAN WESTBERRY

The new start that Wyman Westberry (this is his real name) made did not involve moving somewhere else. He has lived in one corner of southeast Georgia for nearly all of his life. But he saw the possibility of inventing a new society where he lived, and he succeeded in doing so.

I met Westberry in the summer of 1970, when he was twenty-eight. I was just out of college and was in Savannah with several other students, launching what was in retrospect an amazingly presumptuous project for Ralph Nader. Savannah, like Charleston, is a graceful city full of elegant antebellum houses. It also contains one of the world's largest paper mills, specializing in brown kraft-paper grocery sacks. The members of the Nader team were supposed to study all the aspects of the mill's influence on the town — environmental, political, economic, social. Then we were to report to the townspeople about what they had gained and lost through their association with the mill.

The one lasting result of this project was to provoke Wyman Westberry into action. Westberry lived about two hundred miles south of Savannah in a tiny town on the Florida border named St. Marys. When Nader announced the Savannah project, Westberry read about it in the paper. A few weeks after we began, he called late one evening and, sounding very much like Gomer Pyle, said that he had something very interesting to show us in St. Marys.

Sometimes clichés come to life, and in St. Marys a hoary southern cliché did. When we drove there to meet Westberry, we found an isolated, feudal, suspicious mill town, like the setting for *Tobacco Road*. The only way into town was by a long dead-end cutoff from the state highway; it ran through groves of pine pulp-wood trees planted in rows for easy harvesting. St. Marys was built around one large paper mill, where nearly everyone in the town worked. The mill's degree of political control was almost comic. The mill's attorney was also the city attorney, the county attorney, and the attorney for the school board and the hospital board. He was also the state legislator for the district, and his brother published the local newspaper. The city's mayor was the president of a sweetheart union at the mill. And the real power in town was the mill's manager, usually referred to as the Big Man or King. He was a major landowner and the biggest shareholder in the local bank. He wore dark glasses indoors and out, and his bearing was very much like George C. Scott's in *Patton*. His eventual undoing began when TV crews got into town and put him on the air.

The natural result of this concentration of power was a completely controlled society. There was a noticeable climate of fear. Westberry was the bravest man in town, but the first time he met us he drew all the shades in his house before he began to talk. Later he took us to another house, where all the lights had been turned out and the occupant was waiting for us to creep in through the back door.

By the time he read about Ralph Nader, Westberry had apparently decided that it was time to change the rules of life in St. Marys. He had worked at the paper mill for several years in a skilled technical job, as a millwright. He had grown up in a working-class family in the nearby town of Jessup, had finished high school, and had briefly gone to college in Savannah. He was drafted into the army in 1964 and gave a preview there of what he would later do in St. Marys. When he saw a crew of mess sergeants and officers stealing food from the mess hall, he immediately turned them in. He was harassed and shunned, but he stood by his accusations, and the thieves were finally cashiered.

Westberry's sense of justice became offended in the mill town as it had been in the army. He claimed that he decided to begin his crusade when he went waterskiing one afternoon on the St. Marys River and noticed that the water was as sudsy as if the river were a washing machine. The foam and scum came from the millions of gallons of effluent the mill put into the small river each day. "At first I wondered why I was the only person doing any waterskiing," he said. "When I came out of the water, I found out why. It took a long time to rub that foam and chemicals off my body."

Over the next five years, Westberry devoted nearly all of his time, energy, money, and emotions to changing the traditions and rules of life in St. Marys. He learned, through his contacts with Nader and by poring over law books, that the plant put out far more effluent than the state's clean-water laws allowed. He pestered state officials, trying to draw their attention to St. Marys. He dug up tax records that showed a variety of provisions favoring the mill, such as one that froze its tax assessments at the 1958 level. These he passed to a friend, a local doctor, who had challenged the mill's attorney for a seat in the Georgia legislature. In the 1970 election, Westberry's friend edged out the attorney and began promoting tax-reform bills once he took office. Westberry realized that pressure from outside St. Marys was the only force that could offset the mill's influence within the town, and he showed great ingenuity in attracting outside attention and support. Two of the Nader officials wrote an article in *Harper's* about the mill's political and economic control. That, in turn, lured Mike Wallace's *60 Minutes* crew, which scored a coup by capturing the Big Man on tape in his dark glasses. The national publicity increased the pressure on the state government, which pushed the mill harder to clean up the river, and on the state legislature, which continued to eliminate the mill's special tax breaks.

The mill officials took a while to comprehend the gravity of Westberry's challenge. They had been surprised in September 1970, when Westberry's doctor friend beat the mill lawyer in the Democratic primary. A week before the general election, the wanton-looking teenage daughter of a mill worker announced that the doctor had raped her while she was in the hospital for a tonsillectomy. The doctor still won the election and was later officially cleared of the charge, but his reputation never fully recovered.

Through the next year, the legislature, the clean-water agency, and the press all made life difficult for the mill. By the beginning of 1972, its officials realized that Westberry was the ultimate source of their problems. And so they decided (according to federal prosecutors) to have him killed.

This stage of the drama also resembled a familiar stereotype, but it was *The Lavender Hill Mob* or *The Gang That Couldn't Shoot Straight* rather than *The Godfather*. The intended hit man was an improbable character named Lawrence Brown, a 260-pounder who looked like a member of the rap group The Fat Boys. Later, when the whole plot had unraveled and was being sorted out in court, Brown claimed that he'd never really intended to kill Westberry. He said that when he received the attractive offer from the mill officials — $1500 in cash, in exchange for gunning Westberry down in a parking lot — he saw only dollar signs, and intended to leave town when he got his advance payment. He said that a mill supervisor had first suggested the deal early in 1972. Brown told him that he wanted more reassurance, straight from the Big Man, that he wouldn't be caught or prosecuted — and while waiting to get that, he also told a friend of Westberry's about the offer. The friend told Westberry, who immediately (and predictably) drove across the bridge to Florida, making it an interstate case, and called the FBI. The fat man was fitted out with a body bug, he met the Big Man, the mill lawyer, and the supervisor in a hideaway, and he recorded their instructions to get rid of Westberry. "I'm ready, I'm ready for him," Brown kept saying on the tape while the others told him to "cool it" until the FBI got out of town. Shortly afterward a federal grand jury was secretly convened to take testimony about the murder conspiracy against Westberry.

The dénouement of the case was long and almost impossible to understand. Three years after Westberry first called the FBI, the federal government indicted the Big Man, the mill attorney, and the mill supervisor on various charges arising from the conspiracy to kill Westberry. A jury eventually found them guilty on all counts. An appeals court then reversed the conviction, despite the seemingly damning evidence from the body bug, mainly because the star witness, Lawrence Brown, had changed his story so many times. (First he'd said there was a conspiracy to kill Westberry, then that there wasn't and Westberry was trying to frame the Big Man, then that, really, there *was,* and he'd been bullied into telling a lie. Brown himself became a dubious illustration of the ever-open possibility of starting a new life in America. He was described during the trial as a man "who could tell 45 different stories to 45 people and keep them all straight," but shortly afterward he turned up in a small town in northern Georgia as a deputy sheriff.) But even before their trial, the mill and the three officials had settled a $2,225,000 damages suit filed by Westberry for trying to kill him.

The obvious solution to the Westberry problem would have been simply to fire him, but his union, the International Association of Machinists, had put ironclad job-security clauses into its agreement with the mill. In the fall of 1972, after the humiliating *60 Minutes* report on St. Marys but before the murder plot was unveiled, a reporter for the *Atlanta Constitution* learned about the federal grand jury's investigation. He published a front-page story about it, and a week later Westberry finally lost his job.

The mill needed to show cause to fire a union member, and it did. Several years earlier, someone in the plant had poured acid over a black employee who was sitting in what had been a whites-only toilet stall. The culprit was never caught. But in a dismissal letter to Westberry, a mill executive said that the company had just learned that Westberry had poured the acid, so in the interests of racial harmony he had to go.

This case too became almost unbearably complicated. In the end, Westberry was fully cleared of the acid-pouring charge. A federal arbitrator ordered the company to restore his job, his seniority, and his back pay. But it took more than a year for Westberry to be vindicated. During that time he was out of work, unpaid, ostracized — yet, it seemed, totally determined to get his way. He told me at the time that he knew he was right, they were wrong, and he was not going to let the company unfairly drive him out. "A lot of people felt there's no way under the sun you can beat those people, with all the power they've got. It felt good to show them that as long as you're right, there's some justice in the world. What amazes me about people in general, when something happens to them and you talk to them about getting a lawyer and going to court, they say, 'Oh it's just not worth it.' Well, I wanted to show them that was wrong."

The striking part of Westberry's story is not the melodrama or his phenomenal stubbornness and blunt sense of right and wrong; it is that this one man was able, through cleverness and force of will, to transform a closed, unfair society that might otherwise have persisted for years. By the time the various lawsuits and indictments had been sorted out, St. Marys had, because of the disruptions that Westberry had put in motion, become a different town. The Big Man was gone from the mill, having resigned as soon as a federal court agreed to hear Westberry's suit for damages from the murder plot. He was replaced by a more conventional, lower-profile corporate manager. The mayor was gone, replaced by a local shrimper who was one of the few people in town whose livelihood was independent of the mill. A new city council was elected, and it changed the tax laws. When the state pressed for further pollution controls, two hundred mill employees, including white-collar salaried workers, signed a petition asking the mill to cooperate. "Ten years ago, you could have held a gun on a salaried employee and not got him to sign," said Russell Tyre, a friend of Westberry's who had been elected to the reformed city council. "There's a far more relaxed atmosphere in town and at work. If people have gripes, they're not afraid to stand up and say things should be changed."

There was, in the drama, a deus ex machina, which set the seal on the changes Westberry had started in St. Marys. Through the mid 1970s, the U.S. Navy had been assessing sites on the East Coast for its new fleet of Trident submarines. In December 1976, just after Jimmy Carter's election as president, the navy announced that it had chosen King's Bay, Georgia, just outside St.

Marys, as the new home for its Tridents. There would be a huge
naval base and thousands of jobs. People would at last have a
choice about where to work. The naval base would have changed
the balance of power in St. Marys anyway — but Wyman Westberry, believing he could control his fate, had already done so on
his own.

THE NGUYEN FAMILY

The classic form of starting over in America is of course immigration. Men and women leave the old country; they sacrifice
and endure; eventually they prevail. Yet this classic pattern
seems a little antique. Mario Cuomo and Michael Dukakis talk
about their immigrant backgrounds, but it was their parents who
came, to an older, simpler, and more spacious America. Perhaps
the success of Dukakises and Cuomos says something about the
way America used to be, before the empty spaces were filled up.
Almost a hundred years before Dukakis ran for president, the
young historian Frederick Jackson Turner delivered his famous
paper "The Significance of the Frontier in American History."
He said that vacant land had been the key to American opportunity. Now that the U.S. Census Bureau had declared the frontier
closed, as it did in 1890, Turner said that America would become
a more subdued, less hopeful place. He turned out to be wrong
in his prediction, since the American frontier involved something
more than vacant land. Although the first Dukakises and Cuomos
arrived after the bureau's frontier was closed, they found no
shortage of opportunity.

The example of the Nguyen family shows that the frontier is
still open. It was not some lost feature of turn-of-the-century
America that allowed earlier immigrants to succeed, or any trait
in particular about Greek or Italian or Polish immigrants. The act
of immigration itself made the difference.

I met the first arrival from the Nguyen family late in 1982, just
before I met Buddy Ginn. I was in Southern California, the center
of modern American immigration, interviewing new arrivals from

Indochina, the Philippines, and Mexico. In a refugee-resettle-
ment office, I asked a man, who was short and slight even for a
Vietnamese, to help me locate some families of refugees. He gave
me a list of names and addresses of new arrivals, several of whom
I later interviewed. Then he said, "Also, there's our family."

The Nguyens were typical of the first wave of Vietnamese
refugees. During the war there were fourteen Nguyens living in a
household in Saigon. Among them were six children, ranging in
age from the teens to the early thirties. The family business was
a small import-export firm. Most of the children had been educated and held good clerical or semiprofessional jobs. Two of the
sons were in the South Vietnamese army (Army of the Republic
of Viet Nam, or ARVN); one of them had been drafted out of law
school. Another son was a draftsman. Two daughters worked as
secretaries, one in a South Vietnamese government ministry and
the other at the U.S. embassy.

When Saigon fell, the crucial member of the family was obviously the daughter who had worked at the embassy. This gave
the family a claim on evacuation, or so it thought. In the spring
of 1975, the North Vietnamese and Viet Cong forces closed in on
Saigon much faster than anyone, including the communists themselves, had predicted. In the last days of April, most of the
Nguyens could not force their way into the embassy compound
to be evacuated, as they had hoped to be. Only the son who'd
been drafted out of law school into the ARVN, Nguyen Dong,
scrambled to the American air base at Tan Son Nhut and got a
place on an evacuation helicopter. (His is the only pseudonym in
this account.) He was thirty years old when he left, and he did
not speak any English.

Refugees, like prisoners, often have suspiciously pat-sounding
life stories, since they've had to tell them so often and they know
what themes and emphases pay off. When I was interviewing
Haitian refugees in Miami, several who obviously had just arrived started saying, in Creole that was very similar to French
and was easy for me to understand, that they'd left because they
wanted to make more money and rejoin their families. My "interpreter," a politically involved Haitian priest, gave them a glare
and gravely told me, "They say, 'We left because we could no

longer endure the repression of the unjust Duvalier regime.' '' I suspected that they would have a different story to tell the next time a visitor stopped by. Nguyen Dong's story, too, was neat-sounding, with a clear moral shape, very much like the *Autobiography of Benjamin Franklin*. But, as with Franklin and Poor Richard, that imposed moral shape was probably more important than the literal accuracy of the details. The story that Nguyen told was the classic version of the American dream.

As an early arrival, Nguyen went through the makeshift camps that were set up to process the first flood of refugees. He went from Clark Air Force Base, outside Manila, to Guam, and finally to a big refugee center at Camp Pendleton, the marine corps base north of San Diego. He was there for six months, getting English lessons and courses in "cultural orientation" — how to get a driver's license, how to apply for a job. Like many refugees who show aptitude for English while in the resettlement camps, he worked as an interviewer, taking down people's life stories so that their families could be traced and their claims to refugee status assessed. Initially he worked without pay, but just before he was released he was paid $5.00 a day. After Nguyen had been there six months, the Pendleton resettlement camp was closed, and he was on his own in the working world.

Like Buddy Ginn in Houston, Nguyen Dong scoured Los Angeles for any kind of job. He drove in a borrowed car or rode buses all day, and at night he stayed with Vietnamese friends or at flophouses. After a month he was hired at a waterbed factory in El Segundo for $2.10 an hour, which was then the minimum wage. He rented a single room for $120 a month and had $10 a day left for food, transportation, clothing, and everything else.

When he reached this point in his story, Nguyen looked reflective and made sure the moral of perseverance was clear. "I was miserable and lonely. I was working *hard* for $2.10 an hour. In those factories, you can't slow down. They expect you to work like a machine." His spirits rose only when he caught glimpses of other Vietnamese, who were drifting into this factory and doing strong-back jobs like his. "You see one person in the corner, you know you have more education than him, more talents than him, and you tell yourself, He survived, I can survive. You see someone, he may have been a farmer in Vietnam, and he survived. I told myself, I can survive.'' After three weeks assembling waterbeds, Nguyen heard that RCA Records was hiring. He assumed they wanted people to work in studios, so he told the personnel man that he'd had experience on broadcasting stations in Vietnam. When he reported for work, he was shown to the stockroom and told to put labels on records for $3 an hour.

Nguyen began to dwell on another American lesson: the value of money. When he was released from the camp, he had been entitled to a $300 resettlement bonus, but out of showy self-respect he had turned it down. "I did not want to touch it. I had pride. I wanted to feel that I had made it without any help." But with each hard day at the waterbed works he regretted his grand gesture. "I learned that money is really valuable in this country. You pay for it with blood and tears. I started thinking about that $300. Money is money. Why not collect it and put it in the bank and earn interest instead of just ignoring it?''

When he went in to collect the money, he had a stroke of blind luck, like those in Horatio Alger novels. In the resettlement office he bumped into an American refugee official whom he'd known in the camp. She said they needed more office workers to handle new arrivals. Although Nguyen still did not speak English smoothly, she agreed to put him in language school while starting him at $660 per month.

From this point on, the Nguyen family saga had all the classic elements of the Cuomo or Dukakis family's rise: sacrifice, study, ambition, frugality, achievement based on family pride. For the first two years, he was the only member of his family in the United States. Just after the fall of Saigon, most Vietnamese with American or ARVN connections were hustled off to "re-education camp," a combination of labor gulag and brainwashing center. So far, the brother who had been a draftsman, Nguyen Ninh, had kept out of camp because he was needed to help keep an electric power plant running. The other brother who had been in the ARVN (or "puppet forces," as they were now known), Nguyen Viet, had been sent off to a camp in the jungle. After two years of captivity, he escaped and sneaked back into Saigon. He found his brother Ninh and they planned to get out by boat.

Some boat escapes from Vietnam are well-organized commercial projects, with advance bookings and deposits (in gold) required. This was a rushed and amateur attempt. The brothers and several friends bought a tiny skiff in the countryside and tried to study seamanship from books. In the fall of 1977, after the summer monsoon storms, the seven men set out in a fifteen-foot boat.

They wanted to sail down the South China Sea to peninsular Malaysia, but the winds were blowing hard the wrong way. The nearest landfall in the direction they were moving was in the Philippines, about three times as far away as Malaysia. They cruised without really knowing where they were going, and on their eighth day at sea the motor stopped.

"After the broken engine, we figure 99 percent we die in the ocean," Ninh said several years later, obviously not for the first time. "Most people who go from Vietnam on a boat die." These sea lanes are very heavily traveled, especially with oil tankers heading toward Japan. But commercial ships generally steered away from the boat people, since picking them up meant endless legal complications. The Nguyen brothers' boat began to leak; it took on water and then, they said, it sank. They were left to swim in the sea.

At this point, according to the Nguyens, the captain of a commercial ship saw men floundering in the water and decided that he had to save them. A large dark shape loomed up, proving to be a freighter from Kuwait. It took them aboard. The Nguyen brothers and their friends were spared from drowning, but this was not quite the end of their problems. At the freighter's next stop, Singapore, they weren't allowed off the boat. Once it got to Kuwait, they were thrown in jail and told they'd be sent back to Vietnam on the next boat heading east.

From jail, the Nguyens managed to contact Western embassies, the UN refugee office, and the Red Cross. They found their brother's address in Los Angeles and sent a letter to him. The original Nguyen used his connections in the refugee bureaucracy to have the UN pay attention to his brothers' case. They were classified as refugees, sent to a holding camp in Greece, and admitted to the United States about a year after they left Vietnam.

These brothers also spoke no English when they showed up. At their brother's prodding, they began learning while scouring the town for work. All three brothers shared Nguyen Dong's tiny apartment, the two new arrivals chipping in for the rent when they found work and listening to his ceaseless lectures about frugality and discipline. All of the brothers fanatically saved money to help the rest of the family buy its way out of Vietnam. "I tell them, 'Honey, you don't have anybody to support but yourself, you put your money into savings,' " Nguyen Dong said.

Viet, the former ARVN lieutenant, found a minimum-wage job with a valet-parking outfit at the L.A. airport. Ninh became a carpenter's helper. A few months later, he found a place as a trainee draftsman with a machine-tool company. "We were three single men living together then," Nguyen Dong recalled. "We put our money together and save. If we are bringing home $1000 a month each, total $3000, we can save $2000 a month. Soon we have money. The way of living in our country is so different. We have a tradition of sticking together. We need much less." Another Vietnamese man told me at about the same time, "We have one suit of nice clothes. We put it on to go to the good grocery stores. We go back to the butcher section and say casually, like we are rich, 'Excuse me, please, could I have some scrap meat for my cat?' We could get the hearts, the tripe, the other things they would not sell — and we cut them up and get protein."

Four sisters and a nephew were the next Nguyens out. They went as boat people to Indonesia, were admitted to a refugee camp, and in 1979 were sent to join the brothers in Los Angeles.

Then the last two sisters escaped. One, Hai, had been a student when Saigon fell; the other, Mai, had been the U.S. embassy employee. By 1980, they'd had enough of Ho Chi Minh City and set out on foot. With two children in arms, they walked for seven days through Cambodia to the Thai border. After six months in a Thai refugee camp, they were admitted to the United States, arriving about the time Ronald Reagan was elected president.

It was only five years since the first Nguyen was a refugee himself, but he had adapted at a daunting rate. He had just finished his civics course and become a naturalized citizen. He had married another Vietnamese refugee. He and his brothers had entered the Southern California real estate market; they bought a small house in Downey, a respectable middle-class suburb that quickly became largely Asian. After they got the house, Viet still had $3000 in savings left from his $1000-a-month job at the parking lot. He made a down payment on a small furniture store in Hawthorne, a tough district in L.A., and went into business. Just before the deal went through, Viet started to worry. What if he lost everything he'd saved? The first Nguyen scolded him for being fainthearted. If he lost the money, he could always earn it back, but if the gamble paid off, he'd have "financial independence." By the time the store opened, Nguyen Ninh had moved up to a job as a professional draftsman, at $10 an hour.

Nguyen Dong was naturally eager to see his newly arrived sisters start pulling their weight. Hai took a course in accounting and wound up working for a Vietnamese dentist in a crumbling ghetto of Long Beach, where other Vietnamese were moving in. Nguyen Dong steered Mai toward one of the many "colleges of cosmetology" in Los Angeles. She lacked enthusiasm but he pressured her to finish. She did and soon had a job in West Los Angeles, the richest part of the city, a thirty-mile commute each way. Her business went well, and by the end of 1980 she was earning $1500 a month. Some of her clients were real estate ladies from West L.A., one of whom mentioned that a beauty shop was going on the market. On her $18,000 a year, Mai had so far saved about $5000 in cash. She borrowed $2000 from Nguyen Dong and $5000 more from the bank, and she had the down payment. Eighteen months after leaving the refugee camp in Thailand, she opened Mai's Beauty Salon in Beverly Hills.

At about the same time, the Nguyen family's father finally arrived, having first escaped to Belgium, where his knowledge of French made him feel somewhat less lost and where he learned an entirely new trade: bakery work. In the United States he started out as a cook at a hospital and then moved to a bakery that, a few years later, he unaccountably did not yet own. He and his children were still saving money in the hope of buying exit visas for their spouses and siblings stuck in Vietnam. (Vietnamese refugees generally seem confident that they can get money back to relatives in the country. The relatives put it to work by bribing officials to get exit visas or paying for places on a boat.)

As the members of his family began appearing in Los Angeles, Nguyen Dong was constantly improving his own position. He rented the original house in Downey to the eight other members of his family. They paid him $100 a month apiece, which covered the mortgage. "That is the beauty of the American way, everybody sharing!" he said. He and his wife bought a second house nearby on his earnings as a resettlement officer and hers as a chief teller at a branch of the Security Pacific Bank. They had calculated exactly how much leeway their earnings gave them, even for having a child. "I have been Americanized about that," he said in 1983, when he was thirty-eight years old. "In Vietnam, you have children right away. If my wife is pregnant, she stays home. My salary cannot support us now. My wife and I, we each bring home $1000 a month. The house payments are $1000, and $1000 is for living. But we will pay off the second mortgage on the house in three years. Then my salary should be $1500, and the house payments will be down to $600. That will leave $900. We could do it. We can have children in three years."

The first time I visited the house in Downey, home to nearly a dozen people including the children, I was prepared for a sense of confinement, or of stoic endurance amid squalor, or of relentless striving, or of huddled-immigrant scenes like those from the Bettmann Archives, or for practically anything except the semi-elegant serenity I found. The house sat among other unexceptional modern California ranch houses, with a vista of a freeway, on a street like a thousand others in greater L.A. Inside the house, the sisters and brothers began arriving after long commutes. Several changed into Vietnamese pajamas and relaxed in the living room. Delicately colored prints of Asian scenes hung on the walls. The dining table stood on a platform with a canopy overhead, like an indoor gazebo. The only external indications of their nonstop struggle to get ahead were the half-dozen cars that jammed the driveway and lined the curb. I listened to the adults' stories, trying to make them out through the heavy accents. Two elementary school children appeared, saying good night in natural-sounding American English.

Nguyen Dong beamed as he heard them talk. He said that he tells the refugees who still arrive that they must adjust to the "new life" as soon as possible, like him. "I tell them, 'Good advice does not mean an easy life now and a bad life in the future.' I say, 'If you go on job training, you will learn the English faster. Welfare will make you lazy. You will hesitate to work and hesitate to speak English.' "

Several years after I first met the Nguyens, I came to understand more vividly the urgency that drove them once they reached the United States. In the summer of 1988 I was in Vietnam, for the first time, on an endless trip in a decrepit Russian bus. The journey went from Hué, just south of the former demilitarized zone, along Highway 1 down the length of what had been South Vietnam to Ho Chi Minh City.

In Ho Chi Minh City, I walked with my wife to the former U.S. embassy, where so many Vietnamese like the Nguyens had struggled to get over the wall. The building was decrepit and looked boarded-up. The iron railings were still bent and broken, showing the marks of the human assault in the final days. The only sign of activity there was a homeless family, of the Cham ethnic minority group, who had slung hammocks across the front gate and built a cook-fire on the sidewalk.

Across the street from the embassy, we saw four men in their early twenties, one more group of the half-American Amerasians who turn up all over Saigon. Two obviously had black fathers; two, white. Like most of the other Amerasians, they looked much more Western than Vietnamese. From a glance at their faces it was easy to imagine exactly how their fathers had looked.

The young men beckoned us over, and one of the blacks said hello. As soon as we heard him, my wife and I stood dumbstruck. This Vietnamese citizen not only spoke fluent English but spoke with a faultless black American accent. Anyone who had run into him in West Chicago or Washington, D.C., heard him talk, and watched him move would have taken for granted that he'd always lived there. "How ya doin," he said. "You got to help me get out of here."

He said that he called himself Raymond because that was the name of his father, a military policeman from Philadelphia. The son said he was born in 1964 on a U.S. Army base and lived there with his father and Vietnamese mother until he was four. Then his father went home, passing him and his mother on to another American soldier, also black. Raymond said that he'd grown up on the base, never going to school but being taught to read and write by the soldiers. When he was eleven, just before the fall of Saigon, he said, his mother had sent him to Pleiku to stay with an aunt. A few weeks later, when he came back to the city, his mother shunned him, because he was such flagrant evidence of her fraternization with the Americans. The police rounded him up and sent him to re-education camp, and there he stayed for the next twelve years. He said he'd been released the previous fall, at the age of twenty-three. By the time he got out, his mother had died, and since he lacked any proper household registration, he was an illegal citizen in his own country.

Nearly everyone in Saigon has a story to whisper to visiting Americans about the deep ties to the United States that qualifies him as a refugee, and visitors quickly become skeptical about these self-serving tales. Raymond's story had some holes: he said he'd never tried to contact his father because he "didn't have the money for stamps," even though he had the money for a pair of blue jeans. Some of the other Amerasians muttered that Raymond's father was French, and Raymond was trying to weasel his way into the "desirable" Amerasian status, which should eventually entitle him to an exit visa from Vietnam. Given the way Raymond looked, his father had to have been black; and given the way he sounded, Raymond must have spent much of his childhood among Americans. In any case, the details of his parentage were not that important. Other Vietnamese treated him as an Amerasian, and Raymond considered himself such — which is the crucial ingredient in American identity, unlike Vietnamese or Japanese or French. (An earlier refugee, the Austrian-born movie director Billy Wilder, once said, "If you want to become a French citizen, a Swiss citizen, they say: 'What do you mean? We were born here.' If you don't want to become an

American citizen, they say, 'What's the matter? Aren't we good enough?' It's the basis of my love for America.'')

At some point, Raymond is likely to end up in America. The U.S. government has agreed to accept Amerasians, and Vietnam is supposedly willing to let them all go, although it has been very slow about issuing the exit visas. Whenever Raymond does get out, I expect him to eclipse even the Nguyens. He is totally bilingual; he has survived tests that most refugees (to say nothing of most Americans) have been spared; he has invented a new life for himself even more dramatically than Nguyen Dong did. ''I will make it in the States,'' he said. He will, like most other people who have been through the transforming process of becoming immigrants.

NOT KNOWING OUR PLACE

In historic terms, there is nothing at all surprising in hearing that America has made room for adaptable people. The success of the Nguyens and the Ginns is part of a long-established pattern. ''The data unequivocally show that migrants have more successful careers than men still living in the region of their birth,'' Peter M. Blau and Otis Dudley Duncan wrote in their classic study, *The American Occupational Structure,* published in 1967. ''It appears that something either about migration or about migrants promotes occupational success.'' Blau and Duncan were writing about Americans who moved from one part of the country to another, like Buddy Ginn, but the same logic and evidence are appropriate for immigrants from overseas — and even, in a way, for people like Westberry, who wholly changed his society from within. In every U.S. Census for more than a hundred years, a higher proportion of immigrants than of the native-born has been self-employed. (In the U.S. population as a whole, roughly one worker in sixteen is self-employed. Among Korean immigrants, for instance, it's about one worker in eight.) Sons and daughters of immigrants, people like Cuomo and Dukakis, generally earn more money than people of the same age and education whose parents are native-born. Several Asian immigrant groups have higher average incomes than native-born whites.* "As self-selected persons of high motivation and ingenuity, [immigrants] tend to plan, save, invest, and contribute disproportionately to entrepreneurial activity," said the Select Commission on Immigration, a U.S. government panel set up to recommend immigration reforms in the early 1980s. "In any group of people, the ones who choose to leave are likely to be the most productive," Ray Marshall, a former secretary of labor, told me in 1982.

"Migration . . . is the oldest action against poverty," John Kenneth Galbraith wrote in *The Nature of Mass Poverty*. "It selects those who most want help. It is good for the country to which they go; it helps to break the equilibrium of poverty in the country from which they come."

What is striking and impressive is that this historic pattern still holds. In the America of the 1980s, with its deficits and its deindustrialization and its reports of a shrinking middle class, the

* Andrew Hacker reported this comparison, based on data collected in the 1980 census:

GROUP	FAMILY INCOME	PROPORTION FOREIGN BORN
Japanese	$43,493	28.4%
Asian Indian	39,739	70.4
Filipino	37,662	64.6
Chinese	35,869	63.3
White	33,412	3.9
Korean	32,530	81.9
Hawaiian	30,522	1.6
Cuban	29,010	77.9
Mexican	23,476	26.0
Eskimo	21,988	1.5
American Indian	21,748	2.5
Vietnamese	20,415	90.5
Black	20,077	2.8
Puerto Rican	17,067	3.0

"Black Crime, White Racism," Andrew Hacker, *The New York Review of Books*, March 3, 1988, p. 40. The Vietnamese average is low mainly because there were so many new arrivals at the time and because fewer of the newcomers were already educated, like the Nguyens.

Nguyens made a place for themselves as the Cuomos and Dukakises did earlier. In different ways, the Vietnamese immigrants, Buddy and Judy Ginn, and Wyman Westberry all exemplified the fundamental virtue of America. They were people who did not know their place — and who helped themselves and enriched America by inventing new roles to play.

American society works best when people are in flux. When they stop feeling that they can control their luck, the basic glue of American society no longer holds.

CHAPTER SIX

Static Societies

IF AMERICA has always meant the constant chance of movement, what happens when that chance is denied? Then our society becomes crueler, since some of us are stuck in place. A rigid
America is also weak and vulnerable, because it sacrifices its
unique strength: the energy of people who think they can always
make something new of their lives.

American rigidity sounds like an abstract problem, but it is at
the heart of our most troubling defects. Here are three illustrations of what happens to our country when its people conclude
that they can't control their fate.

DISPLACED WORKERS

In the early 1980s, at about the time the Nguyen family was
getting established and Buddy Ginn was becoming a tool pusher,
heavy industries in the American Midwest were entering their
darkest days. The high dollar, resurgent Japan and Korea, aging
American equipment, inflexible union work rules, managers who
concentrated on mergers rather than manufacturing — all these
familiar forces led to plant closures and layoffs across that sec-
tion of the country.

Eventually much of "smokestack America" rebounded. After the dollar fell in the late 1980s, American exports became more attractive, and U.S. economic growth was for a while actually led by manufactured exports from the Midwest and Northeast. But by that time several powerful waves of "creative destruction" had battered the old industrial areas, and much of the existing social structure was swept away.

One of the places most dramatically changed was South Chicago, which had once been the center of America's greatest steel-producing area. The crescent along the southwest shore of Lake Michigan, running from Hammond and Gary west to Chicago, contained the densest concentration of steel mills in the world. Like St Marys, South Chicago was in many ways a stereotype brought to life, in this case a stereotype of the stable, rooted, blue-collar community rather than of the company town. The rows of bungalows in communities like Hegewisch, Iron Dale, and Mill Gate were dwarfed by the mammoth steelworks and the heaps of slag that glowed red at night. Apart from the mills, the biggest structures in South Chicago were, appropriately, St. Michael's Roman Catholic cathedral and the United Steel Workers' union hall. Neighborhoods were rigidly stratified, separated not just between blacks and whites but into Polish, Croatian, Bohemian, and Mexican zones. South Chicago's most famous local politician was Alderman Edward (Fast Eddie) Vrdolyak, a sharp-tongued voice of the white ethnics who became the chief tormentor of Chicago's first black mayor, Harold Washington, and then switched to the Republican Party. Families in South Chicago had sent men to the mills for two or three generations, starting with immigrant workers at the turn of the century. The unions were strong, and labor-management relations amounted to class war. In 1937 there was a bitter strike at Republic Steel, and a crowd of demonstrators was gunned down by the police. Nearly fifty years later, at a time when most Americans would have been hard pressed to find Vietnam on a map, let alone the Sudentenland or other landmarks of the 1930s, teenagers from steelworking families could point out exactly where the Republic Steel martyrs fell.

South Chicago's steel mills started running into trouble in the late 1970s. In the face of foreign competition, they gradually retrenched and retreated, apparently believing they could not beat the Japanese or Koreans head-on. The Wisconsin Steel works, for instance, had been one of the area's most successful and harmonious mills. It was run as a profitable captive supplier by International Harvester (now Navistar), and its employees were represented by a company union rather than the somewhat truculent United Steel Workers. By 1976, however, it was losing money, and Harvester sold it to a small California company, Envirodyne, which had no previous experience in running a big steel mill. After various restructuring schemes, applications for federal loans, and optimistic speeches by the peppy new managers, the mill began losing even more money than before. The killing blow was a five-month-long strike at Harvester in 1979, which eliminated Wisconsin Steel's main market. At the end of March 1980, with no advance word to the thirty-four hundred workers, Wisconsin Steel was padlocked and shut for good. The Chase Manhattan Bank, which had financed part of the sale to Envirodyne, apparently figured out what was going to happen before the workers did. In a charming touch, it froze the company's assets so quickly that the paychecks issued on the final day bounced.

The biggest mill in South Chicago suffered a similar fate. During World War II, sixteen thousand workers had toiled at the mighty South Works of US Steel, turning out metal for ships and tanks. By the early 1980s, the work force had gradually shrunk to about seventy-five hundred. US Steel (now USX) was in this period shifting away from the steelmaking business toward oil and other areas that seemed more promising. After long, bitter negotiations with the union and the local governments, which hoped and thought the company would refurbish the mill, US Steel shut down the South Works early in 1984.

The mill closings were, of course, calamitous to people who had always taken steel jobs for granted. On the South Works's last day of operation, March 30, 1984, a "funeral" cortège of about sixty cars drove through South Chicago from the union hall to the South Works, mourning the death of the mill. Men walked around carrying signs saying, "Machine Shop Rest in Peace,"

"Welding Shop Rest in Peace." Then they went back to the union hall to hold a wake and listen to speeches urging everyone to hang on until the business turned around. South Chicago's Local 65 of the Steel Workers Union had been famous as the home base of Edward Sadlowski, the firebrand reform candidate who barely lost the race for the international union presidency in 1976, when he was thirty-six. The Local 65 union hall, named after Hilding Anderson, one of the Republic Steel martyrs, had been built for a membership of ten thousand. After the South Works closed, there were only eight hundred members left, and the local set about the grim business of selling its hall.

At Wisconsin Steel, the traditional, compliant union organization had disintegrated after the shutdown. An informal relief group sprang up around a sixty-four-year-old veteran worker named Frank Lumpkin. Lumpkin, who was born in Georgia as a black sharecropper's son and had come north to Wisconsin Steel in 1950, put together the Save Our Jobs Committee. From the spring of 1980 on, it did what it could to mitigate the damage done to its community.

Lumpkin was as forceful and determined a man as Wyman Westberry, and he tried to keep his group of laid-off workers busy and engaged. They marched with placards in front of the Harvester/Navistar headquarters in Chicago's Loop. They rode buses to the state house in Springfield to meet legislators and ask for loans or other help to reopen the mill. They wrote letters, attracted press coverage, and initiated lawsuits. Lumpkin collected free government-surplus cheese to pass out to his men.

In the end, the Save Our Jobs Committee did win an important moral victory. When Harvester sold the mill, it asserted that it had also sold its way out of its obligations to the pension fund that workers like Frank Lumpkin had built up over the years. When the mill failed, tiny Envirodyne could not begin to cover the pensions. In addition to losing their jobs and their medical insurance, then, most workers suddenly lost their pensions too. Soon after the shutdown, Save Our Jobs contacted a young lawyer named Thomas Geoghegan, who filed a suit against Harvester demanding that it cover the pensions accrued during its long ownership of the mill. For the next eight years, Geoghegan persisted with the suit. In early 1988, as the case oozed its way toward the top of the court docket, Harvester/Navistar agreed to settle for $14.8 million. It did not amount to much money when divided among the Wisconsin Steel workers. The largest award was about $17,000 and the smallest was $200 — and this after eight years of waiting. At least six hundred of the workers had died before the money was distributed. When the suit was settled, there was a flurry of coverage in the Chicago papers. Frank Lumpkin was described in the *Chicago Tribune* as "probably as close to a saint as Chicago has these days." Geoghegan was "the only other real hero of the case," praised even by the judge for pursuing an unpopular case for so many years for so little money. But despite this late vindication, the stories made clear that much of South Chicago had died and most of the workers had never recovered from the shutdown.

Very few of the workers ever came up with jobs remotely as attractive as those at the mill. To reporters and to those conducting surveys, the workers said that they were doing part-time construction work, working in supermarkets, or collecting aluminum cans from trash cans and along the side of the road. The laid-off South Works employees I spoke to said they had given up hope of finding jobs anywhere else in the country, because prospects looked bleak all over. Everyone seemed to have heard a story about a friend or nephew who drove to Houston or Denver, found himself stacking bottles at the 7-Eleven or competing with illegal Mexicans for construction jobs, and drove back home. It happened even to Ed Sadlowski's son. "My kid took one of those treks down to Texas," he told me, half embarrassed and half righteous about his son's comeuppance. "He went to Houston, worked construction. One day he called up and asked for bus fare home. The contractor owed three or four weeks' wages to thirty guys, and he skipped town. Maybe my son learned something from it."

This side of the deindustrialization story has become familiar to Americans. It runs from TV news reports through Bruce Springsteen's "My Hometown." But there was a side to the story not so often reported, which was the way certain cultural forces greatly compounded the steelworkers' problems and seemed to make the classic form of American adaptation impossible for them.

Even when the Chicago mills were closing, America had not become a hopeless, doomed economy. This was the very same period in which the Ginn family and the Nguyens were on their way up. Nor was the sort of disruption that affected South Chicago that unusual in American history. A hundred years earlier, the mill towns had arisen because of large-scale economic changes that were dismantling other communities. "This community is suffering from the same process that built it," said Dominic Pacyga, who grew up in South Chicago and has directed oral-history projects about the steel communities. "It benefited from the search for cheaper labor and less taxation that has driven capital all along. The very movement that gave it birth is now killing it." The shock to South Chicago was much more abrupt and brutal than it needed to be, because of the highhandedness of the companies as they closed the mills and, in Harvester's case, tried to escape their pension obligations. But the basic fact, that a community had lost its traditional industry, is not exceptional in American history: it has been the unfortunate norm, even during times of America's most robust overall growth. What was exceptional, and tragic, was that so many forces kept so many workers from adjusting to a different role.

Some of those forces were political: conceivably the government could provide more job-matching services to make the search for new work less hit-or-miss. Certainly the government should keep companies from running away from their pension commitments. Some of the forces were practical: the Wisconsin Steel work force was older than usual, and workers in their fifties and sixties understandably thought it was too late to start over with blue-collar jobs somewhere else. Moreover, when the steel industry collapsed, it brought the local real estate market down with it, and even younger workers were stuck with homes they couldn't sell.

But there were also powerful, destructive cultural forces at work. The life of the steel communities was dominated by big, unwieldy institutions: the church, the schools, the army, the union, the mill, the Chicago political machine. Despite their many differences, they all taught one lesson: people should know their place. Nothing about the environment encouraged people to believe that it paid to invent roles for themselves or step out of line. On the contrary, the unions, the military, and the political machine demonstrated that the man who bucks the system is the man who gets slapped down. It was a Japanese-style lesson of teamwork, obedience, and conformity ("The nail that sticks out gets hammered in") inflicted on people who eventually would be expected to adjust in a non-Japanese, individualist culture.

"Some people will even tell you that the workers can't change because they're lazy and shiftless," Bill Koziarski, a burly, red-haired South Sider in his mid thirties told me soon after the South Works shutdown. Koziarski came from several generations of South Chicago steelworkers but was the first in his family to finish college; he later became a journalist. "They're not lazy at all. But their whole life has been channeled in a certain direction. It's like a football player who's been tracked since the eighth grade to play football. Everything's arranged for him — and suddenly he has to do something else. It's comfortable being tracked. I remember when I used to wonder how I was going to use my English degree in the mill. That was in the period when I hadn't realized that I didn't have to go back.

"The biggest difference between growing up there and some other place was that you didn't *consider* doing anything else. If you came from some other place, you always considered some options, even if it was just a different factory."

"That's the thing about these towns," another man told me. "They let you know exactly what your place is."

A sense of place is important even to Americans, and old, dense, settled societies like South Chicago's are as legitimately and nobly American as a trailer park outside Houston. Machine-style politics, in which institutions take care of individuals, is a basic part of the American (and especially the immigrant) way. "These are good, stupid, hard-working people, if you know what I mean," Joe Mulac, a laid-off Croatian steelworker, said one day as he drove past rows of South Chicago bungalows. He pointed to the parish school and said, "The note on that school was paid off the year after the cardinal blessed it. That's how stupid we are." "It is *such* an institutionally rich place," said

Dominic Pacyga. "Even now there are hundreds of clubs and organizations — chambers of commerce, ladies sodalities, rosary clubs. The connection with the parish is so intense. It's more than a place of worship — it's a library, a center for all sorts of organizations."

But this dense, tightly connected society has become very vulnerable. We have always lived with economic shifts; it's highly unlikely that that will change. So we rely on our people to remain flexible and mobile. If they can't, they suffer, for the whole society can't adjust to accommodate the few. The grandparents of today's steelworkers all came from different jobs in different places, as presumably the workers' children will hold different jobs in different places. But the inevitable changes would be easier on everyone if local cultures did not teach their members to know their place — and if, as will be seen in the next chapter, the outside culture can be made more open to blue-collar workers who want a second chance.

LEARNING TO FAIL

The group that is most permanently and disturbingly left behind as the rest of America adapts is the black underclass. It is a special case, but in essence the forces that imprison it are the same ones that hampered many of the steelworkers. These forces constitute an internal culture of resignation bounded by external barriers.

American society must at some level be open to talent regardless of color. After all, black-skinned immigrants from the Caribbean and Africa are generally successful, like other immigrants, and more successful on average than native-born American blacks. By some measures of education and income they are more successful on average than native-born whites.

It is conceivable that black immigrants do better than American blacks because, as foreigners, they may encounter less prejudice, or prejudice of a different kind. The more likely explanation, however, is that roughly similar degrees of prejudice affect the two groups, immigrant blacks and black Americans, in very different ways. In much of Southeast Asia, the Overseas Chinese minority is even now subject to considerable legal and social discrimination. The same has obviously been true of the Jewish minority in Europe and North America for centuries. But in these cases, the discrimination was not built on a message of inferiority and was not taken as such by those discriminated against. Jews and Overseas Chinese may feel that they are destined to be persecuted, but not that they are destined to fail. Antiblack stereotypes in the United States seem to affect black immigrants and many black Americans in this same way. They are inconvenient and unfair, but they can be overcome. The effect on the black underclass, most of whom are descended from slaves rather than northern freedmen or postslavery immigrants, is much more damaging. Racial prejudice boils down to the deeply anti-American message that some people are born to fail.

In the hallway of a public high school in Miami, I once studied the pictures of students that lined the walls. Along one wall were photos of the student honor court, those with the best grades. Along the other wall were pictures of the basketball team. All the faces in the pictures were black, and it would have been very difficult to tell by looking at them who was from what country. The names, however, were different. On the first wall were the likes of Jean-Louis and Roland and Marie, the names of Haitian immigrants. The students on the other wall, wearing basketball uniforms, were native-born Americans.

I mentioned the pictures to Irving Hamer, the headmaster of the Park Heights Street Academy in Baltimore. Park Heights, located in a spruced-up row house in the Baltimore ghetto, is a private school designed to give a second chance to students who seem bright but have run into trouble in the public schools. Hamer, who was raised in central Harlem by his mother, is a tall, broad-shouldered black man who was then in his late thirties. He said that what he fought at his school, every day, was the idea that blacks should not try because they could not win.

"When you watch these young men playing sports, you *know* the enthusiasm, the creativity, the competition, and the standards are all there," he said. "Sports is different, because it's the one place where adolescent black males believe that they'll get a fair test. The determination and energy they show there doesn't translate itself into other areas because they think they're unavailable. Can you doubt their creativity and vigor when you see what they do on that court? You can hear it in their banter — it's very witty, extremely fast and competitive. But it's not defined as 'useful' or 'creditable.' Apart from sports, there's nothing that brings them the message that an upbeat approach can pay off. By the time they are twenty-four years old, it's over. The competitive spirit is there — how could it be more obvious? — but we don't have a way to fire it up. The message that leaps from their experience and reinforces their self-hate is that they shouldn't even try."

I visited Park Heights in 1984, during Jesse Jackson's first campaign for the presidency. One wall of Hamer's office was dominated by a life-size portrait of a dignified-looking Jackson. "Why do you think he's getting all the votes around here?" Hamer said. "He sends a message that you can succeed.

"It is a killer to have those immigrants come in and do so well," Hamer said, speaking not just of the Haitians but also of the Korean merchants in the ghetto. "The Haitians, they may have been oppressed, but they don't have a psychology of oppression. They felt they could make their lives better here.

"The students here have some very skewed information," he continued. "Their analysis of the black condition can become apologetic and excuse-ridden. They've learned to look for external circumstances as a way of getting us off the hook. That's the trap: if all these conditions prevent us from making it, then the fact that we don't make it is okay."

"People are always saying, 'Why don't these local blacks try harder, when so many of the black-skinned immigrants do so well?' " Juan Williams said soon afterward. Williams, a reporter for the *Washington Post* then in his early thirties, is himself a black-skinned immigrant, born in Panama and brought by his mother to Bedford-Stuyvesant when he was two. "When people do well, it's because their parents gave them the feeling that great things were expected of them and were within their grasp. My older sister went off to a fancy college and came home all fine and uppity. It makes you think, I want that too. I can do that too. What mattered was having practical models of what you could achieve."

The aftereffects of slavery are America's peculiar social burden, but they also illustrate a broader point: the violence that a static culture does to the American ideal of constant mobility. When people think they can't control their fate, that they can't play by the same rules as everybody else, they fail. From outside the country, it is obvious that America's greatest strength is its willingness to keep opening itself to the ambitions of new people, and that its greatest vulnerability is the barriers that keep other Americans out. Outsiders looking at Japan can easily see the talent it wastes by barring half of its population, its women, from contention for the best jobs. Much more than Japan, America has grown strong by giving ordinary people a chance to rise without limits. The black underclass is an example of what happens to America when people feel they can't change.

THE CLASS WAR

American society is not egalitarian, but it is democratic. There has always been a class *structure* — the distribution of income between rich and poor has been surprisingly constant through the years — but not a powerful class *system,* since continually changing groups have occupied the various tiers. Because of the impermanence, Americans don't have an ingrained sense of rank and deference. Some people may be richer or more famous than others, they may be cleverer and quicker, but most Americans will be damned if they'll admit that the successes are better people. Even though Ross Perot and Bill Gates (the young founder of the computer-software giant Microsoft) have made a billion dollars each, everyone still expects them to behave like average guys.

The idea that some Americans *are* better than others is ruinous to America. It strikes at our cultural core, the belief that anyone can try and that all will play by roughly the same rules. It also lies behind the most poisonous episode of America's mid-twentieth-century history: the class-war aspect of the Vietnam War. I know about this at first hand.

I started college, in 1966, with a genial indifference to the war. I didn't know much about it, I didn't complain, and I certainly never expected it to last long enough to have anything to do with me. But, in the most trite portion of my life story, over the next four years my thoughts changed. By the time I began my final year at Harvard, in 1969, I'd been to lots of marches and written lots of antiwar material for the college newspaper.

As the months went by during that last year, the rock to which I had instinctively anchored my hopes — the certainty that the war would be over before I could possibly fight — began to crumble. It shattered altogether on Thanksgiving weekend of 1969, when, while riding back to Boston from a visit with my relatives in Philadelphia, I heard that the draft lottery had been held and my birthdate had come up number 45. I recognized for the first time that if I didn't want to be drafted, I had consciously to find a way to avoid it.

At that place and at that time, every choice had barbs. To answer the call seemed unthinkable, not only because, in my heart, I was sure I would be killed, but also because among my friends it was axiomatic that one should not be "complicit" in the "immoral" war effort. Draft resistance, the course chosen by a few principled members of the antiwar movement, meant going to prison or leaving the country. That is what I should have done — formally resist, taking a stand and accepting the consequences of my views — but I didn't. I wanted to go to graduate school, to get married, and to enjoy the bright prospects I thought I'd earned.

I learned quickly enough that there was only one way to get what I wanted. A medical deferment would restore things to the happy state I had known during four undergraduate years. The barbed choices would be put off. By the impartial dictates of public policy I would be free to pursue the better side of life.

Like many of my friends whose numbers had come up wrong in the lottery, I set about securing my salvation. When I was not participating in antiwar rallies, I was poring over the army's code of physical regulations. I was very skinny, and my normal weight was at the cut-off point for an "underweight" disqualification. With a diligence born of panic, I lost ten pounds in two months to make sure I would have a margin. I was six-feet-one at the time. On the morning of the draft physical I weighed 120 pounds. I knew some students who were going the other way, trying to break out of the height-weight limits at the top end. I'd see them late at night, madly gorging on pizzas and milkshakes.

Before sunrise on the morning of the draft physical, I rode the subway to the Cambridge City Hall, where we had been told to gather for shipment to the examination at the Boston Naval Shipyard. The examinations were administered on a rotating basis, one or two days each month for each of the draft boards in the area. Virtually everyone who showed up on Cambridge day at the Naval Shipyard was a student from Harvard or MIT.

There was no mistaking the political temper of the group. Many of my friends wore red armbands and stop-the-war buttons. Most chanted the familiar words "Ho, Ho, Ho Chi Minh, NLF is gonna win." One of the things we had learned from the draft counselors was that disruptive behavior at the examination was a worthwhile political goal, not only because it obstructed the smooth operation of the criminal war machine but because it might impress the examiners with our undesirable character. As we climbed into the buses and as they rolled toward the Naval Shipyard, about half of the young men brought their chants to a crescendo. The rest of us sat rigid and silent, clutching x rays and letters from our doctors at home.

Inside the Naval Shipyard, we were first confronted by a young sergeant from Long Beach, a former surfer no older than the rest of us and seemingly unaware that he had an unusual situation on his hands. He had just started reading out instructions for the intelligence tests when he was hooted down. It is easy though unpleasant to imagine the reaction of a roomful of Harvard and MIT seniors, in 1970, to the prospect of an army "intelligence" test. The sergeant went out to collect his lieutenant, who clearly had been through a Cambridge day before. "We've got all the time in the world," he said, and let the chanting go on for two or three minutes. "When we're finished with you, you can go, and not a minute sooner."

From that point on the disruption became more purposeful and individual, largely confined to those whose deferment strategies were based on anti-authoritarian psychiatric "problems." Twice I saw students walk up to young orderlies, whose hands were extended to receive the required cup of urine, and throw the vials in the orderlies' faces. The orderlies looked up, initially more astonished than angry — but then plenty angry — and went back to towel themselves off. Most of the rest of us trod quietly through the paces, waiting for the moment of confrontation, when the final examiner would give his verdict. I had stepped on the scales at the beginning of the examination. Desperate at seeing the orderly write down 122 pounds, I hopped back on and made sure he lowered it to 120. I walked in a trance through the rest of the examination until the final meeting with the fatherly physician who ruled on marginal cases like mine. I stood there in socks and underwear, arms wrapped around me in the chilly building. I knew as I looked in the doctor's face that he understood exactly what I was doing.

"Have you ever contemplated suicide?" he asked after he finished looking over the chart. My eyes darted up to his. "Oh, suicide — uh, yeah, I guess I've been feeling very unstable and unreliable recently." He looked at me, staring until I returned my eyes to the ground. He wrote "Unqualified" on my folder, turned on his heel, and left. I was overcome by a wave of relief that revealed to me for the first time how great my terror had been, and by the beginning of the sense of shame that remained with me for years.

It was, initially, a generalized shame at having gotten away with my deception, but it came into sharper focus later in the day. Even as the last of the Cambridge contingent were throwing their urine and deliberately failing their eye tests to prove they were color blind, buses from the next board began to arrive. These bore the boys from Chelsea, thick, dark-haired young men, the white proles of Boston. Most of them were younger than we were — they had just left high school — and it had clearly never occurred to them that they should look for a way out of the draft. Some may have felt trapped into serving, and some — probably more — may have been proud; others may have felt that they were just doing their duty to their country. In any case they were on their way. I tried to avoid noticing, but the results were impossible not to see. While four out of five of my friends from Harvard were being deferred, the figures for the Chelsea boys were being reversed.

We returned to Cambridge that afternoon not in government buses but as free individuals, liberated and victorious. The talk was high-spirited, but there was something close to the surface that none of us wanted to mention. We knew now who would be killed.

I wrote about this episode in 1975, five years after it happened. I described the difference between my friends from my home town, where hundreds were drafted and about two dozen killed, and my classmates from Harvard, very few of whom were forced to put themselves on the line, either by going into the military or officially refusing induction. In a fifth-year reunion report, to which just under half of the twelve hundred members of the class of 1970 responded, fifty-six said they'd been in the military in some form; two specified service in Vietnam. Seven said they had performed alternative service as conscientious objectors, and though no one reported going to prison, one wrote from England that he had been a "draft resister, beat the rap on a legal technicality." On the other hand, I was stunned to learn the name of one of the handful of Harvard graduates from the late 1960s who had been killed. He was also from Redlands, and his parents lived a few blocks away from mine. He had started college a year before I did. I had barely known him before college, because his parents had sent him east to prep school, but I worked alongside him one summer at the Redlands post office and saw him frequently in Cambridge. He was the son of a career military officer, and had gone to Harvard on an ROTC scholarship. He was a shy, gentle, droll person and as unlikely a soldier as I had ever met. Usually I'd run into him on the Larz Anderson Bridge when I was heading across the Charles River to the sports fields and he was walking back from ROTC drills. His uniform cap was usually askew and his collar points curled up. He died two years after graduation. If there had to be an exception to my sense of the class-war pattern, it was heartbreaking that he should have been the one.

When I wrote the article, I emphasized why it mattered, for

America in the 1960s and early 1970s, that so many privileged people had had an easy way out of the war:

> Not everyone at Harvard opposed the war, nor, I suspect, did even a majority of the people throughout the country who found painless ways to escape the draft. But I did, and most of the people I knew did, and so did the hordes we always ran into at the antiwar rallies. Yet most of us managed without difficulty to stay out of jail . . .
>
> It may be worth emphasizing why our failure to resist induction is such an important issue. Five years after Cambodia and Kent State, it is clear why the war could have lasted so long. Johnson and Nixon both knew that the fighting could continue only so long as the vague, hypothetical benefits of holding off Asian communism outweighed the immediate, palpable domestic pain. They knew that when the screaming grew too loud and too many sons had been killed, the game would be all over. That is why Vietnamization was such a godsend for Nixon, and it is also why our reluctance to say No helped prolong the war. The more we guaranteed that we would end up neither in uniform nor behind bars, the more we made sure that *our* class of people would be spared the real cost of the war. (Not that we didn't suffer. There was, of course, the *angst,* the terrible moral malaise . . .)
>
> The children of the bright, good parents were spared the more immediate sort of suffering that our inferiors were undergoing. And because of that, when our parents were opposed to the war, they were opposed in a bloodless, theoretical fashion, as they might be opposed to political corruption or racism in South Africa. As long as the little gold stars kept going to homes in Chelsea and the backwoods of West Virginia, the mothers of Beverly Hills and Chevy Chase and Great Neck and Belmont were not on the telephones to their congressmen, screaming *You killed my boy;* they were not writing to the president that his crazy, wrong, evil war had put their boys in prison and ruined their careers. It is clear by now that if the men of Harvard had wanted to do the very most they could to help shorten the war, they should have been drafted or imprisoned en masse.

If I were telling the story for the first time now, almost twenty rather than five years after the event, I would sound more knowing about a number of things. I realize now that my fears of getting shot were naïve. If physical safety had been my only concern, I could have aimed for a safe, college-boy berth in the military, perhaps at language school. ("I got a lucky draft, number 13. That was good for six months in the Reserves," one classmate wrote in the fifth-anniversary report. "There I got in-depth training on how to be a 'Petroleum Supply Storage Specialist,' i.e., a service station attendant.") Everyone now knows that the threat of communism to the people of South Vietnam was real, not "hypothetical." The threat to the other "dominoes" of Southeast Asia, on the other hand, was wildly exaggerated — and in Vietnam now, twenty years after the peak of American involvement, there is very little sign that the United States was ever there. All the blood and all the money seem only to have delayed the North Vietnamese communists' victory for about a dozen years. Indeed, from Asia it is clear that the Vietnam War will be important in history mostly for what it did, internally, to the United States, not what difference it made in Indochina.

I would also, now, avoid the role I took on for a while in the late 1970s: that of the publicly repentant performing-bear draft dodger. I was on panels about the "meaning of Vietnam" and said time and again what I still believe, which is that the surest way to prevent future Vietnams is through a universal draft without student deferments. This would make all classes of society hostage to the nation's policy and would increase the likelihood that the public will support whatever wars we get in. Assuming this identity became a big emotional problem for me. I had always been vain about following the honorable, the self-abnegating, the Episcopal course in life, which in this case I manifestly had not done. I nearly went berserk when a newspaperwoman concluded that I'd written about the draft in order to earn big bucks and get on TV. Couldn't she see, I wailed, that in coming clean I was letting the public service side of my character reassert itself?

Nearly all of the reactions I received, positive and negative, were from people who'd been in Vietnam, or from their families. I almost never heard from people who had avoided the war, which made me think that many people were uncomfortable with their dirty little secret of the war years. Unfortunately, in the early 1980s that discomfort started to be expressed in the least self-aware form imaginable. About the time that President Reagan declared Vietnam a "noble cause," many former college boys began lamenting that they had not experienced the thrill of combat or racked up an admirable service record. In real life, Sylvester Stallone spent the war years working at a girls' school in Switzerland; in fantasy life, he was Rambo. John Lehman, like Dan Quayle, spent the war in the National Guard, but as Ronald Reagan's first secretary of the navy he was usually photographed in a flight suit alongside a navy jet. My point had been the opposite of combat envy: I said that I regretted not paying the price by formally refusing, and that millions of college boys who one way or another failed to pay a price had unintentionally prolonged the war.

It wasn't until I visited Vietnam, twenty years after Tet, and heard the Vietnamese reminisce about the war that I began to comprehend one of the most destructive aftereffects of the way we fought the war. Even as Vietnam veterans got more "attention" and "sympathy" in the United States, starting with the dedication of the Vietnam Veterans Memorial, the prevailing emotion remained just that — sympathy, verging on pity, for people who'd been through something terrible. The presumption was that most or all had been damaged by it. America still seemed to view its Vietnam veterans more or less the way Japan views people killed or maimed by the atomic bombs: innocent victims, but victims nonetheless. I was startled to hear that when the Vietnamese described "the American war," they did not speak in contemptuous or pitying tones at all. They said they had felt sure they would win, since they were willing to outsacrifice any foreign foe. But they were proud of themselves for overcoming the "formidable" American presence and the "terrifying" American firepower, not scornful of the men they had fought against. Except for a few novels, such as John Del Vecchio's *The 13th Valley,* that view is not yet part of America's political and cultural attitude toward the Vietnam War. The "great" Vietnam movie, *Platoon,* once more presented most of the soldiers as victims and a few as monsters.

But the main thing that has changed since I first wrote that article is that now, twenty years after the class war, a different question seems more compelling: not what choices people made during the war years, but how the whole situation could have happened. How *could* the middle-class, democratic America of Norman Rockwell, Frank Capra, and the Hardy boys have tolerated such a blatantly unfair system? Of course the United States had fought poor-men's wars before. During the Civil War, which was as "good" and necessary as a war can be, there were draft riots in the North and a system of hired replacements, in which a reluctant man with money could hire a substitute or simply pay a fee to be exempted from service. The first northern draft call, in 1863, covered 300,000 men. Of them, 9 percent hired substitutes, 18 percent paid $300 and were exempted, and 70 percent were disqualified on medical or other grounds. Only 3 percent were left to be drafted. Oliver Wendell Holmes made such a big deal out of his wartime service because, for people of his class, it was a rarity. Military historians contend that the World War II draft, not the draft for Vietnam, is the great exception, because the rich and privileged have managed to stay out of most wars.

Still, the Vietnam draft was blatant and destructive — and it was tolerated by respectable opinion until the very end. It grew from assumptions similar to those which would later restrain the steelworkers and exclude the underclass blacks. All these manifestations of a static society were logical extensions of a trend that had begun a hundred years earlier, when some Americans really were recognized as being "better" than others.

CHAPTER SEVEN

Confucianism Comes to America

THE CONCEPTS that now keep Americans in place began to develop a hundred years ago. In the late nineteenth century, school started to become the key to American mobility, and the qualities that made for success in school — high IQ, the right study habits, good family background — became more and more closely linked with success in life. This connection sounds obvious, commonsensical, and unavoidable, but it is not any of those things, and it was not inevitable that schools should have taken on the role they now play.

The effects of this change on modern America are profound. The emphasis on formal schooling has introduced an unnatural "Confucian" element into an American culture that is based on the radically non-Confucian promise of constant, unstructured change. Confucian societies are meant to be static. They honor the scholar, place great emphasis on credentials and academic degrees, teach children always to defer to parents and social inferiors to their superiors, and assign people very early in life to the rank they will hold as adults. This package of values may be suitable for Japan, China, and Korea, although even in those countries the system of rote, memorized education is stifling and oppressive. In America, the Confucian idea that society should be more orderly is an unhealthful, alien influence.

America's Confucian values unfolded in three stages over the last century. The first was the expansion of expert professions, which artificially strengthened the connection between advanced schooling and economic success. The second was the notion that certain people simply could not succeed in school and were therefore destined to lead lower-class lives. The third was the use of government power to steer people toward the careers and social class that their background seemed to dictate. The cumulative result of these changes showed up in South Chicago, in the ghetto, and during the class war: people who were born wrong, and had been to the wrong schools, did not have the American opportunity to start their lives over again.

THE GROWTH OF MODERN GUILDS

Between the end of the Civil War and the beginning of World War I, American society was in constant tumult. The nation's population grew faster and migrated more frequently than ever before or since. Tens of millions of people passed through Ellis Island into the New World. Millions more left farms in Wisconsin and Tennessee to work in the stockyards and steel mills of the new boomtowns — Chicago, Cleveland, Detroit. Men and women who had grown up in homey small towns found themselves being bossed around by foremen and mixing with people just off the boat from Calabria or Minsk. As the railroads were completed, the country developed a truly nationwide market. Small-town merchants suddenly had to compete with mail-order houses in Chicago and New York. American grain farmers were affected by harvests in Canada and South America. Huge new industries rose up and fell; farmers endured booms and busts. This was American flexibility at its most creative and destructive.

"An age never lent itself more readily to sweeping, uniform description: nationalization, industrialization, mechanization, and urbanization," wrote Robert Wiebe, a historian, in his classic study of the era. "Yet to almost all of the people who created them, these themes meant only dislocation and bewilderment. America in the late nineteenth century was a society without a core." Wiebe's book was called, significantly, *The Search for Order*. That was what different layers of society tried in different ways to find: some protection against the unpredictability and disorder of the outside world. Aristocrats tried to slap down the vulgar nouveaux riches who were springing up around them. Farmers expressed their discontent through the Populist movement. Workingmen formed unions. Nativist groups tried to turn back the floods of immigrants. Whites in the South tried, through the Klan and Jim Crow laws, to return blacks to their pre-Reconstruction place. And, less conspicuously than any of these other groups, a fledgling middle class tried to protect itself too.

At the time, middle-class Americans were as vulnerable as all the other groups. Their problem was not simply that anyone could move into town, set up a store, and compete with established merchants. There was also the risk that anyone could move into town, pronounce himself a teacher or doctor or lawyer, and compete with the upper middle class as well. Virtually no occupations were regulated by the government. Practitioners could come and go as they pleased, and customers took their chances. This made the market for middle-class services almost as unpredictable as the world market for grain. "The concept of a middle class crumbled at the touch," Wiebe said. "The so-called professions meant little as long as anyone with a bag of pills and a bottle of syrup could pass for a doctor, a few books and a corrupt judge made a man a lawyer, and an unemployed illiterate qualified as a teacher."

The response of white-collar workers and imperiled professionals was not surprising in its nature. They tried to restrict competition, as almost everyone would like to do. Industrial workers were doing the same thing through the union movement, farmers through the demand for parity, manufacturers through the creation of trusts. But the professional movement succeeded more sweepingly than any of the others and had a more lasting effect on the nature of American mobility.

In his influential volume on economics, *The Rise and Decline of Nations,* Mancur Olson of the University of Maryland described how this self-protective process works. Any society is more productive if every group in the society is exposed to competition — but each group is better off if it's not. American quotas on imported sugar hurt America but help its sugar growers. Japanese laws forbidding chain stores hurt Japan but help its small shopkeepers. Sometimes, Olson said, small groups can shield themselves from competition on their own, through private, informal, or even cultural means. Big steelmakers can tacitly agree to raise their prices all at the same time. The caste system in India is a form of private action against competition, since it excludes most people from certain jobs. Prejudice against minority groups has the same effect.

But, Olson said, these private steps are always more effective if they are backed up with government action. Tariffs are the most obvious form of protection the government can offer, but not the only one. The form of protection that was crucial to the professions was licensing: certification by the government of those who could practice a certain trade. If anyone can open a barber shop, the cost of a haircut will be lower than if all barbers must be graduates of barber college. The barber colleges would, of course, claim that their graduates give better haircuts, but for the moment the point is the economic effect. As with any other kind of constraint on competition, professional licenses raised prices and incomes for those inside the profession.

The idea of licensed occupations — the practice of law, accounting, optometry, psychiatry — is now accepted so unquestioningly that it is startling to realize how recent it is. Very few of the licensing organizations existed a century ago, precisely because "professional" services were then as open as any other kind of business. Practitioners of almost every occupation now thought of as a profession organized themselves around the time of the Civil War. Dentists, in 1840, were the first; medical doctors banded together soon after, in 1847. A generation later, dozens of other groups had become licensed professionals: architects, accountants, lawyers, chemical engineers, and many more. "For the American aspiring to middle-class status, the generation between the Civil War and the turn of the century was a 'guilded age' . . . in addition to being a 'gilded age,' " Burton Bledstein wrote in *The Culture of Professionalism*.

Perhaps more important, the government began backing these

groups in their desire to restrict competition. Initially the organizations of doctors, architects, and engineers had been purely private associations. Their only tool was to give certification or approval to their members in the hope that customers would seek them out for higher standards. But with government licenses, private organizations could legally forbid outsiders from competing; it was as if, to use a homely example, the roughnecks of Texas had lobbied the state legislature to pass a certification law for rig work that would exclude competition from "unqualified" applicants like Buddy Ginn. Since, in nearly all cases, the government let the organizations themselves determine the standards for a license — so many years of school, so many tests passed — licensing essentially gave small groups the right to regulate their own competition.

Again, the tools of licensing — above all, the requirement for a certain amount of schooling — have come to seem entirely natural. But they were put into the private organizations' hands in one sudden burst early in this century. Before World War I, not a single state required its lawyers to have attended (let alone have finished) law school; and the American Bar Association asked only that prospective lawyers have finished high school before they took the bar exam. But after World War I, educational requirements suddenly cropped up everywhere. By the early 1970s, it was virtually impossible to practice law without both a college degree and one from a law school. The next chapter will consider whether these changes were necessary for technical reasons or for protecting the consumer. At the moment, however, it is worth noting that the practice of law in England never went through this shift. There, law school is an alternative to college, not a course for college graduates only — and in any event a degree is not strictly required for solicitors and barristers. It's hard to find evidence that the average standard of practice in America is higher than in England.

Medical education changed even more rapidly and dramatically. The crucial event occurred in 1910, when a layman named Abraham Flexner published his famous report *Medical Education in the United States and Canada,* commissioned by the Carnegie Foundation. At the time of the Civil War, medical training lasted two years at most, and many doctors simply learned their skills as apprentices to established doctors. By the turn of the century, the typical course was four years long, but most schools were fly-by-nights, of the sort that, if they existed today, would advertise on matchbook covers. Flexner visited all of the schools then operating and recommended that most be shut down. "The country needs fewer and better doctors," his report said; "the way to get them better is to produce fewer."

The country did as Flexner said: it got fewer, better, and much better paid doctors. The principal means was to increase dramatically the number of years prospective doctors had to go to school. Before Flexner's report, two thirds of all North American medical schools didn't even require a high school diploma for admission. Soon after Flexner, nearly all schools required at least two years of college, and the most prestigious schools wouldn't let in anyone without a four-year college degree. Before Flexner, there were 155 medical schools in the United States and Canada; ten years after, there were fewer than 40. At the turn of the century, most doctors enjoyed only mediocre status and income. By 1925, a poll on the prestige of various occupations showed doctors at the very top, a position they have held (or alternated with Supreme Court justices) ever since. Probably the most dramatic illustration of the restrictive effect of licensing is what happened to American medicine immediately after Hitler came to power. The surprise is that nothing happened: Jewish professionals, including large numbers of doctors, were pouring out of Germany, but the number of foreign doctors licensed to practice in the United States in the five years after 1933 was the same as in the five preceding years.

The connection between going to school and getting a professional license spread through many other fields with less obvious scientific basis than medicine (including, of course, the law). Through the late nineteenth century, people who wanted to become business managers typically started as clerks or secretaries; they were apprenticed on the job rather than trained in school. As late as the Great Depression, only about half of all businesses insisted that prospective managers be graduates of high school. After World War II, the supply of college graduates surged, and so did the jobs reserved exclusively for them. By 1967, according to a regional study conducted in California, nearly half of all managerial jobs required that applicants hold at least a B.A. and preferably a postgraduate degree. In the early 1960s, about seven thousand students received M.B.A.s each year. By the mid 1980s, seventy thousand did. By the 1980s, some 490 different occupations became subject to licensing or state regulation. (As S. David Young pointed out in *The Rule of Experts,* "Few Americans would guess that in some states falconers, ferret breeders, and eye enucleators are also subject to some form of government regulation.") In most cases, the licensing requirements include a certain minimum time in school.

Even the civil service became a kind of profession. In the generation before the Civil War, it had been taken for granted that the spoils system was the lubricant that kept American politics and government running. It may have had its excesses; for instance, after the Union Army was routed at Bull Run, Artemus Ward wisecracked that the soldiers had run away because of a rumor of three job vacancies in the New York Custom House. But it was the only obvious way for politicians to reward their supporters, and most of the jobs didn't seem to require expert technical preparation. But after the assassination of President James Garfield by a man invariably described as a "disappointed office seeker," the nation was on its way to a "reformed," professionalized civil service. The civil service dampened competition as effectively as the other guilds had done. When Abraham Lincoln took office, he fired nearly three fourths of all civilian federal employees in Washington and replaced them with his own supporters. By the time Ronald Reagan arrived, he could not legally fire more than one in a thousand. Under the spoils system, political patronage had been like capitalism or like the nineteenth-century professions, with much churning and change. Under the civil service, it was more orderly and tame.

Choosing public servants through tests was, of course, the essence of the old Confucian system. Passing written tests, which concentrated on the mastery of Chinese characters, was how Mandarins earned their positions of power in China and Korea. America's system was not exactly Mandarin; in old Korea, for example, the only people eligible to take the test were members of the aristocracy, whereas in principle any American could take the civil service exam. But the "professionalization" of the civil service was part of a general step away from a creative destruction concept of how people found jobs. Under the old American idea, jobs were not very secure, but people could always switch to another field, in which they might succeed or fail. Under the new system, it was harder to become a member of a profession — you had to have the right credentials — but it was safer and more profitable once you got in.

One effect of licensing is obvious and beyond dispute, at least among economists. By reducing competition, licensed professions have increased their members' earnings. A study of eyeglass prices found that when states prohibited advertising (that is, treated the making and selling of eyeglasses as a licensed profession), prices were 25 to 40 percent higher than in states where eyeglasses were sold over the counter, as part of a normal, competitive business. Depending on state laws, contact lenses are sometimes fitted by ophthalmologists (medical doctors), sometimes by opticians, and sometimes by employees of big commercial optometry chains. In a survey of eighteen cities, the Federal Trade Commission found that lenses from opticians and optometrists cost about a third less than those from ophthalmologists, even though the standard of fitting (as judged by a professional panel) was the same. In states where real estate agents are licensed, houses stay on the market longer, and the market clears at a higher price. To put it another way, when the real estate market is more competitive, buyers get more house for the money. States that don't recognize out-of-state medical or dental licenses have higher average professional fees than states that allow the additional competition. States that license electricians have found a higher rate of death by electrocution than those which don't: the licensing raises the cost so much that many people try to fix wires by themselves.

But the rise of licensed professions also had an enormous effect on social mobility. The old unregulated days were chaotic and in some cases dangerous, but they were open. Anyone could try to be an architect or engineer. Thomas Edison had almost no formal training. Frank Lloyd Wright and Ludwig Mies van der Rohe were not in school long enough even to qualify for today's architects' certifying exam. Before licensing existed, the test of who could remain in a profession was the same as the test in sports, entertainment, politics, or journalism today: performance and marketplace success. Even those who were not geniuses like Edison or Wright or Mies van der Rohe could make their way into skilled fields by learning on the job.

With the rise of educational requirements and licenses, the formula for success and mobility changed. How someone prepared for a job became at least as important as how well he actually did it. If he hadn't been in school for the right number of years, he would never have a chance to show what he could do. The only people who can show their skill at teaching public school are those with a degree from a college of education. The only people allowed to show their skill in courtroom argument are those who invested the time and money to finish college and law school. The military now requires most of its pilots to have finished college, a requirement that would have eliminated Chuck Yeager (and, for that matter, George Bush; he was the navy's youngest aviator in World War II before he graduated from Yale). To see how harmful these barriers are to national productivity, imagine the condition of the American computer industry today if hardware designers and software engineers were licensed, like accountants, and had to pass a qualifying exam drawn up by IBM. There would have been no Steve Jobs, no Steve Wozniak, no Bill Gates, probably no industry. To see how harmful it can be to American mobility, think again of the steelworkers. Because they had not stayed in school ten or twenty years earlier, it was impossible for them to start over in a number of jobs in which they might have been able to succeed.

The emphasis on preparation is to some extent natural. Because it is often hard for outsiders to judge whether a professional knows how to do his job, training may seem the best measure. Indeed, one academic has argued that the reason engineers don't make as much money as doctors is that outsiders *can* judge their work. When a patient dies, laymen can't be sure whether the doctor is to blame, but when a bridge falls down everyone knows the engineer made a mistake. Therefore, engineers are subject to something like the test of the market and have less freedom than doctors to set their own rules and rates.

But whether or not it was natural, the emphasis on preparation marked a radical shift in the American model of second chances and constant change. After all, you can spend your youth preparing only in a certain way. If you start down the wrong path early — as you may well do if you don't begin with the right values or advantages — you will have a hard time changing course later.

In real life, there is a tremendous span between activities in which "preparation" really matters and those in which it is irrelevant. A coach choosing a team for the Olympic Games doesn't care where his athletes went to college — or even where they're from, since immigrants and defectors like Navratilova and Lendl would be welcome on an American Olympic tennis team. An editor choosing a short story to publish rarely wonders what the writer was doing ten years earlier; he cares only whether the story is any good. An American choosing a spouse usually does not care very much where his or her parents are from: Nancy Davis, stepdaughter of a wealthy doctor, married Ronald Reagan, son of a drunk.* An executive hiring a sales staff is mainly interested in finding people who can close deals. On the other hand, Americans voting for president are properly concerned about candidates' life stories, since the details of each one's character are potentially so fateful.

Although the importance of preparation varies widely in most areas of life, academic preparation has come to be the dominant factor in a person's moving up to the most prestigious, best paid jobs. The rise of licensed professions meant that many of America's most desirable jobs were reserved for people who had made the right choice early in life, by going to the right schools. The second chance was remote. There was a distinctly pro-Confucian, anti-American cast to the rise of the professions. Shortly after the Civil War, Charles William Eliot, newly installed as

---

* I say "an American" doesn't care because many other cultures care deeply. Japan has a thriving industry of investigators hired to research the full family background of any prospective mate.

president of Harvard, complained in his inaugural address that "as a people we have but a halting faith in special training for high professional employments." He meant this as a criticism, even though he was talking about a basic national trait. Eliot said that there was "national danger" in the "vulgar conceit that the Yankee can turn his hand to anything, [which] we insensibly carry into high places, where it is preposterous and criminal. We are accustomed to seeing men leap from farm or shop to courtroom or pulpit, and we half believe that common men can safely use the seven-league boots of genius." This "vulgar conceit," of course, is what makes America unique and strong.

The rise of professions, in short, enhanced the importance of schools in determining how Americans rose and fell. The emphasis on education helped some people, who could overcome racial or social prejudice by proving themselves in school. It hurt others, who neglected their schooling early and then found that their options were closed. But in all cases it pushed the crucial life decisions to a much earlier point in each person's life, because success or failure in school counted so heavily.

The second step toward a more rigid society complemented the first. It was the idea that certain people were born to succeed or fail in school, which had come to mean success or failure in later life.

THE IDEA OF ABILITY

At about the same time that the guilds and professions were forming, another development that is now a familiar part of the landscape was taking shape. It was an outgrowth of the "science" of psychometrics — mental measurement — now known to everyone in the form of IQ testing and college entrance exams. Combined with the new emphasis on schools, it threatened to make America a much less flexible society than it had been.

Every society has had a way to place people into more and less desirable categories, and everyone knows that there are differ-

ences in raw intellectual talent. What made the psychometricians' work significant was what they claimed to be able to do.
Before their science took form, most ability tests were like the
first civil service exams, or like Japanese school admission tests
even today. They straightforwardly measured what you knew,
not necessarily how smart you were. The new IQ tests, in contrast, were supposed to be a measure of ultimate ability: they
would show not only what a person knew but how much he was
capable of ever knowing.

This is a fairly dramatic difference. What someone *knows* can
always be changed; what he *is* obviously cannot. In Japan, passing tests and getting into the right schools are more important
than in America, but the idea of ultimate ability seems to matter
less. When someone does poorly on a university entrance exam,
he doesn't necessarily tell himself he's stupid. He and his parents
are more likely to say, "Pass with four, fail with five!" — referring to hours of sleep the candidate is allowed each night while
cramming for another try at the exams. Such effort would be
pointless if the tests were thought to measure raw ability. But the
Japanese assumption is that just about everybody has "enough"
ability; what the tests really measure is determination. Therefore,
students have a reason to try their best. American IQ and Scholastic Aptitude Tests convey the opposite message: Don't worry
about cramming, students. This is a measure of the real you.

Where did Americans get the idea that there were precise,
innate, very important differences in ability, which could be used
to direct people to the right role in adult life? Partly it came from
the universal human impulse to put people into hierarchies and
to prove that whatever hierarchy exists is fair. But there were
some more specific causes too.

One was the nativist reaction in America to the seemingly un-
stoppable flow of Southern and Eastern European immigrants at
the turn of the century. The rate of arrivals was much higher than
it has ever been since, even during the 1980s. (In absolute numbers, immigration during the 1980s may yet exceed the ten-year
record at the turn of the century. As a proportion of the existing
American population, however, early-twentieth-century immigration was four or five times as large.) Those Italians and Greeks

and Jews looked so different and disturbing and inferior, it was tempting to many people to try to prove that they really were. At this very time, a generation after Darwin had propounded his theories, a number of half-scientific systems for human classification were being thought up. Phrenologists in Europe were trying to figure out who had criminal tendencies by feeling bumps on the skull. Police agencies hired specialists in physiognomy to identify the typical faces of murderers, rapists, pickpockets, and so on. Scientists in America, England, and on the Continent tirelessly measured feet, brains, fingers, and faces in an effort to detect character traits. All this work had its effect. Immigration specialists in the United States said that Eastern Europeans needed to be kept out, because "races may change their religions, their form of government, and their languages, but underneath they may continue the PHYSICAL, MENTAL, and MORAL CAPACITIES and INCAPACITIES which determine the REAL CHARACTER of their RELIGION, GOVERNMENT, and LITERATURE."

It would not be fair to say that IQ tests are pure quackery just because they arose from these practices; still, that is how they started. And of all the human-classifying devices developed at the turn of the century, mental measurement is the major one to have survived.

The man who created the first intelligence test, the French psychologist Alfred Binet, viewed his tests in a way that would surprise most twentieth-century Americans who have taken them. Binet devised the test because the French Ministry of Instruction asked for a way to identify children who needed remedial help. He came up with a list of simple tasks that would indicate the child's "mental age": a normal three-year-old should be able to point to different parts of his face; a normal ten-year-old should be able to make a sentence using several specified words. The ratio between mental age and chronological age would be the intelligence quotient, or IQ, with 100 defined as normal.

Neither Binet nor the French ministry saw this test as a way of classifying normal children or testing to see whether one was smarter than another. It was to be more like a medical diagnostic procedure. White blood cell counts, for example, aren't meant to show whether one healthy person is healthier than another, but only to identify the ones who are sick. Binet thought of mental measurement in the same way, as a means of selecting those who needed treatment. He also went to some lengths to rebut the idea that an IQ score was something permanent. When he was a young student, Binet had been told that he would "never" have a true philosophical spirit. His dissatisfaction with this verdict apparently stayed with him, and he said he didn't want his tests used the same way. Instead — again like a blood cell count — they were to be guides to therapy and recovery.

But, of course, as Binet's tests were put into practice around the world, neither his cautions nor his therapeutic vision went with them. In both England and the United States, the IQ test often became a means for measuring precisely the long-suspected mental differences among individuals and races. Before the tests, Americans who thought immigrants were defective had to rest their argument on cranium measurements and the like. The IQ tests showed the same thing, but now with hard proof.

In the United States, the pivotal figures in the transformation of IQ were Henry H. Goddard, Lewis Terman, and Robert Yerkes. Their good fortune was to live at the moment when the first mass intelligence tests were administered to American inductees in World War I, yielding the first "hard" data about intelligence. As the great wartime mobilizations began, Yerkes, who had been a psychologist at Harvard before the war, persuaded the Army to give mental tests to men being screened for induction. The Army Alpha was the standard intelligence test, based on written questions; Army Beta used pictures and was for illiterates or those who did very poorly on Army Alpha. Yerkes collaborated with Goddard, Terman, and others to develop the tests, and then, as a newly commissioned colonel, he oversaw their administration. By the end of the war, mental measurements of 1.75 million American men were available for analysis and cross-tabulation by race, ethnic group, and geographic and social background.

Much of the work of the early psychometricians makes easy sport today. The tests they used were, to put it politely, imperfect gauges of innate talent. One typical Army Alpha question was "The Brooklyn Nationals are called the *Giants Orioles Superbas Indians.*" Another, " 'There's a reason' is an 'ad' for a *drink revolver flour cleanser.*" But despite flaws in his testing procedure that now seem laughably easy to detect, Yerkes created a huge sensation when he published his nine-hundred-page analysis of the test scores in 1921. "Psychological Examining in the United States Army" confirmed what some people had suspected: that immigrants and blacks were overwhelmingly subnormal, the most recent arrivals being the worst. Yerkes and his colleagues wrestled with one perplexing finding: tests showed that immigrants who had just arrived were feeble-minded, even though others of the same "race" who had been in America longer had edged back into the normal range. Four fifths of all new Hungarian arrivals, and five sixths of new Jewish immigrants, tested as feeble-minded, but Jews who had immigrated earlier had higher scores. Of all the possible explanations for this pattern, the psychometricians settled on the theory that the old immigrants must have been smarter than the new ones. That change, in turn, could be explained by the steady decline in the proportion of "Nordic" stock among the immigrants and the corresponding rise of the Mediterranean and Semitic "races."

An even more depressing implication of the studies was that most people, "real" Americans as well as immigrants, seemed to be subnormal; America was the opposite of Lake Woebegon, where all the children are above average. The average mental age for adult white draftees was thirteen, just a shade above the cutoff point for "moron." Yerkes concluded, "Thus it appears that feeble-mindedness . . . is of much greater frequency of occurrence than had been originally supposed." Yerkes's colleague Henry Goddard said that the tests called the whole idea of American democracy into question. How could the country run on principles of majority rule when the average American, according to the tests, was too limited to make his own decisions and, according to Goddard, was "vastly better off when following directions than when trying to plan for himself"?

All this examination of American mental capacities had two lasting effects. The first was the idea that what was being measured was something inborn and unchangeable, like eye color. The second was that these innate qualities were very important in daily life.

Of course, talent and intelligence have been important in all societies. People differ in their temperaments and abilities, and some of the differences seem to be inherited. Some people are stronger, faster, better-looking, and cleverer than others — and their children may be the same. Life is unfair. But there is a difference between such fact-of-life observations and what mental measurement added to the American system. Indeed, there are two differences. The first is that psychometricians claimed that intelligence was an entity, like weight or height, that could be measured on a single scale. The second is that the resulting number pretty much determined what a person could do — especially whether he was up to the challenge of schooling for jobs in the modern world. People who didn't have enough intelligence were not to aim too high; they would be like midgets trying to make the basketball team or people with astigmatism trying to be pilots.

Later we'll return to these two claims and see whether they were realistic. For the moment, my point is that they had an effect. While the early supporters of IQ testing often spoke in terms that now make them look ridiculously snobbish and class-bound, the real significance of their work was not snobbery but something more destructive: the idea that inherited, precisely measurable abilities were the main limit on what people could hope to do. The whole idea of starting over was not valid if people's innate abilities determined what jobs they could hold.

The rise of professions had heightened the importance of school, and the rise of mental testing indicated who was destined to do well in school and therefore in life. America was moving toward a Confucian model without a Confucian society (racially homogeneous, conditioned to obey authority and be content in lowly ranks) to back it up.

GOVERNMENT CHANNELING

One further step nudged America toward an inappropriate, static, Confucian-style merit system. The government reinforced the move by adjusting the school system to steer different people toward their predicted destinations. Ideally, American schools, in addition to helping people live happy, meaningful lives, should equip them to start over as easily as possible whenever they have to do so. Instead, schools were pushed to do the opposite, to put people on the track that their background and ability dictated.

Through the eighteenth and nineteenth centuries, the schools had only modest influence, since so few people went for more than a couple of years. Before the Civil War, compulsory-attendance laws were practically unknown, and only about 2 percent of the school-age population went as far as high school. By the turn of the century, more than half the states had passed attendance laws, and the long nineteenth-century crusade for publicly financed "common schools," open to the general public, had succeeded.

The very success of this campaign created new complications. Back when only a few Americans, largely from the upper classes and the cities, finished even grade school, anyone who learned to read and write well had a good chance of escaping factory or farm work. But as more and more people went to the common schools, that expectation had to change. By the early twentieth century, school systems needed (as David Nasaw, a historian, put it) to "bring as many 'plain people' as possible into the high schools and keep them there through their teens, but in such a way that their expectations for life after graduation would not be inappropriately raised."

One solution was to separate schools into categories, each of which would serve a different social and educational function. In 1912, the National Association of Manufacturers, drawing on the fast-developing science of mental measurement, recommended schools that would serve children according to their abilities — that is, their fate in life. It said that the only realistic approach was to develop three kinds of schools for children who would

end up in three different kinds of work: highly skilled professional work, ordinary jobs, and unskilled jobs. According to the
NAM report, fully half of the nation's children were destined for
the bottom category of school and work.

The point of these distinctions is that the schools were enlisted
in the channeling effort that the mental measurers had asked for.
Each child was "supposed" to end up in a certain kind of job
because of the talents he had been born with (or without), and
the sooner he got pointed in that direction, the easier it would be
on everybody.

There are obvious tensions between channeling and the American ideal that anyone can grow up to be president. Channeling
was not only at odds with the notion that Americans should always have a second chance; it meant that many Americans didn't
have even a first chance. Therefore, it is not surprising that the
most dramatic steps in the direction of channeling took place
under wartime pressure, when everyone agreed that normal rules
might have to be suspended for a while. The mental-measure-
ment campaign had taken big leaps during World War I, and
manpower channeling did the same during World War II.

Because the United States was late to enter the war against
Hitler, its strategic planners, in their frenzy to make up for lost
time, tried to use human resources as efficiently as rubber or tin.
There wasn't enough time to let people figure out where they fit
in — at an aircraft factory, at Los Alamos, on Omaha Beach.
The government did its best to decide on appropriate destinations, and it sent people where they belonged.

The main channeling tool was the government's power to draft
some men and defer others. Especially in light of what happened
during the Vietnam War, the World War II draft has come to look
remarkably broad and fair. In many ways it was. The registration
bill approved after Pearl Harbor eventually covered all males
between the ages of eighteen and sixty-four, theoretically including President Roosevelt himself. But because not even a two-
front total war required all men to be in uniform, the central
drama of Selective Service was the selection of who would serve
where.

During the war, that decision was based in large part on what people could already do. In most cases, the government didn't waste time wondering what a young man's future ability might be; it just looked to see whether he already had a job at Lockheed or US Steel or on the farm. There were only a few student deferments, mainly for men who were just about done with specialized training in science or medicine. The military came up with its own programs for providing promising young men (identified through qualifying exams) with advanced scientific training, in exchange for later service. But in their emphasis on those with high "potential," these programs were the exception.

After the war, predictive efforts became the norm. The draft flickered into and out of existence in the late 1940s, coming to stay in 1950. General Lewis B. Hershey, the half-blind regular army officer who directed Selective Service from its glory days in World War II to its depths during Vietnam, initially pushed a minimal-deferments policy like that used during the war. "I don't know what in a democracy you can do if you do not require each citizen to take all of his responsibilities," Hershey said in 1947. People, smart and dumb alike, had the same obligations. When draft calls for the Korean War began, Hershey overcame the American Medical Association's opposition and convinced Congress to draft doctors, pointing out that medical students had been deferred during World War II, and now their turn had come. Later, as Congress backtracked and began larding the draft code with other deferments, Hershey said caustically that the United States was moving toward the kind of draft used by Chiang Kai-shek's Nationalist Chinese government: "I don't know exactly how it works, but the ones who get inducted are always coolies."

But prevailing opinion — including Hershey's own when he saw which way the Congress was moving — began to drift in the opposite direction, toward the idea that smart people and dumb people should have different responsibilities. Even before the Second World War, a panel of experts from the Social Sciences Research Council had warned that the country could no longer afford the "wasteful process in which a person had to try and fail in a number of different activities before finding the one for which he was best suited." This "wasteful process," like Charles

Eliot's "vulgar conceit," is of course what had built the country and made it different from the Old World. "It is difficult to over-estimate the importance of utilizing to the fullest possible extent the most accurate and discriminating prediction instruments available." After the war, the pressure for accurate prediction became heavier. "We are short of people," the National Security Resources Board reported during the Korean War. "If we are to do everything we need to do for ourselves and for others, every person must count. We can afford no slippage." As Representative Mendel Rivers of South Carolina once put it, "Korea has taught us one thing if it has taught anything. You don't need a Ph.D. degree to fight those Chinks."

Late in 1948, an advisory committee recommended that Selective Service invent a new draft deferment, open to any young man "whose educational aptitude suggests he is of potential special value." Students had to get good marks in college or do well on an IQ-style test to qualify. When Hershey called men for service in Korea, he accepted a compromise version of the plan for deferments according to test scores. He contracted with the Educational Testing Service, by now famous as the creator of the Scholastic Aptitude Tests, to produce the deferment examination.

In a way, the deferment plan was just a symbol. The number of deferments for married men and fathers, members of ROTC, and those classified 4-F was much greater than those given through the IQ test. And the student deferment was in those days really a deferment — not an exemption — since most of the students were drafted after graduation. (Of all the men who reached age twenty-six in 1958, 70 percent had been in the military at some point.) Still, it was a potent symbol. The deferment examination was the first time the U.S. government had put its muscle behind the idea of channeling different people toward different fates, depending on their innate and scientifically determined merit.

All in all, the rise of professions and schools, the emphasis on "intelligence," and the broad use of channeling in the last century represented a big change in the American ideal of mobility.

Now it was more important to be born with the right abilities and harder to start over or switch tracks later in life. The American "merit" system of earlier times had been like a sporting competition: a team wins the World Series one year, but it has to prove itself again the following spring. Everyone can say, Wait till next year. The professional merit system was more rigid. It was still possible for someone to overcome a lack of schooling or a bad start, but it was hard. The radius of trust was smaller, because some Americans were simply better than others. And the average American's belief that he could control his fate naturally decreased.

The worst part about these changes is that they were completely unnecessary. There is no good reason for modern America to sort people into categories early in life. Even the most advanced, technological, and internationally competitive parts of American life can be open to newcomers making new starts.

CHAPTER EIGHT

What Morons Could Do

THE SYSTEM that I've been calling Confucian sometimes goes by the weightier name of "the meritocracy." The term was popularized thirty years ago by the English sociologist Michael Young, who introduced it in his short satire, *The Rise of the Meritocracy*. Taken literally, meritocracy means "rule by the meritorious," and such a system is what America, among other societies, has always dreamed of attaining. Many people assume, even without thinking, that the current system of school tracking, tests, and professional organizations is about as efficient a meritocracy as we're likely to devise. Some people who have thought about it have come to the same conclusion. R. J. Herrnstein, in *I.Q. in the Meritocracy,* made the case that a system like the current one is inevitable. "The ties among I.Q., occupation, and social standing make practical sense," he wrote. "If virtually anyone is smart enough to be a ditch digger, and only half the people are smart enough to be engineers, then society is, in effect, husbanding its intellectual resources by holding engineers in greater esteem, and on the average, paying them more."

But is the connection between intelligence and success really so necessary and natural? It is not, as an examination of the meritocracy's premises will show.

"LINEAR" IQ

The starting point for today's meritocracy, of course, is the idea that intelligence exists and can be measured, like weight or strength or fluency in French.

The most obvious difference between intelligence and these other traits is that all the others are presumably changeable. If someone weighs too much, he can go on a diet; if he's weak, he can lift weights; if he wants to learn French, he can take a course. But in principle he can't change his intelligence. There is another important difference between intelligence and other traits. Height and weight and speed and strength and even conversational fluency are real things; there's no doubt about what's being measured. Intelligence is a much murkier concept. Some people are generally smarter than others, and some are obviously talented in specific ways; they're chess masters, math prodigies. But can the factors that make one person seem quicker than another be measured precisely, like height and weight? Can we confidently say that one person is 10 percent smarter than another, in the same way we can say he's 10 percent faster in the hundred-yard dash? And can we be confident that two thirds of all people have IQs within one standard deviation of the norm — that is, between 90 and 110 — as we can be sure that two thirds of all people have heights within one standard deviation of the norm for height? Yes, they can, and yes, we can. Those, at least, are the answers that the IQ part of the meritocracy rests on.

Think for a moment about the difference between measuring intelligence and measuring anything else. We know that some natural traits are distributed according to what the statisticians call a "normal distribution," better known as a bell curve. Height is the classic example. If you randomly chose a thousand American men and measured them, you'd find that most would be slightly over or under six feet, smaller numbers would be four inches taller or shorter, and only a few would be at the top and bottom of the scale. Many other natural characteristics — the number of hairs on a person's head, the size of fish in a lake — follow a normal distribution. But some other, equally natural features, don't. Hair color among Japanese citizens does not have a normal distribution: almost everyone's is black. The ability to walk is another example. It is not "normally" distributed, since the great majority of people can walk without difficulty, and a minority of those who are too old, too young, or too sick cannot.

There is, then, nothing in nature that dictates that intelligence be distributed along a bell curve, with the normal proportions of geniuses and morons and people with average IQs. So how can we be sure that intelligence really is distributed that way? In fact, we can't; no one is sure just how it is distributed. The bell curve was invented for analytic convenience, not because anyone knew that it resembled the real, underlying pattern of intelligence. The physicist Philip Morrison, of MIT, once wrote an essay about the difference between measuring intelligence and measuring other natural phenomena. When scientists measure speed or size or weight, they make their readings without worrying about what pattern the results are supposed to fit. Otherwise, they're hardly scientists. It was different with measuring intelligence, Morrison said. Ever since Binet, IQ tests have been designed to produce a predetermined pattern of results. That is, if test makers produced a set of questions, but students' scores on the test did not follow a "normal" distribution, then the questions themselves must be bad. A good set of questions was one that yielded a bell-shaped curve. The logic was obviously circular, Morrison concluded, but it was the way IQ tests were actually produced. At the headquarters of the Educational Testing Service, I observed this process in action: a team of experts drew up what they thought were "challenging" or "serious" questions for inclusion in the Scholastic Aptitude Test, but they couldn't tell which questions were "valid" indicators of intelligence until they saw the results of a pretest (when the new questions were included in the normal SAT). Any question that produced the desired normal distribution was valid; all the rest had to be thrown out.

IQ scores now fall into a bell curve mainly because that is where the original English and American psychometricians thought they should fall. But suppose they'd started out with different preconceptions. Suppose they believed that "intelligence" was something like "health": some people were weak and some were strong, but most people were "healthy enough." Their bodies may have been shaped differently, but one type couldn't be called healthier than another. In that case, the distribution of IQ scores would have been very different. Indeed, it would look more like the distribution in Japan, where the prevailing idea is that intelligence (among Japanese) *is* like health. Most people are thought to have "enough."

Suppose the psychometricians thought that intelligence was like patriotism. Most people are loyal, but a few are traitors and a few are potential heroes. With that model in mind, psychometricians might have concluded that most people have enough intelligence for normal modern life, but a few do not and a few have extra capacity. We wouldn't bother with more precise rankings for intelligence any more than we do for patriotism. Suppose, to turn this around, that government started ranking people according to their patriotism quotient, or PQ. Schoolchildren could be given tests and then ranked on a bell curve. Half of them, by definition, would have PQs below 100, and everybody would be slightly more or less patriotic than everybody else. It's hard to think of a more destructive test the schools could administer — yet from a scientific point of view the PQ curve would be every bit as valid as today's IQ.

IQ AS IRON LIMIT

So maybe raw intelligence does not divide people into many small categories of greater and lesser ability. Or maybe it does. No one really knows, which is the point. It is interesting that the qualities that each society chooses to measure often say more about the society's preoccupations than about the traits that are supposedly being observed. The Spanish colonialists in Latin America, for instance, had a system for classifying minute distinctions along the scale from pure-blooded Spaniard to pure-blooded Indian. The racial distinctions weren't any finer than they are now; the Spanish just cared about them more. In today's Malaysia, on the other hand, there is an almost infinite range of skin colors and blood mixtures, but most of the variation is ignored. The distinction that matters in Malaysia is the three-way division among Malays, Indians, and Chinese. A faint difference in coloration and facial features between a southern Chinese and a Malay is tremendously important, but the distinct contrast between a black-skinned Tamil Indian and a pale-skinned Punjabi, or between northern and southern Chinese, is defined as not important. Similarly, America's emphasis on schooling and ability shows up in the precision of its IQ scores.

This brings us to the second question. Whatever intelligence may be and however it may be distributed, is it really the main factor in determining how far people can go in life? Unless IQ is an important limit, the entire tracking system makes no sense. Why start channeling people early if most of them really can handle most jobs? Why not let them end up where they will, by trial or error, or encourage them to keep starting over? Why hive people off to trade school if, given a later chance, they could become scientists, doctors, or inventors? It would be like steering children out of sports because their HQ was too low.

As it happens, there have been some studies designed to test precisely this hypothesis: that only a small fraction of the public is intelligent enough to do complicated professional work. If the hypothesis were true, you would expect to see a correlation between IQ scores and positions on the job ladder. The greatest variety of IQ scores would be at the bottom of the ladder, because people in society's bad jobs would be (a) those who weren't smart enough to do anything else and (b) those who were smart enough but for one reason or another — weak ambition, negligent parents, sickness, alcoholism, character defects, simple bad luck — never fulfilled their potential. At the top of the ladder, there would not be much variety — there couldn't be, since only those with high IQs could handle professional or managerial work. If you met a manager, a professional, or a skilled technical worker, you could be sure that he or she came from a small group near the top of the IQ scale. Otherwise he couldn't be there.

In *I.Q. in the Meritocracy,* Herrnstein discussed one important study that confirmed this expectation. He compared the intelligence test scores given to tens of thousands of recruits during World War II with the jobs they'd held before induction. As he had predicted, there was much variety at the bottom and less among those in good white-collar jobs.

But Herrnstein's subjects were young, just starting out in life. When Michael Olneck, of the University of Wisconsin, and James Crouse, of the University of Delaware, worked from data that followed men later into their careers, they found just the opposite. Their principal source of information was the "Kalamazoo brothers" study, one of sociology's longest-running and most thorough surveys, which followed thousands of boys from their childhood in Kalamazoo well into adulthood. Because the study lasted so long, early guesses about the boys' potential could be matched against the way their careers actually turned out.

When Crouse and Olneck compared men's first jobs with their test scores, they found a pattern like Herrnstein's. But the longer they followed the subjects, the more the pattern changed. Of the Kalamazoo brothers who ended up as professionals, 10 percent had been considered "high-grade morons" as boys. Their childhood IQs were below 85, putting them in the bottom sixth of the population. One third of all the adult professionals, and 42 percent of the managers, had childhood IQs below 100. On average, managers were smarter than normal, but many managers were dumb. The greatest diversity of IQ scores was not among unskilled laborers, as Herrnstein had predicted, but among those in professional jobs. "While men with quite high test scores would rarely be found in undesirable jobs, men with low scores are represented in desirable jobs in fair numbers," Olneck and Crouse said. Men in the highest category, "professional, technical, and kindred," had a mean IQ of 107.5, but the lowest score in this category was 62, often classified as "imbecile." The standard deviation of IQ scores was greatest at the highest levels; the most homogeneous groups were the ones with the lowest scores, laborers and farmers.

"Rather than high cognitive ability being essential for successful performance in desirable jobs, it appears that the capacity to succeed in such jobs is rather widespread, and is not confined to men who score well on tests," Olneck and Crouse concluded.

Here is an implication worth chewing on. The ultimate justification for a semi-Confucian system with early tracking is, again, that we're chronically short on intellectual talent. Pretending that a low-IQ student can ever do a professional job, runs this argument, is like telling people that they can eat sand. They can't, and it's both cruel and inefficient to mislead them. Yet Olneck and Crouse's findings indicated that the basic reasoning was wrong. Many men who'd been classified as "subnormal" and "morons" did fine in jobs demanding high skill, once they *got* the job. Perhaps they had managed to raise their previously low IQs, or perhaps what the tests measured was not really significant. In either case, the "limits" imposed by low IQ did not seem to be natural.

There is an even more familiar (and more emotionally charged) example of the same principle: the story of the G.I. Bill.

As World War II ground toward its close, the concept of the G.I. Bill was taking shape. The government decided it could reward the returning veterans, and help the economy digest hundreds of thousands of demobilized men, by offering a free or subsidized college education to every G.I.

The most prestigious members of the educational hierarchy thought this was a preposterous idea. Robert Hutchins, of the University of Chicago, warned in 1944 that when the G.I.s came home, "colleges and universities will find themselves converted into educational hobo jungles." In the same generous spirit, James B. Conant, the president of Harvard, said in 1945 that the bill was "distressing," because it did not "distinguish between those who can profit most by advanced education and those who cannot." The bill was clearly a scheme to push people beyond what their intelligence permitted. What Conant would have preferred, as Keith Olsen wrote in his history of the G.I. Bill, was a program restricted to a "carefully selected number" of the most able veterans. Otherwise, Conant feared, "we may find the least capable among the war generation . . . flooding the facilities for advanced education."

In one way — but not quite the way they intended — people like Conant and Hutchins were right. By promoting the idea that everybody should go to college, and that any trade worth learning (accounting, phys. ed., journalism) should be learned in a university, the G.I. Bill magnified the importance of academic credentials and diminished the purely academic role of the university.

But Conant and Hutchins could not have been more wrong about the G.I.s. When the 2.3 million veterans enrolled, they turned out to be phenomenally successful. Older, less flighty, more seriously motivated than ordinary students, the early G.I. Bill scholars became the most successful group of students American universities had ever seen. By 1947, the *New York Times* was reporting that "the G.I.'s are hogging the honor rolls and the dean's lists." *Newsweek* reported that not one of Columbia University's 7826 veterans "was in serious scholastic difficulty at the last marking period." *Fortune* said that the class of 1949, 70 percent of whom were veterans, was "the best . . . the most mature . . . the most responsible . . . the most self-disciplined" in history. About half a million of the G.I.s who went on to college were not from traditional "college prep" backgrounds. They were older than the average G.I., had been out of school longer, had served longer overseas, and were more likely to be married and to have children. But, according to researchers who assessed the G.I. Bill's effects, these students did better in course work than many veterans who had planned to go to college anyway.

The G.I.s' success might seem surprising to anyone who took the shortage-of-talent hypothesis seriously. But it was wholly consistent with several other major trends in American and world history. During the two and a half centuries before the G.I.s went to college, the Western world accomplished its Industrial Revolution. At the beginning of that process, most people lived on the farm. IQ tests almost always show that rural children are less intelligent than urban ones; the scores typically go up when the families move to town. If widespread IQ testing had been available in the early 1700s, it would surely have shown that there weren't enough intelligent people available to do advanced industrial work. Yet somehow people adjusted; as more demanding, complicated jobs opened up, more people learned how to do them. IQ testing was used widely on the immigrants at the turn of the century, and it showed that America's intelligence level, low enough to begin with, was being dragged down by the brutes from overseas. But somehow America rose above that limitation too. Since 1900, the proportion of "intellectually demanding" professional and managerial jobs in the United States has quadrupled, yet Americans rose to the task. Somehow children raised in the Sicilian village or on the Indiana farm managed to become engineers and schoolteachers and pharmacists, once the changing job market let them do something besides slop the hogs.

It is theoretically possible that now, in the late twentieth century, we've finally reached the precise equilibrium point. Perhaps we have exactly as many smart people as we have difficult jobs. If this is so, then it makes sense to channel people as early as possible. Why fool them with unrealistic expectations? Why let talent dribble away?

This is theoretically possible, but it's absurd. It's easy to tell in retrospect that there was a lot of unrecognized talent in the American hinterland of 1900; there is also talent in the ghettoes and steel towns and backwoods today. Japan's theory of intelligence is designed to make everyone rise to challenges. That country is often, and accurately, described as having the "best bottom 50 percent on earth." America's theory of intelligence writes off the supposedly untalented bottom ranks.

INPUT EQUALS OUTPUT

There is a third presumption shoring up the school-based meritocracy: that if we didn't have a more or less rigid channeling system, modern society couldn't function. America had to steer people to the appropriate destinations during World War II, and America may have to do the same thing today. How can we be sure that we have competent engineers, teachers, air-traffic controllers, and lawyers if we don't insist on their having gone to the best schools?

This idea sounds even more logical than the first two. But it is not any truer. To see what is wrong with it requires a look at the difference between "competence" and "ability."

In 1973, ten years after he published *The Achieving Society,* David McClelland wrote a short article about precisely this distinction. "Testing for Competence Rather than 'Intelligence' " appeared in a professional journal, *American Psychologist.* McClelland, who had spent many years investigating why people "succeeded," asked in this article whether it made sense to devote so much effort — through testing, tracking, and requiring academic credentials — to predicting who would succeed.

It was certainly true, McClelland said, that IQ tests helped predict who would get good grades in school. This was not exactly a surprise, since grades and test scores measured similar skills. He said there was also a statistical correlation between doing well in school and succeeding later in life, since in twentieth-century America you had to get through school to enter a profession or get a managerial job. But did being good at school in itself, apart from its value in getting a person a job, usefully predict how well he'd do the job? McClelland's answer was no.

McClelland said that most researchers had failed to find a connection between good grades and good professional performance, once they removed the effect of the credential itself. People who got good grades at one level of schooling usually did well in the next level too, but that was about as far as the correlation went. The most impressive part of the findings, McClelland said, was how hard they were for most academic officials to accept: "It seems so self-evident to educators that those who do well in their classes must go on to do better in life that they systematically have disregarded evidence to the contrary that has been accumulating for some time."

McClelland added that in the 1950s, he chaired a committee of the Social Science Research Council, investigating the correlation between grades and occupational success. It found that college graduates predictably got better jobs than nongrads, but that academic differences among college graduates did not seem to matter very much. McClelland said that even he balked at this conclusion until he went back to study the postcollege careers of some of his own students. He dug out his grades books from Wesleyan University, where he had taught in the 1940s, and got the names of the eight best and eight worst students in his class. He traced their careers through the early 1960s, at which point he found no difference between the two groups. The better students had gotten into better graduate schools, but they had not necessarily proven more successful in their working lives.

There was, of course, a technical problem with McClelland's survey of his former students. When you are measuring a group that is already unusual in a certain way, the true significance of its unusual trait may be obscured. For instance, if you are studying professional basketball players, who are already much taller than average, you may not see a clear correlation between height and skill. (Many players were taller than Larry Bird, few were better.) Similarly, when you study college students, who already have higher than average IQ scores and school grades, the correlation between grades and later success may not look as strong as it really is.

Still, McClelland had more than these thumbnail bios to go on. And he and a number of other researchers who have been interested in why people succeed, not in how smart they are, have emphasized that ability and competence are two different attributes, not always related. Ability is theoretical potential; it's similar to some nightmare version of the Soviet Olympic-training system, where grade school children have their muscle fibers and body fat tested to see who is the most promising natural athlete. Competence is what you can actually do today; it's the idea behind the summer training camps held by National Football League teams, where the coaches see whether the promising rookies and the veteran stars are up to snuff this year.

The Soviet Olympic-training system may be fine for the Soviets, but the summer training camps are closer to the American ideal of how a merit system should work. Everyone has a chance; no one can coast for long; there's always next year. To reflect America's goai of openness and also to ensure skillful performance, an American merit system should pay more attention to competence than to ability. But McClelland and others have shown that the emphasis on professions, occupational licenses, and educational requirements rewards ability more and competence less.

The licensed professions focus attention on how a teacher or accountant or doctor trained for his job — did he go to the right school and get the right credential? — while simultaneously discouraging measurements of how well the people already in the profession do their work. Teachers' unions, for example, fight hard to keep "unqualified" people, those without education degrees, out of their profession, and then fight equally hard against competence tests and outside assessments of how qualified today's teachers are. The IQ and tracking systems strive for more and more refined predictions of who will succeed, but make no corresponding attempt to see who is in fact doing a good job. (The most egregious case of concentrating on preparation rather than performance, unfortunately, is found among political reporters. For three and a half years before a presidential election we get endless analyses of who's going to win and why. Most of the guesses, inevitably, turn out to be wrong. Much less effort goes into examining how the candidates perform once they take office.)

There are two separate issues involved in this shift from competence to ability. One is what it does to the American idea of starting over and having second chances. The other is whether it's effective in its stated goal, guaranteeing skillful performance.

The effect on mobility is straightforward: the more we concentrate on ability, the harder it is for people to find new roles. It's all but impossible to think of starting over, when the steel mill closes down, if your big mistake was being in the slow reading group in fourth grade or choosing the wrong parents. Moreover, an emphasis on ability inevitably leads toward a hereditary class structure, since measured IQ is inherited about as consistently as money.

For as long as intelligence tests have existed, they have been directly connected with income and social position. The people with the most money and the highest social standing do best on the tests. For instance, in 1985 a group called Fair Test released a chart correlating family income with SAT scores:

FAMILY INCOME	AVERAGE SAT (combined verbal & math)
Over $50,000	998
$40,000–$49,999	968
$30,000–$39,999	947
$24,000–$29,999	927
$18,000–$23,999	900
$12,000–$17,999	877
$6000–$11,999	824
Under $6000	771

There are dozens of similar illustrations. When the Army Alpha tests were given during World War I, they showed that intelligence varied with both rank and race. Soldiers with Anglo-Saxon backgrounds had IQs higher than the average score for all whites; Irish Americans' scores were below that average; Greeks placed lower still; southern blacks, lowest of all. (Blacks from the northern states, who mainly lived in cities, had higher scores than newly arrived Italians, Poles, and Russian Jews.) The correlation between money and intelligence could, of course, merely indicate that America's meritocracy is functioning perfectly. The smartest people are getting the best jobs, earning the most money, and having the most talented children. But since this pattern showed up with the very first intelligence tests, which were given in the days of Jim Crow laws and blatant bias against immigrants and women, it is hard to believe that pure merit is the true explanation. Rather, the tests seem to measure something closely connected with social standing, so the correlation between IQ and money is a tautology; that is, it's two measures of the same thing.

Whatever the explanation for the link between money and intelligence may be, the effect is clear: an emphasis on so-called ability makes America rigid. People who start out on the bottom have inherently less chance to rise than those placing above them.

The second issue is whether this bias is necessary. Like the destructive side of capitalism, rigidity may simply be the price America must pay for its long-term growth. This, in fact, is exactly the argument that R. J. Herrnstein made in his book about the meritocracy.

But maybe this is not the whole story. Whenever scholars and investigators have looked closely at what people *do* in their jobs, they've found substantial differences between what it takes to get a job and what it takes to do it well. That is, they've found that the complicated and onerous effort to predict who will succeed need not be made at all.

Part of the problem here is that as licensing requirements have become more restrictive and been based even more on schooling, they haven't necessarily been tied to practical job skills. In California, contractors must pass a pencil-and-paper test before they can be licensed to go into business. According to one study, the major effect of this requirement was to spawn a cram school industry that taught people how to pass the test. "Most licensing exams involve written responses to questions and extensive recall of a wide range of facts that may have little or nothing to do with good practice," S. David Young wrote in *The Rule of Experts*. "For example, occupations such as plumbing and barbering rely on written exams devised by state licensing boards that test little more than the ability to memorize irrelevant facts. Another example is the California licensing examination for architects, in which candidates are expected to discuss the tomb of Queen Hatshephut and the Temple of Apollo." Knowing about the tomb and temple would be a plus for anyone; the question is whether it serves anyone's interest, except that of the architects' guild, to keep people who don't know from entering the market.

Moreover, once a person does get a license, he's practically immune from later scrutiny. Daniel Hogan, a lawyer and social psychologist at Harvard, pointed out that in 1972, only 0.1 percent of practicing lawyers were subject to some form of disciplinary action. Yet in another study, 30 percent of lawyers said they were aware of some legal or judicial misconduct. That is, something was seriously wrong with standards of competence and honesty in the profession, but the elaborate system of licensing and credentials did very little to control it. In a typical recent year, only one American physician out of every 710 had his license revoked or suspended; most Americans who have been patients will find it difficult to believe that 709 out of 710 physicians are completely competent. Professionals must put in years of schooling and pass a test before entering the field, but they're usually never tested again. People who have passed the bar exam are licensed to do anything from drafting wills to arguing a case in court, although the skills involved are very different. A person who has not been to law school or passed the bar exam cannot do either, even though he may have exactly the right skills. (*60 Minutes* publicized the case of Rosemary Furman, of Florida, who drew up low-cost legal forms for poor people. No one contended that she was incompetent or had offered bad advice, but she was sentenced to jail for practicing law without a license.) Only those who have been to medical school can prescribe drugs or perform surgery, but psychiatrists, surgeons, and research specialists are legally free to do any of those things. A few professions have accepted "continuing education" requirements, which once more measure "input": the architect or lawyer shows that he has taken more courses, not necessarily that he's kept up his skills.

Those in the growing field of "competence" studies have developed a theory of how modern, complex society could operate without heavy licensing requirements. "All of our work has given me a very strong view," Richard Boyatzis told me in 1985. The consulting firm Boyatzis heads, called McBer, was founded by David McClelland in 1963. It analyzes what people actually do in business jobs — not what their job descriptions say, but how they spend their time and which skills seem most crucial to their success. "I've come to see that whenever a group institutes a credentialing process, whether by licensing or insisting on advanced degrees, the espoused rhetoric is that it's enforcing standards of professionalism. This is true whether it's among accountants or plumbers or physicians. But the observed consequences always seem to be these two: the exclusion of certain groups, whether by intention or not, and the establishment of mediocre performance."

"The assumption that those who do well in school do well on the job is simply wrong," Paul Pottinger, then the director of the National Center for the Study of the Professions, told me. "I've never seen any evidence anywhere that those who do well academically do well in life — except for getting the credential that enables them to hold a professional position."

One of the most exhaustive studies of the difference between preparation and performance, or ability and competence, was undertaken by Daniel Hogan. In 1979, he published a fat, four-volume study called *The Regulation of Psychotherapists*. Hogan's purpose was to compare preparation and performance as carefully and systematically as he could. First he examined the day-by-day workings of psychotherapists at every level, from the social worker to the licensed psychoanalyst and the psychiatrist with an M.D. He devoted hundreds of pages to an analysis and a description of the traits that distinguish a good psychotherapist from a bad one. In deciding which psychotherapists were most effective, he concentrated strictly on "output" — whether the patient got better — rather than on "input" — how much effort the therapist applied, how much he charged, or how long he'd spent in school.

Then, having considered what it took to *do* the job well, Hogan, in the second half of the volume, went through all the qualifications a therapist needed to *get* the job. There was not much overlap between the two lists. To get a license to practice, a psychotherapist had to do well at hard, scientific training, which in most cases was unimportant in doing the job well. (In some cases it was useful, of course; patients with organic causes of their mental conditions could be treated appropriately. But, Hogan said, these were the exceptions.)

"Contrary to much professional opinion," he wrote, "the effectiveness of therapists is more determined by the presence or absence of certain personality characteristics and interpersonal skills than technical abilities and theoretical knowledge." A good psychotherapist, as Hogan identified him, was warm, empathetic, reliable, unpretentious, an astute reader of moods, adept at drawing people out. "The necessary qualities are very similar to those one looks for in a good friend."

It may be hard to measure such skills on a multiple-choice test, Hogan said, but they are real, and they can be measured in other ways. The people who have these skills can, according to Hogan, be effective therapists whether or not they've had a lot of professional training.

Hogan's book was filled with cases illustrating this point. In a study done in 1965, for example, five laymen, only one of whom had finished college, were given less than a hundred hours of training in therapy skills. Then they were put in charge of patients who had been hospitalized, on average, for more than thirteen years without significant improvement. Under their "amateur" treatment, over half of the patients got better.

Another illustration was based on a semideceptive study. Eight perfectly healthy, perfectly normal "pseudopatients" were told to present themselves at mental hospitals for admission. They were supposed to lie about their names and to invent some "presenting symptom" that would convince the hospitals to admit them. But from that point on, they were to stop faking any symptoms and were to behave normally.

"What happened to these normal individuals was extraordinary," Hogan said. "All of them were hospitalized with the diagnosis of schizophrenia, except for one person, who was diagnosed as a manic-depressive psychotic. The total length of hospitalization varied from seven to 52 days, with an average of 19. During the pseudopatients' entire hospital stay, none of the psychiatrists, nurses, or other professionals suspected that these people might be normal. Interestingly, the ward patients were quite suspicious, with 35 of a total of 118 patients voicing their doubts about the first three admittees alone."

"Competence" studies like Hogan's have turned up many other illustrations of the difference between ability and performance — between what it takes to get a job and what it takes to do it. Two other fields are worth discussing: schoolteaching and air-traffic control.

Anyone who wants to teach in the public schools must first be licensed, which means getting a degree from a teacher's college. Sometimes the people who get these degrees are good teachers, but that seems to be largely coincidental. In 1967, Harold Howe II, who was then the U.S. commissioner of education, said that this focus on credentials and certificates was "a bit like saying that Socrates wasn't a good teacher because he had no teaching credentials . . . We have forgotten that Spinoza earned his living as a lens grinder and that Tom Edison quit school at nine." Howe described a woman in her twenties who had lived for several years in Paris, worked for a French magazine, and taught French at a private school when she returned to the United States. But when she applied for a job as a public school teacher, she was turned down flat, because she had not been to teacher's college. Howe concluded, "I probably don't need to tell you, either, that a majority of States do not require language teachers to be able to speak the language they are to teach." Denny Harrah is a former professional football player for the Los Angeles Rams, chosen for the Pro Bowl six times. When he volunteered to help coach a high school football team in Charleston, West Virginia, he was turned down because he was not "certified." One of my children spent a year with an elementary school science teacher who had been shifted from teaching English. She was fully "qualified" to teach, since she had her credentials, but she knew less about science than most of the children did. During that year my son was taught, among other things, that as the moon rotated on its axis, you could see its back side from the earth and that you could go blind from looking at a picture of a solar eclipse unless you protected yourself with smoked glass. My son would check each day's new information with a neighbor who had studied for a degree in astronomy. The neighbor, of course, was not qualified to teach.

Private schools are free to ignore education school degrees, and generally they do. I once observed classes at St. Albans, one of the most prestigious private schools in Washington, D.C. It was obvious that the students were learning more, or at least being offered more, than in typical public high schools. Part of the reason is that St. Albans is a very high-toned expensive school that draws most of its students from professional-class families that stress education. But the school's headmaster, Mark Mullin, said that another factor was more important to the school's quality: "the freedom to hire the people we want. The freedom not to worry about certification, seniority, and all of that. I don't know how we'd do without it. That clearly is number one." Unlike the surrounding public schools, St. Albans could hire teachers who knew French and music, understood the rotation of the moon, and could also show that they had an instinct for teaching and dealing with children.

A few public schools have edged toward the same approach. The Houston school system has had to cope with large and rapid demographic changes, more dramatic than those in many other big-city systems. Only Los Angeles and Miami have had to absorb more immigrants in their schools. But unlike the performance levels in most other big-city systems, those in the Houston schools went up in the mid 1980s. The superintendent of the Houston schools, a back-slapping character named Billy Reagan, said that his crucial advantage was his freedom, within the limits of a public school system, to let talented people teach even if they didn't have the right credentials. In 1986, some New Jersey districts were allowed to hire teachers who had no teaching credentials but were able to show that they really knew their subject. The Rumson–Fair Haven Regional High School District, for example, hired an honors history graduate straight out of college to teach its high school history classes.

An education school dean would probably argue that public schools should put more emphasis, not less, on preparation. If they wind up with science teachers who've seen the dark side of the moon, then the teacher's colleges should add more science courses to their curricula. This is the argument nearly every licensed profession has made when asking the government to stiffen entry requirements. (In the early 1970s, when I was working as an assistant in the Texas state senate, a group of auctioneers demanded that the state government license them. The public was being jeopardized by unqualified auctioneers, they said. Rather than letting just anybody conduct an auction, the state should make people pass written tests and spend a certain period in apprenticeship.) But there is little evidence that the regulations have done what they are supposed to do — that is, protect the public more thoroughly than a simple market test would have done. (In the case of teachers, a market test would mean letting principals and school districts hire people who know their subjects, as private schools do today.) As S. David Young concluded in his book about licensing, "Occupational regulation has served to limit consumer choice, raise consumer costs . . . deprive the poor of adequate services, and restrict job opportunities for minorities — all without a demonstrated improvement in quality or safety of the licensed activities."

If schoolteaching and psychotherapy seem too "soft" to provide a fair test of meritocratic standards, what about air-traffic control? In 1970, in *The Great Training Robbery,* Ivar Berg reported on a study conducted by the Federal Aviation Administration, which wanted to analyze what made the 507 top-ranking air traffic controllers good at their jobs. The question was whether advanced educational requirements would produce more competent controllers; the answer was no. Berg said that the controller's job seemed to demand a high degree of academic preparation. It required an understanding of important mathematical and engineering principles, and it also drew on some of the personal qualities that higher education was supposed to foster: disciplined thinking, reliability, responsibility, and so on. Yet when the FAA studied the backgrounds of its best controllers, it found no correlation between academic training and professional skill. Half of the top-ranked controllers had never gone to college. Many of them had come directly to the FAA from high school or the military service, and had then received rigorous technical training specifically related to their jobs.

When competence really matters — among air-traffic controllers, on the battlefield, in very competitive businesses, in high-powered prep schools — people soon find a way to look past academic preparation and find out who can really do the job. The fastest-growing American companies are much less interested in background than are big, settled institutions in which no one can really be held accountable — such as the public schools. "We have a lot of walk-in talent," I was told several years ago by Stephen Ballmer, then a twenty-nine-year-old vice president of Microsoft. "We ask them to send us a program they've written that they're proud of. One of our superstars here is a guy who literally walked in off the street. We talked him out of going to college and he's been here ever since." Microsoft was growing so fast that it couldn't *afford* to pay attention to academic background: it had to find people who could really do the job.

ABILITY AS A CONVENIENT FILTER

There is one other argument for relying on "ability" and "prep-aration" to steer people toward jobs. They may not be perfect gauges of later competence, but how bad can they really be? Once, while interviewing officials at the Educational Testing Ser-vice headquarters near Princeton, I came to the end of a long discussion with an ETS test designer. Yes, he said, standardized tests often measured arbitrary skills. Yes, they reflected the stu-dents' exposure to literate, upper-middle-class culture during their formative years. No, test performance didn't necessarily have much to do with useful job skills. And yes, children raised in families with the most money consistently did best on the tests, for reasons that seemed to reflect money itself as much as innate differences in talent. "But, in general, the kids who know these things know a lot else," he said. "A *lot.*"

The idea that tests and school credentials are "close-enough" approximations of other, important skills might be satisfactory in Japan. There, everyone seems comfortable with the knowledge that the people — in practice, the men — who get into Tokyo University are the ones who will lead industry and government. The Tokyo University admissions test doesn't measure much that is directly useful to Mitsubishi or the Ministry of Finance. The English-language portion of the test, for example, measures almost nothing that would be useful to people who intend to speak English. (In a sixth-year English class in a Tokyo high school, I once listened to a thirty-minute lecture, in Japanese, about the supposed difference between "attain" and "attain to." Apparently it had been on an admissions test.) But the tests do measure effort, and for the Japanese that's close enough. Con-ceivably the same principle could apply here. Long years in school and good scores on tests may not be directly connected to professional competence, but indirectly they may lead the right people to the right jobs.

The main problem with this reasoning is that it ignores the tremendous damage caused by the emphasis on "ability." If all other factors were equal, then the government may as well limit certain jobs to people who have spent the most years in school; a job would be a kind of delayed reward. But other factors aren't equal. The more that formal schooling matters, the harder it is for Americans to move out of the social class where they were born. For American society, unlike Japanese, schooling and ability should be emphasized only if there's no other way to ensure competence. In fact, as the evidence shows, the educational merit system increases costs and decreases opportunity without noticeably raising the overall level of skill.

The world is full of "close-enough" judgments, which are also known as "prejudice." Statistically, the average American is five hundred times more likely to be infected with AIDS than the average Japanese, and American male homosexuals are many times more likely than anyone else. Therefore, people in Tokyo may be justified, on close-enough grounds, in avoiding touching the commuter strap I'd held in a subway, and heterosexual Americans would be justified in shunning homosexuals altogether. This policy would be close enough, but it would be ugly and unfair. Statistically, the average black American man is more likely to be a criminal, a drug abuser, and a credit risk than the average white American. Therefore, employers would be close enough if they refused to hire any blacks.

America cannot afford to erect barriers that are close enough. America was built by people who broke out of categories, defied probabilities, and changed their fate.

CHAPTER NINE

A New Status System

AMERICA has been more democratic and less class-bound than most other societies, but it has of course had internal divisions of its own. The three traditional forms of American snobbery, which have always been at odds with the American idea that no one should defer or kowtow to anyone else, are those based on race, money, and family name.

The consequences of these forms of prejudice are well known. Racial hostility is America's central domestic problem, and has been for more than two centuries. Gloating about money is not exactly charming, but in its way it's all-American: in theory, anyone can strike it rich and rise to the top. The desire to have an old, aristocratic name seems perversely un-American — but in practice, the yearning to *become* traditional and aristocratic pays homage to the American ideal of inventing new identities for ourselves. Ralph Lauren turns his store into a replica of Blenheim Palace. *Newsweek* ads show George Will, of downstate Illinois, sipping tea in his study and looking as if he's ready to stroll out to his London club. As reported in *The Atlantic*, "When Susan Gutfreund, a former airline attendant and the socialite wife of the investment banker John Gutfreund, receives a compliment about any antique she owns, her response is desperately *faux patrician*. 'Oh,' she invariably replies, 'we've had that forever.' "

The rise of a status system based on education, however, has created another form of American snobbery, another kind of caste division. The new system is based on intelligence and taste. It is related to some of the more familiar forms of snobbery, since people with the most money and with what are considered the best family and racial backgrounds usually have the most education too. But it has special dangers of its own. Discrimination based on intelligence seems more legitimate than other forms. Most college graduates try to conceal their racial or religious prejudices but are not embarrassed to sneer at high school dropouts. A social hierarchy built largely on academic degrees is fine for Japan. Everyone understands and accepts the ranking system, and nearly everyone agrees to perform his duty as part of a group. But a system implying that people with more brains and more schooling are *better* people is a problem for America. It is a direct threat to the essential American idea that anyone can make a new start.

It may seem odd to complain about an overemphasis on "intelligence" at a time when Americans trail the developed world in their knowledge of geography, foreign languages, math, and almost everything else. (Japanese newspapers hooted about a recent survey contrasting high school seniors' attitudes in the United States and Japan. The Japanese students listed grades and university admissions as their leading concerns; the Americans listed sex.) But snobbish exclusiveness based on the idea of innate intellectual superiority is different from real scholarship, and is connected to several harmful cleavages in American culture.

In strictly economic terms, there is still no conclusive proof that America's middle class has shrunk. (That the issue is endlessly debated in economic and political journals illustrates how closely balanced the evidence is.) But in cultural terms, America is much less middle class than it was a generation ago. The prevailing American culture of the 1940s and 1950s encouraged most white people to think of themselves as middle-class Americans, on a common footing with everybody else. Because of the G.I. Bill, college was suddenly open to the average person, not just the "college boy." The suburbs beckoned people whose parents had been cooped up in tenements. The average man could afford a barbecue and a back yard. The most powerful media were mass circulation and middle class — *Life, Look, The Saturday Evening Post*. The leading actress was the girl next door, Doris Day.

Two powerful institutions encouraged the sense that most Americans were part of a single, broad, common culture. One was the public school system, and the other was the pre–Vietnam War draft. Both brought Americans of different classes into face-to-face contact with one another. American men who came of age in the 1940s and 1950s, from Elvis Presley to Philip Roth, generally shared the military experience. By extension, the women in their families felt at least some of the democratizing effect. Joseph Epstein, who later became a professor of English at Northwestern University and editor of *The American Scholar* — that is, exactly the kind of man who would not have been in the army during the past twenty years — was a drafted enlisted man before the Vietnam War. The army was rigidly and harmfully class-bound internally, he said, with its all-important distinction between officers and enlisted men. And yet

> no American institution was, at its core, more democratic . . . As an enlisted man, one was really thrown into the stew of American life. In my own basic-training platoon I lived with Missouri farmers, Appalachian miners, an American Indian auto mechanic, a black car salesman from Detroit, a Jewish lawyer from Chicago, a fundamentalist high school teacher from Kansas, and others no less varied but now lost to memory . . . Although I groaned and cursed, questioning the heavens for putting me through the torture in tedium that I then took my time in the Army to be, I have since come to view that time as one of the most interesting interludes in my life — among other reasons because it jerked me free, if only for a few years, from the social class in which I have otherwise spent nearly all my days. It jerked everyone free from his social class, however high or low that class may have been.

The public schools had a similar effect, imperfect but important. Those who came of age in the 1960s, while less likely to have shared the military experience, were still likely to have gone through public schools. In my own years in the Redlands public schools, in the 1950s and 1960s, my classmates included people who ended up as auto dealers, doctors, labor organizers, actors in TV commercials, blackjack dealers, schoolteachers, rock musicians, tennis coaches, bartenders, orange growers, librarians, contractors, and art historians. They obviously came from a variety of backgrounds and in reality were from different classes, but they didn't think of themselves as being divided into castes.

Neither of these institutions now plays as powerful a unifying role as it did. The military was skewed first by the Vietnam-era draft policies and then by the switch to an all-volunteer force, which has generally kept the college-bound class of Americans out of uniform. "The distinctive quality of the enlisted ranks in modern times has been a mixing of the social classes," Charles Moskos of Northwestern has said. "This was the elemental social fact underlying enlisted service. This is the state of affairs that has disappeared in the all-volunteer Army." Except in small towns, public schools have become more stratified by income and class, as residential neighborhoods have.

At the same time, the popular culture has gone through a comparable change, highlighting the factors that make Americans different from one another and playing down the shared middle-class traits. Almost every form of business has become more segmented than before. General magazines like *Life* have all but disappeared; specialized magazines like *Gourmet* and *Yachting* continue to rise. Department stores lose ground to boutiques. Advertising, both commercial and political, is addressed to narrow slices of America, less often to the country as a whole. This difference is especially apparent in a comparison with Japan. Advertising directors in Japan aim their messages at certain age groups — teenage girls, retired men. But within those categories they address all Japanese, as did American ads of the 1950s. Since American ads are now more carefully targeted by class, American magazines and newspapers compete ferociously to show advertisers that they have the most upscale readership of whiskey drinkers, watch buyers, and foreign-vacation takers. Frank Capra movies emphasized the things that Americans had in common. The closest counterpart might be the first *Rocky* — but though it showed that Average Joe could succeed, it didn't suggest that he had much in common with Americans who'd gone beyond high school.

Of course America still has some important middle-class institutions, such as network TV and *USA Today*. And, as these examples remind us, broad-brush mass-cult institutions don't make up a distinguished civilization all by themselves. But they have been valuable in offsetting the centrifugal forces built into America society, which is why their decay is a problem.

Here we come back to the rise of a meritocracy of education and measured intelligence, which serves, with the other factors, to erode the sense of possibility that keeps America going.

Despite America's traditional, down-to-earth skepticism about pointy heads and ivory tower experts, there are indications that people at all levels of society take their IQ scores and their school backgrounds as valid judgments of their ability. The officials who create and administer IQ tests no longer say what the pioneers of "mental measurement" did at the turn of the century: that what they are quantifying is innate, immutable, unaffected by such factors as family income and childhood advantage. Representatives of the College Board and the Educational Testing Service carefully point out that the tests are intended for one purpose only: to predict who will get good grades in college, so that the colleges can make informed decisions about whom to admit. This is, in fact, what the tests do, as the previous chapters have discussed. But few people who take or design the tests seem to believe it deep inside. ETS officials themselves, at least those I've interviewed, are not eager to reveal their own SAT scores. While researching his book about the SATs, *None of the Above,* David Owen asked a number of famous and obviously smart people, such as George Plimpton, Frances Fitzgerald, and Wilfrid Sheed, whether they would be willing to take the SAT and then announce their scores. He found no takers.

In 1965, the Russell Sage Foundation published a report about public attitudes toward intelligence testing. It said that while the "upper class respondent is more likely to favor the use of tests than the lower class respondent, [the] lower class respondent is more likely to see intelligence tests measuring inborn intelligence." "IQ is enormously influential in formation of self-image," Howard Gardner, of Harvard's psychology department, said in 1987. "It seems that as many people remember their

Scholastic Aptitude Test scores as remember their Social Security numbers." When the Scholastic Aptitude Test was first administered, students were not told their scores. It was thought that the information was so important and so unchangeable that people would be better off not knowing. In 1958, the College Board finally reversed this policy and allowed students to see their scores. When I visited the ETS, one official showed me a comment made by Frank Bowles, who was president of the College Board when it decided to let students see their scores: "I have learned from hearing my own children's conversations that SAT scores have now become one of the peer group measuring devices. One unfortunate may be dismissed with the phrase, 'That jerk — he only made 420!' The bright, steady student is appreciated with his high 600, and the unsuspected genius with his 700 is held in awe."

The yuppie wave of the mid 1980s illustrated the connection between money and intelligence. At one level it was a purely economic phenomenon. It took a lot of money to buy those bench-made shoes and to stock the cellar with wine. In New York, much of the money came from the banking and investment business, which is hardly a licensed profession; but in the country as a whole the money came from "intelligent," professional work, by people who'd done well in school. Moreover, the money was used in a way that said not simply, "I can spend more money than you," which the owner of a Houston well-service company could have said during the oil boom, but also and more cuttingly, "I am smarter than you and can prove it through my superior taste." Being able to afford the right restaurants, coffees, baby carriages, and clothes was part of the battle; *knowing* which ones were right was the other part. If you ate "interesting" bread and wore only natural fibers, you were better than a person who ate white bread and wore polyester — not just because such K mart products were inexpensive but because choosing them made people look dumb.

The impulse to prove ourselves better — more talented, more deserving — than other people may be deep and primeval. But different societies can manipulate its expression in different ways, some of them constructive and some not. Certain basic desires and emotions are better when they are suppressed than when they're given free rein. Anti-Semitism may still be a dirty secret, but it's less harmful as a secret than it was as an acceptable WASP attitude only a generation ago. Men in America and Japan presumably harbor the same abiding interest in sex and the same impulse to paw through porno magazines. But society works more smoothly, especially for women and children, when that impulse is kept hidden than when it's indulged in public — as it is by the Japanese men who stare happily at their "sports papers" in the subway cars, following the latest cartoon-series adventures of a frisky, talking penis.

American society is healthier and more successful when our culture suppresses the instinct to set ourselves apart from one another. Small-town Southern California values blunted the tools of status comparisons and discouraged attempts to categorize people by class. The resulting society had its defects, but it was a better-functioning and more "American" culture than, say, the New York of *The Bonfire of the Vanities*. Wolfe's New York may be cartoonlike, but it shows what happens to an every-man-for-himself society, one in which people no longer think they're all playing by the same rules. The class-war aspect of the Vietnam draft highlighted the same problem in the 1960s. The school-busing controversy, in which professional-class judges and experts deployed children from working-class black and white families, was the illustration in the 1970s.

Unfortunately for England, it provides one of the most searing examples of what can happen to a society when it gives the snobbish impulse free rein. In *The Great War and Modern Memory,* Paul Fussell said that one single day marked the end of the innocence and optimism of Britain's imperial age. The day was July 1, 1916, when the British launched their suicidal assault at the Somme. At 7:30 in the morning, waves of British soldiers came out of their trenches and began marching toward the German lines. At 7:31, the Germans began firing their machine guns, and for the rest of the day they mowed down the British boys. Of the 110,000 British soldiers who joined the attack, 60,000 were killed or wounded on this one day.

"The disaster had many causes," Fussell wrote; the British

suffered from poor military planning and utter lack of surprise. But in the end, their catastrophic failure had a simpler cause. It was, he said, traceable to the class system and the assumptions it sanctioned.

> The regulars of the British staff entertained an implicit contempt for the rapidly trained new men of "Kitchener's Army," largely recruited among workingmen from the Midlands. The planners assumed that these troops — burdened for the assault with 66 pounds of equipment — were too simple and animal to cross the space between the opposing trenches in any way except in full daylight and aligned in rows or "waves." It was felt that the troops would become confused by more subtle tactics like rushing from cover to cover, or assault-firing, or following close upon a continuous creeping barrage.

The "implicit contempt" that caused the slaughter at the Somme was part of the English snobbery, based on class and family, that Americans like Fussell can easily detect from outside. Our own recent divisions, wrapped up in questions of taste and intelligence, are harder for us to see but could become as poisonous.

The idea that people on the top of a society are better than others — not just richer or luckier but *better* inside, because they're white or smart — creates another problem for the American ethic of constant possibility. It discourages the "bad" people and makes even the "good" people lose their nerve.

The protagonist of Somerset Maugham's novel *Of Human Bondage*, Philip Carey, is an orphan who wishes he had been born into the upper class. His resentment increases when he ends up at a school with his social betters. One of them takes him aside for a little chat on career choices. If Carey had been an aristocrat, the friend says, only certain callings would be appropriate for him — the church, the army, the City (London banking), the bar. But since he didn't have a family name to protect, Carey was free to do what he wanted — even, in theory, to go into trade. Clearly the well-born friend wished no such humiliating freedom for himself.

Outsiders can instantly see how such prejudices weakened England. There is nothing necessarily wrong with the handful of professions considered acceptable to the upper class. A country needs competent clergymen, soldiers, financiers, and lawyers. But the whole idea of "gentlemen's work" pushed much of England's best-trained talent into a tiny funnel, diverting it from science and, most of all, from manufacturing. England would be healthier today if its most fortunate people felt they had a broader choice in life.

The aristocracy of intellectual merit poses a similar danger to America. Like inherited money or family position, intellectual merit should always be liberating. But like money and family, often it is not. All of these forms of inherited advantage should make it easier for people to start over, to recover from early mistakes, to define roles for themselves. But in practice, each can be constricting. Certain occupations, mainly in the professions, have become our version of "gentlemen's work." For smart people they offer the most secure and predictable financial returns, and the most prestige. As with gentlemen's work in England, there's nothing inherently wrong with these professions. But as was the case in England, this sort of snobbery narrows choice and weakens the country. It steers well-trained people away from some of the most creative and useful jobs; it undermines the American belief that anyone can do anything.

The rewards of advanced education and intellectual ability can be great — if you stay on a certain path. When I was living in England, I once saw a catty story in a London paper about Johnny Carson. He was annoyed to find that when he walked down the street in London, nobody noticed him. Since the *Tonight* show was not shown in England in those days, Carson, who was lionized at home, in London became merely another American tourist. There's a similar phenomenon with meritocratic talent. In certain quarters it entitles people not simply to respect but also to a good living, a kind of sinecure. But outside those quarters — anywhere except America, to use the Carson metaphor — the financial reward dramatically falls off. In business, teaching, politics, publishing, the arts, and most forms of science, a good educational pedigree cannot be predictably converted into high earnings. In law, medicine, and a few other licensed professions, it can: getting into one of the professions puts you on a particular plateau. Professionals don't become the richest people in America, but they have a more risk-free place near the top than almost anyone else.

As a result, the "best," most talented people in America are offered a bargain as attractive to themselves, and as distorting for the country, as the one Somerset Maugham described. Rational people find the temptations hard to resist. In theory, Rhodes scholars, like prewar English aristocrats, should have limitless freedom of occupational choice. But in practice, at least a third of them use that freedom to become lawyers. (In the 1940s, it was only an eighth.) Similarly, Phi Beta Kappa members should have wide opportunities in a society that places such emphasis on academic preparation. Of Phi Beta Kappa members who graduated from college in the late 1940s, 5 percent became lawyers or judges. Of those who graduated in the late 1970s, 20 percent did.

There is nothing wrong with people becoming lawyers or doctors. It could also be argued that, since so many well-trained people are shunted away from the hard sciences, teaching, manufacturing, and so forth, there's more room in these fields for ambitious newcomers, immigrants, and members of the "untalented" class. Still, no one contends that, in the abstract, America should be sending so many of its best-educated young people into such a narrow range of professional jobs. From the whole country's point of view, the incentives are perverse — as they were for England, when the best-trained people were, through class snobbery, diverted from careers in business or technology. The rewards offered for education and pure ability are greatest and most reliable in the narrowest, most conventional range of jobs. Societies work best when individual and collective interests overlap. The temptations of the meritocratic life make them diverge.

The distorting effects of this meritocratic bargain reach right down to elementary schools. In the big cities during the 1980s, pressure mounts to get your children on the right private school track, without delay. Sometimes this is a straightforward matter of educational quality, but it's often something more. My wife and I lived in Washington, D.C., when our sons started elementary school. The public elementary schools, in the well-heeled part of town where we lived, were in no detectable way worse than the private schools. The difference was the parents' desire to extinguish risk. Those who got their children into private feeder schools at the age of three or five minimized the risks their offspring would face later on. About the time our first son, aged five, was starting public kindergarten, I read a story in the *Washington Post* about a woman whose five-year-old had just been admitted to the Sidwell Friends School. "Somebody who gets their kid into Sidwell Friends at age 5 doesn't have to think about it again until Harvard," she said with relief. Another parent was quoted as saying, "I think the anxiety of parents is ridiculous. These people are convinced that unless their kid gets into the very best kindergarten, the child will be handicapped for life."

I can't criticize anyone for wanting to minimize risks. It's dangerous to experiment with children's lives. In a way, the anxiety about school admissions is a sign that America is a fluid society: if parents *knew* where their children would end up in life, as aristocrats in Indonesia or even France do, they would not have to worry so much about aiming them toward prep schools and the Ivy League. But it is depressing to see children learning, so early, to be so cautious — to expect the greatest rewards from the narrowest path, to have their fate determined when they are young. It isn't the American way.

CHAPTER TEN

The Reopening of America

AMERICA is strongest when it is most open and optimistic. This sounds like a platitude, but it has important practical effects. When ordinary people believe they have a fair chance, they usually do their best, and the whole country benefits from their efforts. The interests of individual Americans are well matched to the society's collective good. But if Americans think they are trapped, cheated, stuck, or doomed, most of them do not try.

The classic American success stories of the twentieth century illustrate what people can do when they think they can change their fortune. Some of them have already been discussed. The immigrants at the turn of the century were dispossessed in Europe and scorned when they reached New York, but within a generation they'd assimilated and succeeded. In the few areas where blacks have had a chance to compete fairly and be judged strictly on how well they perform — in the military, in sports, and in show business — they've tried hard and excelled. The "unsuitable" scholars sent to college by the G.I. Bill became the best that America's universities have ever seen. Half a century ago, Hitler had contempt for Jesse Owens, and the fascist leaders of Japan had contempt for the will power of America's "mongrel" population. When the first Vietnamese refugees arrived just after the fall of Saigon, news analyses predicted that they were destined to become America's new underclass. As politicians, Ronald Reagan and Jesse Jackson both rose to prominence in ways that other cultures would never have allowed. Modern America's major "failure story," the black urban underclass, illustrates the same point, but in reverse. Although black-skinned immigrants from the Caribbean and Africa have generally succeeded (despite their recent prominence in the drug business), the underclass has been moving toward a separate, worse existence. Theories about the growth of the underclass differ, but they have one theme in common: the teenagers, young mothers, and adult men in the underclass don't feel they have a reason to try (because of racist barriers, because they're coddled by welfare, because the only jobs available pay "chump change," or whatever the reason is said to be).

The way to make America more like us, then, is to allow more people to believe that they can control their fate. Sometimes America needs big, well-organized projects to get its work done, as when mounting the invasion of Normandy or the trip to the moon. Some steps to correct America's trade imbalance may also require government coordination, from improving the public school system to funding certain kinds of research and development.* For the reasons explained earlier, Japan has a natural tendency toward running huge, chronic trade surpluses. Perhaps the United States can live indefinitely with such an imbalance, if it clings to the pure capitalist view that the consumer's welfare matters more than anything else. (An American trade deficit, after all, means that Japanese and Korean workers are toiling to subsidize us.) But if the United States decides that the deficit is

---

* This is not the place for a long argument about "industrial policy." There are two basic points to bear in mind. One is that the United States has always used government money to foster certain industries. It does so now mainly through the military budget (which has helped make America the world leader in the commercial aviation business), Medicare and other health programs (which affect the pharmaceutical and medical technology business, apart from their obvious impact on doctors and hospitals), agricultural policy, and scientific research funds. The second point is that certain other nations, notably Japan and France, use their money more explicitly to promote crucial industries. The strongest argument for an American industrial policy is that since we are destined to spend the money anyway, we may as well do so with a plan in mind.

a problem, coordinated government effort is the only way to steer the two societies away from their natural paths. One way to balance world trade is for Japan to become "more like America," with open markets and a proconsumer outlook on life. Most of the movement in that direction has come only after wheedling and pushing from the U.S. government. The other, more regrettable solution is for the American economy to become more like Japan's, deliberately holding out imports (which means holding down the standard of living) to improve its balance of trade. This would even more obviously require government effort, since there is no other way to keep Americans from buying attractive goods. The government could also change tax incentives to make savings more attractive and pure financial speculation less alluring, and it could improve America's competitive standing in hundreds of other ways.

Still, America's long-term prosperity depends on millions of people being motivated to try their best day by day. Therefore, the crucial up-or-down test for government policies or shifts in values should be this: anything that encourages people to believe that they can start over or change their lives strengthens America. Anything that convinces Americans that they have been denied a fair chance weakens the country and exposes it to the many divisive forces built into a big, disorderly, untraditional, multiracial society.

To make America as productive, happy, and decent as it can be, we need to remove the barriers that keep people from imagining and making new places for themselves. These are some steps that would help.

SHIFTING PUBLIC SPENDING FROM "ENTITLEMENT" TO "INSURANCE"

America's debts and deficits have become familiar (and tedious) topics. The most obvious reason for the budget deficit, the trade deficit, and America's international debt is that America has been "overconsuming," enjoying a higher standard of living than it should, theoretically, have been able to afford. But these conditions can also be thought of as limiting our flexibility, exactly the predicament America does not want to be in.

The federal budget deficit (and resulting increase in federal debt) leads to much higher interest payments by the government. In the late 1970s, interest payments on the federal debt came to about 1.5 percent of the gross national product. By the late 1980s, they had risen to nearly 4 percent. Interest payments are not evil in themselves, but they're as constricting as a huge mortgage is. America's strength is its freedom of action, but past debt leaves the country that much less room to decide to do something new. In an ideal world, the "something new" could be a positive initiative, such as space exploration. In the real world, it will probably be the need to respond to an emergency — grappling with the environmental threats that have become more critical in the late 1980s, covering the financial costs of AIDS, coping with the American underclass. (Whether the last is done through more schools or more jails, it will cost money.)

In another, less obvious way the federal budget leaves America less choice. More money than Americans *pay in taxes* is already committed to "automatic" spending — on interest payments, the military, and retirement programs, mainly Social Security and Medicare. If the government spent on absolutely nothing else — if it financed no research programs, no highways, no FBI, no Centers for Disease Control, no national parks, no NASA — it would still be in the red.

Of course any of these items should be controllable in the long run — military by a change in the international climate, interest by a rise or fall in the level of debt, everything by shifts in policy. But the natural tendency of American politics makes it, in fact, very difficult to control them. The main problem is not the Department of Defense budget: as a share of the gross national product, it is lower in the late 1980s than it was in the 1950s, when the government had only a negligible deficit. Also, it's too simple to say that the problem was excessive tax cutting during the Reagan years. Under Reagan, the federal government collected about 19 percent of the GNP in taxes, more than it did in the 1950s or 1960s. The difference is that in the 1950s and 1960s, the government only spent 19 or 20 percent of the GNP; now it spends about 25. That's where the federal debt — and the limit on future freedom of action — comes from; where most of the spending, in turn, comes from is middle-class entitlement programs, such as Social Security and Medicare.

The problem of Social Security financing has also become familiar, but its essential element is often overlooked. In many ways, the universal retirement programs represent American mobility, decency, and openness at their best. The fear of poverty in old age trapped parents and children alike. Insurance against financial disaster gives a society flexibility, since people can take risks without fearing that they'll be destroyed if they fail. (In the poorest peasant societies, farmers are notoriously reluctant to experiment with new strains of rice. If the experiment should fail, their families will starve.) Because American retirement programs are universal, there's no shame attached to anyone's accepting benefits that he or she is considered to have "earned."

The problem is one of proportion. The middle-class entitlements have become less like insurance against difficulty and more like a guaranteed subsidy or reward. The financial structure of Social Security and Medicare has been so designed that the typical beneficiary is paid much more than he and his employer contributed. A man who retires in 1990, having earned the average wage all his life, can expect to receive about 50 percent more in Social Security benefits than his contributions (and his employer's contributions) would have earned during his career in a normal pension plan. There's nothing wrong with this in principle, and if the nation's growing work force or productivity could sustain this kind of dividend to all retirees, the system would be ideal.

But guaranteeing a subsidy to everyone, not just to the people who need the protection that an insurance system would offer, reduces everyone's flexibility. Payroll taxes (to support Social Security and Medicare) have risen dramatically. The maximum annual tax was only $45 in 1950, and did not exceed $1000 until the late 1970s. As a result of the 1983 reforms, designed to make the system cover its costs for baby boom retirees, the maximum tax is nearing $4000 per year in the late 1980s and will keep going up. Most Americans pay more for retirement programs than they do in federal income tax. Since the Social Security tax is regressive — a janitor pays a higher proportion of his earnings than an investment banker does — and since the portion of the population over sixty-five is richer than the population as a whole, part of the system amounts to a subsidy paid by working-age people to retirees, who, as a group, need the money less.*

Moreover, a rising payroll tax increases the obstacles facing small businesses that are trying to start, survive, and grow. The corporate income tax is a tax on profit; a struggling young company doesn't pay it. The payroll tax, of course, is a fixed cost: a company must pay the tax from the day it opens its doors. As the payroll tax rises in importance relative to the income tax, the government penalizes new businesses relative to large, established ones.

The current entitlement system makes America less open than it could be in one other way. The cost of guaranteeing some benefit to everyone is so large that the people who most need help can't get enough. Although retired people as a group are wealthier than the whole population, some old people are very poor. (In the early 1980s, half of all single women above the age of sixty-five lived on less than $5000 per year, and for most of them, Social Security benefits were their only income.) Because benefits are tied to previous wage levels, it turns out that the smallest Social Security benefits go to those who depend on them most. The largest go to those most likely to have other retirement income.

The point is not that Social Security and Medicare are problems. They are huge successes and the most popular programs

---

* As the economist Michael Boskin has written, "Above and beyond replacing income for low-income retirees, Social Security is transferring billions annually from the general taxpaying working population to well-off retirees . . . It would be hard to imagine Congress explicitly voting to transfer $800 billion to well-off elderly individuals over the next several decades, financed by a flat-rate payroll tax (with no exemptions or deductions) on the general population. Yet that is exactly what our current Social Security system does!" *Too Many Promises: The Uncertain Future of Social Security,* Michael J. Boskin (Homewood, Ill.: Dow Jones–Irwin, 1986), p. 48.

the federal government runs. But the imbalance in the systems is making America less open than it could be. Federal debt reduces our choices and limits our freedom in the long run; entitlement spending is the main reason for federal debt; rising taxes handicap the poorest workers and the smallest firms. On balance, the country would be more flexible if payroll taxes were lowered and benefits were used more as insurance for people most in need. The Congress took a step in this direction in 1983 by making Social Security benefits partly taxable for retirees whose income was above a certain level. We should continue in that direction, making benefits fully taxable as the fairest and least obtrusive form of "means testing." Then, for the same level of taxes, benefits could be generous for people who really need them — or, for the same benefit schedule, payroll taxes could be held down. At the same time, it makes sense to raise the retirement age gradually. In the 1930s, the average life expectancy was only a year or two longer than the standard retirement age of sixty-five. Now, many people live well into their eighties, but most retire at sixty-two. When the government helps spread the risk of modern life through social insurance, Americans can experiment and adjust without fearing that they'll be ruined if their gambles fail. But when the government tries to guarantee too much to too many people, it gums up the process of American adjustment.

DEALING WITH THE LEGACY OF SLAVERY

Racial diversity is not America's problem, no matter what the Japanese think. American society has absorbed people of all backgrounds, including many thought un-absorbable when they arrived. The first major U.S. immigration law was the Chinese Exclusion Act, a flat prohibition on Asian immigrants that reflected a powerful racial prejudice of the time. Now Asian Americans are considered to be America's "model immigrants." One of the most popular American books of the World War I era, *The Passing of the Great Race* by Madison Grant, said that the Italians, Greeks, Polish Catholics, and Russian and Polish Jews then

streaming in were "sweeping the nation toward a racial abyss."
The young Progressive reformer Robert Hunter, in a famous
book entitled *Poverty,* published in 1904, wrote that the "peasantry from other countries, degraded by foreign oppression, are
supplanting the original stock of this country. This is the race-
suicide, the annihilation of our native-stock, which unlimited immigration forces upon us." Somehow the Republic survived.
Black immigrants from Africa and the West Indies have encoun-
tered prejudice but, like other immigrants, have generally succeeded.

But of course race is behind America's major social problem,
which began in the seventeenth century, with the arrival of
slaves. Apart from Native Americans, the African slaves were
the only involuntary, nonimmigrant members of this open, mobile society. It seems extreme to say that sins committed several
hundred years ago must be atoned for now, especially by people
whose ancestors, including mine, were nowhere near America at
the time. But it is not outlandish to believe that slavery, which
ended only 125 years ago, and legalized segregation, which ended
only a generation ago, contributed to a culture that still leaves
people feeling trapped and helpless. (Many Japanese intellectuals, after all, say that their culture is still feeling the aftershocks
of Commodore Perry's first visit to Japan, which occurred at
about the time of our Civil War.) Racial prejudice, in the form of
slavery and segregation, was a necessary condition to the creation of today's underclass, but as the success of black immigrants
and the black middle class shows, it was not sufficient. The culture left over from slavery also played a part: it convinced people
that they would never be allowed to rise.

Working out solutions to the growth of the underclass is America's most complicated challenge, much harder than dealing with
the Russians or the Japanese. My intention in raising the issue is
to show its connection with the general theme of American mobility. In keeping with the idea that America works best when
Americans believe they can control their fate, I can emphasize
two points that should be considered in dealing with the problem.

One is that welfare should be tied to work. Just as everyone
should be entitled to insurance against disaster but not to guar-

anteed subsidies, everyone should be expected to work in exchange for benefits paid for by other Americans.

This sounds like the familiar conservative corrective for welfare chiselers, but there's an important difference. The right-wing "get a job" thesis assumes that the government can wash its hands of all responsibility to the people who are now on welfare. The most probable results of such a cold-turkey policy would be like those of the "deinstitutionalization" of mental patients, which started in the late 1960s. Many of the unfortunates "freed" from government control ended up on the streets. Welfare through work would not eliminate the government's responsibility but would redirect it, in a way less likely to have a destructive cultural effect. Instead of offering cash welfare benefits, the federal government would offer jobs to anyone unable to find work elsewhere. This is essentially the approach taken during the Depression, when Franklin Roosevelt eliminated a cash-relief program and replaced it with the Works Progress Administration. The goal would be the same now: to reinforce the idea that the society runs on work, and that individuals are finally responsible for themselves. "The Work Ethic State proclaims the equal dignity of all who work, an idea that seems more Democratic than Republican," Mickey Kaus wrote, in an essay on a work- rather than welfare-relief program. "In any case, it's very American." It is indeed "very American," because it emphasizes that everyone can move up and start over, and that no one should be viewed as permanently dependent.

The other crucial principle is that children should not be hobbled for the rest of their lives because they start out in third-rate schools. Whatever damage today's welfare system may do to the work ethic, today's urban public schools do more grievous harm. Education has a greater importance than ever; bad schools mean that children not only have no second chance in life but have no chance at all. The decline of the big-city schools reflects poorly on just about everyone involved: those whites who pulled their children out at the first rumblings of desegregation, those black parents who don't try to control or motivate their children, the teachers' unions that fight harder to protect teachers from outside evaluation than to protect the children from bad teachers.

The big-city public schools that have, despite the odds, raised standards and maintained discipline usually share one trait: a strong principal who is able to set a prevailing tone and has the power to reward, punish, and encourage teachers. A system that relies on a strong principal has the potential for abuse, but it couldn't damage the country any more than the one that depends on a weak principal and bad schools.

A more dramatic way to shake up the big-city schools is through the use of vouchers. This idea has moved into and out of respectability over the last generation. Under the plan, the state government, instead of guaranteeing a free education to all children, would issue vouchers for parents to use at either public or private schools. The public schools have been so fundamental to American democracy that one hesitates to recommend anything that may damage them more than they've been harmed. But since they are not serving a democratizing function in the ghetto, there may be no other way to get a school system's attention than by giving parents an alternative.

DE-EMPHASIZING CREDENTIALS AND ELIMINATING CONFUCIANISM

A modern society needs good schools. But modern America should not use schools as a filter, sorting people into categories early in life. Since education has always been related to where one stands in regard to the starting line of life, the more that schooling matters, the harder it will be for anyone to overcome an initial handicap. The less that formal schooling matters, the more likely second chances become — and the harder people will try. Americans can easily understand what's wrong with the extreme versions of educational rigidity: the Eton boys who go on to run England, the iron law that says that University of Tokyo graduates will run Japan. The American version is milder, but it is too confining for a country like ours.

In the last decade, the United States has led the way for Europe, Japan, and even parts of the communist world in deregulating business. With exceptions, such as the pointless breakup of AT&T and hands-off airline deregulation, deregulated businesses have generally worked better for everyone. There's been much less deregulation of professions, which at the moment need it much more. In this form of deregulation, the guiding principles should be (a) to ignore educational background wherever possible, (b) to let people perform whatever service or profession they've shown they can perform competently, whether or not they've prepared for it in the conventional way, and (c) to keep judging people on competence even after they've gone into practice. Here is how such steps might change several major professions.

Nursing

Medical care is economically one of the most important professions, but it is probably the most hostile to the idea of the second chance. Future doctors are separated from future nurses very early in the game, and after that it's hard for anyone to make a new start.

Doctors do end up with something that other people lack: the broad base of knowledge that comes from medical school and subsequent training. This prepares them better than anyone else to interpret surprising, atypical, and potentially misleading symptoms. Nurses don't have the same breadth. But many of them have learned to do specific procedures very well and to recognize the most common maladies — which, after all, are what most patients have. Nurses may be better than doctors at many of these procedures. Who would you rather have clean your teeth, the usually rushed dentist or the dental hygienist?

Because nurses and dental hygienists didn't go to the right colleges or professional schools, they can't convert their skills into anything like the money, freedom, and prestige that doctors enjoy. They could come closer to doing so if medical licensing were based not on preparation but on demonstrated skills. In theory, nurses could prove, by passing realistic, rigorous examinations, that they have mastered certain skills — and then be allowed to use them, even if they hadn't gone to medical school. (The exams, of course, would not be "ability" tests designed to measure the nurses' standardized-test skills; they would be competence tests, to see what the nurses can do.) Once they had moved this far, some nurses might want to fill in the missing parts in their general medical knowledge. They could take time off for additional academic training — even though they did not finish college or score well on the Medical College Admissions Test — and then show, by performance testing, that they were ready for another step toward the top. Not all nurses would want to do this or be able to do so, but some would be both willing and able.

A scholar, Randall Collins, has proposed a similar pattern of stepwise advancement for doctors too:

> All medical careers would begin with a position as orderly, which would be transformed into the first stage of a possible apprenticeship for physicians. After a given number of years, successful candidates could leave for a few years of medical school (2 years seems sufficient background for most practitioners . . .) and then return to the hospital for advanced apprenticeship training of the sort now given in internship and residency programs . . . Advanced specialties would be taught as they now are — through further on-job training; only medical researchers would be involved in lengthy schooling.

The point of all these plans would be to separate people into categories no earlier than necessary, to allow them the maximum flexibility later in life, and to base the classifications on actual skill, not on background.

Teaching

This is an obvious and important example. Public school principals should have the leeway most private school headmasters have: to hire people who know their subjects and seem promising *as teachers,* whether or not they've been to education school. Frank Lumpkin would have been an excellent civics teacher in the Chicago public schools, but without credentials he could never get the job.

Of course there are all sorts of ways that a no-credentials system could be abused. The principal could hire cronies; he could browbeat the teachers; he could hire people who didn't have a clue about what they were doing. But private schools, which also run all these risks, somehow survive them. Perhaps some safeguards should be built in: for instance, half the teachers would need the credentials and half could be the principal's choices. Or all those brought in without credentials might have to pass some certification tests over their first five years on the job. But if you've had children in the public schools recently, ask yourself: Do the risks of a more flexible system seem as serious as the risks we run now?

Piloting

Aircraft pilots are as highly regulated as any other professional guild, but in a very different way from teachers, lawyers, accountants, and doctors. Precisely because it's so important that pilots know what they're doing, the pilots' licensing system already puts more stress on real competence and less on academic preparation.

In the early days of commercial flight, the airlines were totally responsible for training their own pilots and assuring passengers that they were trustworthy. The airlines were very nervous about this arrangement, which left them wholly liable if anything went wrong. They soon begged the federal government to issue its own licenses to the pilots so that when planes did crash, the government could share the responsibility.

The government's pilot-licensing system was built on the idea that people needed distinct, different skills to fly different kinds of planes. People can be good at one thing without being good at others, and they should be licensed only for the skills they have mastered. As opposed to other professionals, who receive blanket licenses, pilots must work their way up through four certificate levels, from student to air-transport pilot, and be separately qualified on each kind of aircraft they want to fly. More radical still, a pilot must regularly demonstrate that he is competent — something none of the other big professions requires in such a clear-cut form. To keep his license, a pilot must take a review flight with an instructor every two years, and the pilots of commercial airliners must pass a battery of qualification tests every six months. "A small but regular percentage is washed out each time," John Mazor of the Air Line Pilot Association told me. It is reassuring to know that those pilots are gone, but what about their counterparts around the operating table or in the courtroom?

The results of this licensing scheme are a high level of proficiency — after all, airline travel is very safe — and a profession that is much less class-bound than the others. Most pilots of big jets learned to fly in the military, since that is the least expensive way to put in the fifteen hundred hours of flight time necessary for an air-transport license. The remainder slowly worked their way up, putting in flight time on their own or working for small air-taxi outfits until they could move to the next license level.

Separating Skills and Encouraging Success

It is easy to imagine what a comparable approach would mean in business, the military, engineering, the law. In all cases the central theme should be to make as much room as possible for people who can show their talent, and not lock in privileges on the basis of early schooling (which is a way of saying, on the basis of family background). There are two important subsidiary themes that mark a distinct change from today's licensing schemes.

One is that skills are specific, not general. Today's professional licensing system assumes that "preparation," like "intelligence," is a big, general quality that you either have or don't have. You are licensed as an M.D. or you're not — and if you are, you're legally free to perform all sorts of procedures that you may not have any idea how to do. If you're not licensed, you can't perform any of the procedures, including ones that as a nurse you may have done under supervision dozens of times. If you've passed your bar exam, you are equally free to argue a case in court or draw up a contract, though those skills are very different from each other. If you haven't passed the bar, you're not allowed to do either. Jesse Jackson might do better before a jury than two thirds of all trial attorneys, but because he doesn't have a law degree he's not allowed to try.

In real life, skills are different. In law, medicine, teaching, or sports, there is such a thing as general ability but also such things as discrete skills. Before the 1987 Super Bowl, Pete Axthelm of *Newsweek* wrote about the Denver Bronco quarterback John Elway: "He has been praised endlessly as a quarterback with unmatched 'pure athletic ability,' which is only slightly more relevant than saying that a concert pianist would be terrific in the decathlon." The more an American professional system concentrates on the specific skills people have, the more opportunities it will open up — and the better the level of performance will be.

The other crucial theme, in keeping with all of America's experience, is that when people are given a chance, they can learn. No one can change his family background or where he did or didn't go to college, but people can learn to do surprising things. At the urging of David McClelland and others, several large American companies (and the foreign service) have set up "competency centers," where people are judged on specific skills, required for performing different jobs well, rather than on general ability. In most cases, it's been found that the more specific the focus, the more people suddenly become "talented," because they can focus on learning a skill. This is supply side economics of the most constructive sort: when a company gives up the idea that only a few people are smart enough to do the job, the supply of people who *can* do the job suddenly increases. Richard Boyatzis, of the consulting firm McBer, said, "The most positive message we consistently get is that people do want to improve themselves, but usually they don't know *exactly* what to work on. When you can give them good feedback on specific goals, that releases the natural internal inclination to improve."

As much as Japan, America depends on all of its people being willing to try. The peculiarities of Japanese culture give people a reason to keep trying all life long. The connection between American schools and American jobs tells some people they may as well quit trying. By making room for people without the right background, we can give Americans a reason to keep trying too.

LETTING IMMIGRANTS IN

That immigration is "good" is a quaint American belief that, to most people, seems no more than quaint. "Immigrants" were the doughty grandparents and great-grandparents who came to America eighty years ago; what happened to them doesn't seem too urgent or instructive anymore.

But of course immigration is still going on, and it is important to America in both a practical and a symbolic way. In practical terms, it continues to be America's major advantage over other countries, especially Japan. A disproportionate share of the ambitious people of the world are fighting for a chance to use their ambitions in the United States. Most other countries, with the exception of Australia and Canada, can't use these foreigners' talents. America can. On the symbolic level, America, by remaining open to immigrants, shows that it understands what kind of country it is. It is not a particular ethnic group or the result of a particular tradition; it is an arena, in which new people can try their best.

The economic evidence about immigration, as we've seen, is open and shut. Immigrants are disproportionately entrepreneurial, determined, and adaptable, and through history they have strengthened the economy of whatever society they join. John Higham, of Johns Hopkins University, probably the leading historian of American immigration, has argued that immigrants strengthened American capitalism during its rocky periods at the turn of the century, and that they add crucial flexibility today. "At the simplest level one notes the prominence of the foreign-born among American inventors and also entrepreneurs and technicians in new, high-risk industries such as textile manufacturing in the early nineteenth century, investment banking in mid-century, and movie-making in the early twentieth century," Higham told a congressional committee in 1986. "Migration looses and sometimes breaks the bonds of tradition. It creates needs that cannot be met in customary ways, while throwing together people with rich, unsuspected potentialities."

There are of course objections to immigration, the most familiar of which are these.

Brain Drain

Some Americans say they oppose immigration because it damages the third world countries from which immigrants come. If immigrants really are that talented, why should the United States be skimming them off from countries that need help more? "Out of 5000 impoverished people, we took one, taking the brightest, most able, most energetic, the best organized," a leading anti-immigration spokesman told the Congress in 1981. This would seem to be the strongest argument for more immigration, but he said it made immigration unfair.

Some forms of immigration can represent brain or talent drains. But in most cases, people emigrate precisely because some barrier in the old country kept them from doing what they would later prove capable of in the new country. A lot of people leaving a country indicates the level of frustrated opportunities there. But a refusal elsewhere to take them in does not eliminate the frustration or help anyone.

Population Pressure

There are so many people in the world, and so many of them are poor, that maybe we'll be swamped if we let them come piling in. And anyway, the United States is not the big, open country it was a hundred years ago, when it might have been fine to let immigrants populate the empty land.

Of course there is such a thing as a world population problem, and the United States doesn't need to create one for itself. But the United States does not have an overall population problem. Its population density is among the lowest in the world. If anything, its general demographic problem in the next half century will be a relative shortage of working-age people, as the members of the postwar baby boom retire. America does have local population problems. Some national parks are overcrowded; overdevelopment is a growing worry in Southern California; overintensive agriculture in Colorado, Nebraska, and elsewhere has depleted the underground aquifers. But these population pressures are the result of the distribution of people: too many Americans want to live in Los Angeles or Denver. Cutting off immigration won't do much to solve those imbalances unless we also prevent people in New Jersey or Michigan from moving west.

There is a stupider version of the demographic case against immigration. In the days of the automation scare, people talked about the lump-of-labor theory — the idea that there is a certain amount of work to be done, and if robots did more of it, there would not be enough left for people to do. A similar flawed logic can be applied to immigrants. For instance, the Environmental Fund warned in 1983 that "if two million immigrants settle in the United States every year, the unemployment rate could rise to 15.2 percent by 1990 and 19.1 percent by 2000." Of course, the annual intake of the United States is nowhere near two million people, but even if it were, it would be absurd simply to divide the existing jobs by the expanded labor force and assume that more people will be out of work. In fact, the parts of the country with the highest immigration rates typically have the lowest unemployment rates — exactly the opposite of what the lump-of-labor reasoning suggests.

Hurting Americans

Maybe immigration is good for the immigrants, but what is the point if they're just taking opportunities away from Americans?

This is the more sophisticated and substantial version of the lump-of-labor fear. Increasing the competition, by bringing in all the low-wage Mexicans and the overambitious Asians, may hurt the Americans who are already there — shrimp fishermen on the Gulf Coast, for instance, who suddenly find the waters teeming with Vietnamese. Richard Lamm, a former governor of Colorado, said in 1982 that since the American economic "pie" was not getting larger, we couldn't afford to cut slices for any more mouths. "The unchanging pie dramatically alters an issue like immigration, for now additional people will have to take from that pie rather than contribute to it like those who helped turn a newly found continent into an economic paradise. Who needs additional people when we cannot employ our own citizens?"

But the evidence goes the other way. The record is that immigrants have long been part of *expanding* opportunity; they've helped the pie get bigger for everyone. This was true of the immigrants at the turn of the century, despite widespread Progressive fear that they would hold down the native American working class, and by all indications it's true today. For instance, Southern California has been more heavily affected by immigration than any other part of the country, yet a major economic study, released in 1985 by the Urban Institute, found no indications that the immigrants had hurt anyone already on the scene. "Average income per capita in Los Angeles County . . . grew somewhat more rapidly than in the rest of California and the nation, despite the arrival of 325,000 Hispanics whose current average income is only half that of the average income for the area," said the study. "That the immigrant influx was not accompanied by job losses for other workers as a group is consistent with the experience of prior immigrant waves." Many other studies have come to the same conclusion.

Hurting Blacks

There is an important subclause of the hurting-Americans argument: immigration is another millstone around the necks of unemployed blacks. Yet despite the friction in many large cities between Korean or Vietnamese shopkeepers and their black customers in the ghetto, it's hard to find any proof that the Asians or other immigrants have reduced opportunities for unskilled blacks. "Increased immigration has [had] . . . little if any impact on young black and Hispanic Americans," said Richard Freeman, the coordinator of a National Bureau of Economic Research study. The Urban Institute compared black unemployment rates and the concentration of Hispanics — largely immigrants — in 230 cities in the United States. It found "no statistical relationship between the size of the Hispanic population and black unemployment . . . Even the job prospects for black teenagers do not appear to be adversely affected by the influx of immigrants." Another scholar, who has specialized in studies of Korean immigrants, found no relation between the rate of self-employment among Koreans and of unemployment among blacks. That is, the Koreans were not "soaking up opportunities that blacks would otherwise have."

Illegal immigration probably is bad for working-class blacks and whites, but the crucial variable is the illegality, not the extra people. If one factory doesn't have to obey air-pollution laws, it's hard for law-abiding factories to compete. Similarly, if companies can hire some people without paying the minimum wage or providing health insurance or letting them organize a union, it's harder for other workers to enjoy the rights that the law theoretically guarantees. The answer to this problem, though, is to reduce illegal immigration — through employer-sanctions programs like those begun in the mid 1980s, and to make it easier for people to immigrate legally, even without the family connections that are indispensable under current law.

America's long-term strategic secret is that it can get the most out of people by putting them in surprising situations. Competition from other Americans is the source of most of this ultimately healthful disruption, but a continual supply of new competition is invigorating too.

Fear of the Other

The main resistance to immigration at the moment is not economic but cultural. The strain on the social fabric may seem too great. For each group of Nguyens starting new businesses and working round the clock, there may well be a group of Latin Americans refusing to learn English, or Haitians practicing voodoo, or Iranians preaching Shi'ite fundamentalism — or, more generally, *outsiders* diluting the sense of Americanness.

Language is the easiest aspect of this problem to discuss. About half of today's immigrants, legal and illegal, are thought to be Spanish-speaking. (They are "thought" rather than "known" to be because estimates of illegal immigration are so imprecise.) That is a higher proportion of people in this country from one non-English-language group than ever before. The previous high was Germans, who made up about a third of all immigrants in the mid nineteenth century. In addition, there are now Spanish-language TV stations and bilingual schools, which some see as slowing an immigrant's progression to English; and many of the immigrants are really "sojourners," who travel back and forth to Mexico, with little incentive to learn English.

These omens seem threatening, but in fact there is no evidence that Spanish-speaking immigrants are behaving differently from the way Italian, Polish, or German immigrants behaved several generations earlier. In retrospect it may look as if their transition to English went quickly and easily, but many dragged their feet just as some Spanish speakers do today. According to most studies by linguists, first-generation immigrants typically were not very comfortable in English. The transition came with their American-born children, and much the same pattern seems to hold today. Los Angeles, Houston, and Miami are full of Spanish-language billboards and graffiti, but those are indications of the large number of immigrants who have arrived relatively recently. The people who speak only Spanish are nearly all foreign-born. Their American-born children may speak Spanish as well as English, but that's an advantage, not a problem.

At Miami Senior High School, I talked with a hulking Puerto Rican football player who said he hoped to join the navy after he graduated. I heard his story and then I asked him his name. He told me, and I wrote "Ramon." He came around behind me and looked at my pad. "No, no!" he shouted, making me fear for my safety. "You should have put R-A-Y-M-O-N-D."

The concern that lurks behind language is ethnic, racial, and emotional. America may be a multiracial country, but it has been mainly white and of European origin. Until the immigration laws were made "color blind" in 1965, European countries accounted for more than four fifths of all legal immigration to the United States. In the last twenty years the proportion has switched; Latin America and Asia now account for more than 80 percent of the legal total, split equally between the two areas. That may be economically efficient, because of people like the Nguyens, but is it wise to dilute the country's major cultural identity so rapidly?

Early in 1988, I got a letter expressing these fears from an American friend who had lived for many years in Japan and felt unsettled by what he saw when he went "home." I quote from it because even though I think my friend is wrong, I know that he's not the only one to feel as he does.

> None of the great outpourings of human civilization was, so far as I know, prompted by immigration. In fact, Attic Greece, Imperial Rome, Han China, Renaissance Italy, Bourbon France, Imperial England all were products of a racially and culturally homogeneous people . . . With the most depressing regularity, it seems that great cultures have been the products of single peoples . . . I

think that part of the horror of New York City is due to its ethnic heterogeneity. It is very, very hard to develop a sense of kinship or commonality with people who look, act, and sound so different from oneself. Where there is no sense of commonality, there's not even the semblance of order, and where there is greatness there is always a strong sense of commonality . . .

Just ask the Tamils, the Karens, the Ibos, the Kurds, the Armenians, the Palestinians, the Assamese, the Khmers Rouges, the Afghans, the Acholi and the Baganda, the Hutu and the Tutsi, the Kosovo Albanians and the Sikhs what they think with. They think with their blood and with little else. That's why they are so ready to spill it.

As a description of what the rest of the world does, "thinking with blood" may be correct. Certainly there is little evidence in Asia or Africa that people can rise above racial, ethnic, or tribal divisions. But, to return to the point on which this book began, America *is* abnormal. It faced the challenge of immigration in much more intense form a century ago; and instead of being weakened, it was enriched. By all accounts, the immigrants from Eastern and Southern Europe seemed more threatening and alien to the Americans of the late nineteenth century than Mexicans, Vietnamese, and Ethiopians do to the white and black Americans of today. No president of a major university would say today what Francis Walker, the president of MIT, said at the turn of the century: the Italians, Greeks, Poles, and Russian immigrants were "beaten men from beaten races, representing the worst failures in the struggle for existence." No one has contended, as the scientific experts of the day did then, that the new arrivals were inherently less intelligent than the native-born. Many of those now considered to be part of "mainstream" white American culture are descended from people seen as totally alien when they poured in. Was there less "real" difference between those Greek, Italian, and Russian immigrants and the native stock at the start of the century than there is between today's Americans and the Hmong? Maybe, but it doesn't matter: racial difference is in the eye of the beholder. (To outsiders, the Ashanti and Ewe tribes of Ghana look very similar. To each other, they are hostile foreigners, for all practical purposes different "races.")

That is, America has been through worse racial disruption than any risk posed by today's immigration, and it emerged as the strongest, most dynamic, and most open society in the world. The disruption was worse then because the newcomers seemed more foreign and because the flow was proportionately much greater than it is today. (At the turn of the century, the annual influx of immigrants was as high as 1 percent of the existing population. During the 1980s, the peak has been less than a third of 1 percent, and the average has been about a fifth of 1 percent.) We've already proven that we are the great exception and can withstand strains that other societies could not tolerate. The racial problem that afflicts America has nothing to do with immigrants, whatever their color or origin. Indeed, it arises from the one great exception to voluntary immigration in the peopling of America.

Completely open immigration would be too great a strain even for American society. At the beginning of the twentieth century, when the relative flow was three to five times greater than it is now, the backlash was widespread and severe. It led to the "national origins" laws, which essentially restricted immigration to people from Western Europe. These laws, together with the Depression and World War II, dramatically slowed the influx for the next thirty years. The backlash that would result from extreme, rapid change is the main argument for limiting immigration at all. Like totally open capitalism, without safety standards or child-labor laws, totally uncontrolled immigration is too raw for modern societies to accept. But short of open immigration, the United States should keep taking at least as many people as it does now — somewhere between 600,000 and 800,000 per year, depending on surges of refugees and other factors — and should feel grateful for the new blood, rather than resentful of it.

One sort of immigration should be increased. The fundamental purpose of opening the country to immigrants, of course, is to offer a new chance to people from around the world and to let America take advantage of the ensuing human efforts. But the law is skewed in a way that distorts this purpose. Of the immigrants the United States admits legally each year, virtually all fall into one of two categories: refugees from Indochina and from

Soviet-bloc countries, and relatives of people already in the United States. The refugee policy is arbitrary in its effect: people who escape by boat from Vietnam have a good chance of eventually being admitted to the United States as refugees, but those who escape from Burma, where life is just as chaotic, miserable, and oppressive, have almost no chance. The arbitrary effect of the family-preference policy is more broadly damaging. Parents, minor children, and spouses of American citizens are admitted without limit, which makes humanitarian sense. But the law also contains such heavy preference for more distant relatives that there is very little room for anyone else. Long lines snake outside the U.S. embassies in Manila, Mexico City, and Seoul. The cousins and in-laws of earlier immigrants complain that they may have to wait five or ten years for their turn. But people who are *not* cousins or in-laws have to wait forever. Through the late 1980s, only about 10 percent of American visas have gone to "independent" immigrants, the often-skilled and always-ambitious people who epitomize the desire to make a new start. A change in the law could push the "independent" proportion as high as a fourth. It should go higher still, to at least half of the legal visas.

MORE LIKE *US*

Japan is strong because of its groups; America, because of its individuals. Men and women who believed they could change their life found America different from any other society, and continue to make it unique.

But no society, not even this one, can survive on naked self-interest. Thomas Hobbes knew about this when he described the War of Every Man against Every Man. We know it now, as we see the effects of the drug economy, of interest-group politics (an attempt to extort the greatest possible benefits from everyone else in the country, via the government), of inside wheeling-dealing, of the inequalities that have left New York's streets as beggar-ridden as Manila's.

Self-interest is the basic energy that has made America go, but it has been tempered and harnessed by other powerful forces. One was the belief in fair play — the idea that there were rules of competition, that they'd be enforced, that everyone was playing on more or less the same field. The other was the face-to-face democratic contact that kept Americans from putting on airs or separating into distinct classes. The calamitous exception in each case, of course, is the long separation of blacks from whites. The balance of these forces — every man for himself, but only according to certain rules — was the basis of America's paradoxical achievement. Our individualism *is* our source of community. We're all doing our best for ourselves, but as players in the same game.

The individual side of this balance has received nearly all the political and cultural attention in the last ten years. The pendulum is ready to swing the other way. Paul Simon of Illinois did not get far in the 1988 presidential campaign, but on withdrawing from the race he summed up the side of our politics that has been neglected. "Americans instinctively know that we are one nation, one family, and when anyone in that family hurts, all of us hurt," Simon said. "There really is a yearning across this land for leadership that appeals to the noble in us rather than to the greed in us."

The institutions that kept Americans in contact with one another — the public schools, the "general" publications, the middle-class army — may be gone beyond recall, another set of victims of America's constant change. But new institutions can be created if we revive the idea that America is one coherent society, with bonds that are stronger than its internal differences. We understood this instinctively during World War II, but not often enough since then. Jimmy Carter used William James's phrase, the "moral equivalent of war," during the energy crisis of the late 1970s, and he was widely misunderstood. Most people thought he was talking about some kind of holy war against the oil producers. What he really meant was that America had to find a way, in peacetime, to inspire some of the moral nobility that people often show in time of war. This was the paradox that William James had discussed in his famous essay seventy years earlier: the worst human activity, warfare, often brings out some of the finest individual behavior. People sacrifice for their friends and families; they always do their best. Societies would flourish, James said, when they found a way to separate the noble behavior from the ignoble cause — that is, to create a moral equivalent of war.

The first sign that America is moving in this direction will be a reawakened sense of *us*. Between 1941 and 1945, Americans thought of each other as us, out of hatred for the Germans and Japanese. We don't need to hate anyone anymore. But we will do better, as individuals, if we realize that we don't simply stand or fall on our own.

I know what that feels like. From outside the country, I see clearly that our society is judged on all its members, not just the rich or successful ones. The Japanese concede that America commands the very heights of luxury and technology and advanced training. But their society as a whole, they believe, works better than ours.

As I walk down a street in Tokyo, I know I'm being judged not just as an individual but as an American. To people who will never know me personally, my honor rises and falls with the honor, creativity, and decency of 250 million people at home. We're all judged this way from outside, whether we realize it or not. It may not be logical or high-minded to feel this way, but it is natural, perhaps inevitable. And it can be useful, because it reminds us that we share certain values and share a fate.

NOTES

Introduction

page

1   The world is full of potential Americans: Residents of other coun-
     tries in the Americas often resent the use of "America" rather
     than "the United States." I am using it deliberately here because
     I am talking about the culture that is America more than of the
     political or geographical unit that is the United States.

2   racism runs through nearly all the world: For instance, Seymour
     Martin Lipset has written, "Stratification correlates with racial
     ancestry in almost all of the [Latin American] nations. That is, the
     privileged classes are largely of white background, and/or are
     lighter skin-colored than the less affluent strata . . . The Carib-
     bean nations, all of which are former European colonies, reveal an
     even greater emphasis on color and race than elsewhere. Whites
     and/or mulattoes occupy the dominant position, even in predomi-
     nantly black societies such as Haiti and Jamaica." In W. Scott
     Thompson, ed., *The Third World: Premises of U.S. Policy* (San
     Francisco: Institute for Contemporary Studies, 1980), pp. 129–
     130.

6   "You've been very slow in recognizing your decline": Quoted by
     Susan Chira, of the *New York Times,* in the *International Herald
     Tribune,* July 1, 1988.

     Nakasone's remarks: Technically, Nakasone was right when he
     said that American blacks, Hispanics, and other minorities score
     lower, on average, on IQ tests than American whites do, and that
     Japanese score higher than Americans as a whole. By most esti-
     mates the average Japanese IQ score is about 10 points higher than
     the American average. In the United States, Scholastic Aptitude

Test (SAT) scores are very closely correlated with IQ scores, since the tests are essentially the same. On the SAT tests the average for blacks and Hispanics is consistently below the average for American whites and Asian Americans.

10   "Well, they're a lot of little swots": Ronald Dore, *Taking Japan Seriously: A Confucian Perspective on Leading Economic Issues* (Stanford: Stanford University Press, 1987), p. 3.

11   "It takes a long time": Rosovsky made these remarks at a conference on industrial competitiveness, held at Harvard in April 1980.

12   Jared Taylor: Jared Taylor, *Shadows of the Rising Sun: A Critical View of the "Japanese Miracle"* (Tokyo: Charles E. Tuttle Co., 1983), p. 307. Emphasis added.

Chapter 1

page

14   "Deep springs in the human mind": W. Arthur Lewis, *Theory of Economic Growth* (London: Allen & Unwin, 1955), p. 14. Shlomo Maital discusses this quote and Lewis's views in his own book about psychological impacts on economic behavior, *Minds, Markets, and Money* (New York: Basic Books, 1982).

17   Daniel Patrick Moynihan: Mickey Kaus cited this in his article "The Workfare State," *The New Republic*, July 7, 1986.

      "Pay attention to the effects": David McClelland, *The Achieving Society* (New York: Free Press, 1961), paperback edition, p. 393. This is one of several quotes also summarized in Lawrence Harrison's *Underdevelopment Is a State of Mind: The Latin American Case* (Cambridge, Mass.: Harvard Center for International Affairs, 1985).

20   Asians' secret weapon: The Asian attitudes — part Confucian, part Taoist, part Buddhist — that show up in Japan, Korea, China, and elsewhere contain ingredients that both promote and retard capitalist growth. The positive elements are the emphasis on study, the ethic of "legitimate" rule under which superiors are supposed to prove worthy of their station, and the ingrained spirit of obedience and hierarchy. But traditional Confucianism had nothing but contempt for the businessman, venerating the scholar and mandarin or bureaucrat instead.

      The Malays had been weakened: "The people who left the shores of China to seek their fortune abroad were hardened and resourceful. Like emigrants everywhere they were the people who were not content with their lot and were moved by a desire for a better life, and obviously by the determination to work for this . . . Hunger and starvation, a common feature in countries like

China, were unknown in Malaya. Under these conditions everyone survived . . . The Malays, whose own hereditary and environmental influence had been so debilitating, could do nothing but retreat before the onslaught of the Chinese immigrants. Whatever the Malays could do, the Chinese could do better." Mahatir bin Mohamad, *The Malay Dilemma* (Kuala Lumpur: Federal Publications, 1970), pp. 21, 25, 85.

21 *Bridge Over the River Kwai:* The moral tension of the book turns on the contrast between the Japanese soldiers, who have dealt the English a temporary setback, and the British soldiers, who are still the better men. Out of pride in a job well done, the British captives help the Japanese build the finest possible railroad bridge across the Kwai. The Japanese finally grow dependent on their captives because of the innate superiority of British skills. Pierre Boule, *The Bridge Over the River Kwai*, trans. by Xan Fielding (New York: Bantam Books, 1957).

"My impression as to your cheap labor": Cited by Robert Klitgaard in private communication. He referred to T. N. Srinavasan, "Comment," in *Pioneers in Economic Development,* Gerald M. Meier and Dudley Seers, eds. (New York: published for the World Bank by Oxford University Press, 1984), p. 53.

22 "British Society was open": David Landes, *The Unbound Prometheus* (Cambridge: Cambridge University Press, 1969), as quoted in Mancur Olson, *The Rise and Decline of Nations: Economic Growth, Stagflation, and Social Rigidities* (New Haven: Yale University Press, 1982), pp. 82–83.

24 Gunnar Myrdal: Gunnar Myrdal, *Asian Drama: An Inquiry Into the Poverty of Nations,* one-vol. edition, abridged by Seth F. King, for the Twentieth Century Fund (New York: Pantheon, 1971), p. 39.

25 "The writer knows of no instance": Ibid., pp. 49–50.

Harrison's list of traits: Harrison, *Underdevelopment Is a State of Mind*, p. 9.

26 "The absence of trust": Samuel Huntington, *Political Order in Changing Societies* (New Haven: Yale University Press, 1968). Harrison discusses this in his book, p. 7.

Edward Banfield: Harrison, *Underdevelopment Is a State of Mind,* p. 30.

Chapter 2

page

28 different brains or intestines: The great crackpot best seller of the late 1970s was *The Japanese Brain,* by a Dr. Tadanobu Tsunoda,

which contended that the Japanese have brains that are differently organized from the rest of humanity's. According to Dr. Tsunoda, all non-Japanese hear vowels in the right hemisphere of their brains, but the Japanese hear them in the left. Since the Japanese also handle consonants in the left hemisphere, they are able to attain a higher unity and coherence than other races, thereby explaining their calm, harmonious civilization.

30   Ernie Pyle: John W. Dower, *War Without Mercy: Race and Power in the Pacific War* (New York: Pantheon, 1986), p. 78.

"The Japanese are just like other people": Edward Seidensticker, *This Country: Japan* (Tokyo: Kodansha International, 1984), paperback edition, p. 332.

31   "Har-rooo!": The American linguist Roy Andrew Miller attacked the belief, widespread among even educated people in Japan, that the Japanese language is "more unique" than other languages and inseparable from Japanese-ness: "Japanese race consists in using the Japanese language. But how does one become a member of the Japanese race? By being born into it, of course, just as one becomes a member of any other race . . . But what if someone not a Japanese by right of race . . . does manage to acquire some proficiency in the Japanese language? Well, in that case the system literally makes no intellectual provision at all for his or her very own existence." Roy Andrew Miller, *Japan's Modern Myth: The Language and Beyond* (Tokyo: Weatherhill, 1982), pp. 147–148.

"In my own case": George Fields, "Racism Is Accepted Practice in Japan," *Wall Street Journal,* November 10, 1986.

no longer quite Japanese: In a book about "returnees," Merry White quoted a Tokugawa-era education code that sums up the view of foreign influence: "Those who take delight in foreign ways end up losing their native Japanese spirit and become weakly cowards, a shocking eventuality against which you must ever be on your guard." Merry White, *The Japanese Overseas: Can They Ever Go Home Again* (New York: Free Press, 1988), p. 50.

32   Japanese ethic of racial unity: Many recent books have explored the evolution of Japan's "myth" of monoracialism. Two recent examples are John W. Dower, *War Without Mercy,* which contrasts the wartime anti-Japanese propaganda in the United States with Japan's own effort to build up racial consciousness, and Ross Mouer and Yoshio Sugimoto, *Images of Japanese Society* (London: KPI Limited, 1986) a dense academic analysis of *nihonjinron,* the Japanese fascination with Japanese "uniqueness."

33   one hundred million with one heart: Dower, *War Without Mercy,* p. 215. Another phrase, introduced the day after the attack on Pearl Harbor, was *susume ichi-oku hi no tama da* — one hundred million advancing like a ball of flame.

34 *madogiwazoko:* This intriguing word literally means "the window-side tribe." It refers to white-collar workers in big companies who are never going to be promoted but who, in the Japanese scheme of things, can't be fired and don't resign. In the typical Japanese office, the best seats are *away* from the window, in the center of the action. The etymology of *madogiwazoko* is obvious to anyone who has spent time in Tokyo. The commuter trains and elevated highways run right next to the upper floors of big office buildings. As you look out from the train, you can see the forlorn "window people," neatly dressed, ready for action, but with nothing to do but read their newspapers or look out into space.

38 to keep farmers from going out of business: As a practical matter, fewer than 10 percent of Japan's rice growers are true farmers. The rest tend the crop on weekends, when they're away from their jobs at factories or offices.

39 "In the most significant decisions": Thomas K. McCraw and Patricia A. O'Brien, "Production and Distribution: Competition Policy and Industrial Structure," in *America versus Japan,* Thomas K. McCraw, ed. (Boston: Harvard Business School Press, 1986), p. 106.

Small retail stores: These figures came from a Japanese chain store executive, Isao Nakauchi, who said, in July 1988, that it was time to break up the small-store network that made Japanese retail costs the highest in the world. "We are undergoing an industrial restructuring, and we cannot simply continue what we had," he said. Reported by Fred Hiatt in the *Washington Post,* July 27, 1988.

40 "A typical American reaction": "Japan Inc.: Consumers Pay for Protection," *MicroNews/Views,* (MicroClear Inc., New York), September 5, 1986, p. 3.

41 "People think I should only": *New York Times,* May 1, 1987.

42 six additional forty-hour weeks: According to the Japanese Ministry of Labor, in 1986 the average Japanese worker in manufacturing industries worked 2512 hours per year, versus 1898 in the United States. Exactly how "hard," as opposed to how long, the typical Japanese employee works is one of those questions which can keep a discussion in Japan going for hours. In most blue-collar jobs, in factories or on construction crews, Japanese workers move with a bustle and diligence unmatched elsewhere except in Korea. White-collar workers who hope to succeed have to put in long hours at the office. But it is not so clear that the longer hours on the job mean that the white-collar employees are actually doing more work. *Being* at work, and being seen to be there, seems to matter more in a Japanese career than what gets done each day. From what I can tell, the average Japanese blue-collar worker does

work harder than his American counterpart. The average salary-man does about the same amount of real work in both countries, but in Japan he lets it take up more of his time.

cordless telephones: The *Wall Street Journal* of March 14, 1988, carried this report about the cordless telephones, which were originally made by Matsushita Electric Trading Company: "Mass merchandisers were re-importing them from the U.S. and selling them for an eighth of the price of similar models that were made for Japan. At first, Matsushita professed not to care. Surely the Japanese would buy the trusted Japanese-market model. Wrong. The re-imports outsold the domestic model by 10 to 1. Suddenly Matsushita wanted them back. To get them away from one of the discounters, Bic Camera, it coughed up Bic's full price."

43 whose interests are at odds with the consumers': "How do the farmers and the construction companies and the shopkeepers maintain all this power?" a Western diplomat in Tokyo once asked me rhetorically. "It's not really because the people are so docile, but because the system is so corrupt. The prime minister is chosen by a handful of people, and the process is controlled by money. Not by big-business money . . . but from the brokers who rely on political protection inside. The farmers and the farmers' cooperatives, who feed their subsidies back in Liberal Democratic Party contributions. The retail-store lobby. The construction industry, which freezes out foreign competitors and leaves people driving on third-rate roads. All this comes out of the hide of the poor salaryman."

44 "The Japanese never really caught up": Ronald Dore, quoted in *The Economist*, May 22, 1987.

45 statement of purpose: Merry White, *The Japanese Educational Challenge: A Commitment to Children* (New York: Free Press, 1987), p. 17.

Robert Whiting's comic masterpiece: *The Chrysanthemum and the Bat: Baseball Samurai Style* (New York: Dodd, Mead, 1977). The title is of course a take-off on the famous anthropologist Ruth Benedict's even more famous study of Japan, *The Chrysanthemum and the Sword: Patterns of Japanese Culture* (Boston: Houghton Mifflin, 1946).

46 "The Japanese exporter": "Japan Victorious," Murray Sayle, *The New York Review of Books*, March 28, 1985.

Chapter 3

page
49 one American family out of thirty: *The Economist*, February 7, 1987, p. 40.

51   "Historically, as new lands": David M. Potter, *People of Plenty* (Chicago: University of Chicago Press, 1954), pp. 96–97.

52   "The first requirement": James Oliver Robertson, *American Myth, American Reality* (New York: Hill & Wang, 1980), p. 148.
     three times as many people worked on farms: See, for example, *Historical Statistics of the United States,* vol. 1, p. 138.

53   three times as many people have been at work: Max Geldens, *Future Employment in the Industrialized Democracies* (New York: McKinsey & Co., 1984).

54   Timber crisis: Sherry Olson's *The Depletion Myth* (Cambridge, Mass.: Harvard University Press, 1971) tells the story of the wood crisis. Another account is in Charles Maurice and Charles V. Smithson, *The Doomsday Myth: 10,000 Years of Economic Crises* (Stanford: Hoover Institute Press, 1984).

55   Electric can openers: This was Charles Killingsworth of Michigan State University, as quoted in Stanley Lebergott, *Men Without Work* (New York: Prentice-Hall, 1964), pp. 55–56.
     every job in America would disappear: Quoted in Lebergott, *Men Without Work,* p. 24. For the productivity figures, and for a general history of the automation crisis, see Charles Silberman, *The Myths of Automation* (New York: Harper & Row, 1966).
     "In its very nature": Jane Jacobs, *Cities and the Wealth of Nations: Principles of Economic Life* (New York: Random House, 1984), pp. 221, 223.

56   until the opponent makes his first move: One of the finest examples of such reasoning in the modern American military is the work of John Boyd, a retired air force colonel. Boyd, who flew fighter planes in the Korean War, soon became the air force's premier theoretician of aerial combat. On the basis of combat-kill results in Korea, Boyd demonstrated that *what* a fighter airplane could do — climb, roll, dive—was less important in combat than how quickly it could *change* from doing one thing to doing something else. A slower and theoretically less capable plane could often beat a "better" plane, if the plane's design or the pilot's skill allowed it to switch quickly from one maneuver to another and catch its enemy by surprise. Boyd demonstrated that a similar principle applied to combat on the large scale: it didn't really matter whether an army attacked by land, by sea, on the flanks, or from the air. What mattered was whether it could change its behavior more quickly than its adversary. His argument is similar to Jane Jacobs's; each concerns competition and concludes that the advantage lies with the more adaptable side.
     "An increasingly productive economy" and "Empty plants": Both of these quotations are from writings by Donald Hicks. The first is from a government report that was released during the final weeks of the Carter administration: *Urban America in the*

Eighties: Perspectives and Prospects, Report of the Panel on Policies and Prospects for Metropolitan and Nonmetropolitan America, President's Commission for a National Agenda for the Eighties, 1980, p. 4. The second is from a book, *Advanced Industrial Development,* A Lincoln Institute of Land Policy Book (Boston: Oelgeschlager, Gunn & Hain, 1986).

57 "Perhaps the most serious impact": Richard Wilcock and W. H. Franke, *Unwanted Workers: Permanent Layoffs and Long-Term Unemployment* (Glencoe, Ill.: Free Press, 1963), pp. 166, 185. The book about factory shutdowns in which it was quoted was Barry Bluestone and Bennett Harrison, *The Deindustrialization of America: Plant Closings, Community Abandonment, and the Dismantling of Basic Industry* (New York: Basic Books, 1982), pp. 65–66.

58 Poughkeepsie examples: Clyde Griffen, "Workers Divided: The Effect of Craft and Ethnic Differences in Poughkeepsie, New York, 1850–1880," in Stephan Thernstrom and Richard Sennett, eds., *Nineteenth-Century Cities* (New Haven: Yale University Press, 1969).

59 Fast-growing Midwestern cities: Glenn E. McLaughlin, *Growth of American Manufacturing Areas: A Comparative Analysis with Special Emphasis on Trends in the Pittsburgh District* (Pittsburgh: Pennsylvania Bureau of Business Research, University of Pittsburgh, 1938), pp. 11–12.

Akron's population: *Population Redistribution in the U.S.: Issues for the 1980s,* Larry H. Long (Washington, D.C.: Population Reference Bureau, Population Trends and Public Policy, March 1983), p. 9. Also, see McLaughlin, *Growth of American Manufacturing Areas,* p. 66.

Transient Bureau: The Transient Bureau started in 1934 and was never very popular. Local officials thought it would bring drifters into town. The program offered relief payments and job counseling to people who, as newcomers, weren't eligible for local relief benefits. The program was dismantled in 1937, but by that time John Webb, a sociologist working for the WPA, had analyzed its effects. In general, he judged it a success. It didn't create a permanent welfare class but seemed to move people into new jobs — when they existed. Webb also found that the migrants were better educated and more highly skilled than the unemployed people who had not moved. The program, and Webb's analysis, were described by Richard Phelps in "Facilitating the Interstate Migration of Unemployed Workers," *The Public Historian,* Spring 1982, pp. 57–69.

"a recent study": Philip E. Ryan, "Relief for Transients," *Survey 76,* September 1940, pp. 252–253, discussed in Phelps, p. 67.

"An overwhelming view": George C. Myers, "Migration and

60

61

the Labor Force," *Monthly Labor Review,* September 1973, pp. 15–16.

"Most new housing": William L. O'Neill, *American High: The Years of Confidence, 1945–1960* (New York: Free Press, 1986), p. 19.

"rolling stone" and "tree hugger": The rolling stone illustrations are from Takao Suzuki, *Words in Context: A Japanese Perspective on Language and Culture* (Tokyo: Kodansha International, 1978), pp. 28–29. The dictionary he refers to is *The Oxford Concise Dictionary.* The implications of "tree hugger" were explained by Anne Soukhanov in the April 1988 issue of *The Atlantic.*

"the 'simple' manner": Fanny Trollope, *Domestic Manners of the Americans* (New York: Oxford University Press, 1982), paperback edition, pp. 37–39.

63

64

"I launched into": Gregory Curtis, "Behind the Lines," *Texas Monthly,* October 1984, pp. 5–6.

"Americans want": Nelson Aldrich, Jr., *Old Money: The Making of America's Upper Class* (New York: Knopf, 1988), p. 38.

"Fine boys": Cited in Robertson, *American Myth,* p. 220. He referred to John Baskin, *New Burlington: The Life and Death of an American Village* (New York: Norton, 1976), p. 113.

65

"When they were built": McClelland, *The Achieving Society,* p. 222.

66

"What a modern society": Ibid., p. 194.

Chapter 4

page

76–
77

Didion article: Joan Didion, "Some Dreamers of the Golden Dream," in *Slouching Towards Bethlehem* (New York: Farrar, Straus, & Giroux, 1968), pp. 3–4.

83

"That's why we have so many nuts out here": *Los Angeles Times,* November 7, 1969.

84

"Among democratic peoples": Alexis de Tocqueville, *Democracy in America* (New York: Anchor Books, 1969), pp. 507, 376. Michael Kammen quotes these passages in his discussion of the absence of tradition in *A Season of Youth: The American Revolution and the Historical Imagination* (New York: Knopf, 1978), p. 4.

Chapter 5

97   The dénouement of the case: The government version of events
was as follows:

   In the spring of 1972, when the legislature was cracking down
on the mill's tax breaks, a mill supervisor named Tommy Thomas
spoke with the would-be killer, Lawrence Brown. Thomas offered
Brown $1500 to kill Westberry. Brown replied that he was worried:
he didn't want to end up on the chain gang. He said he would like
more reassurance — from the Big Man himself.

   At this stage, according to the government, Brown was stringing
the mill officials along, planning to run away with the money. But
before the deal went any further he told Westberry's friend about
the plot. Then the FBI and the Georgia Bureau of Investigation
equipped him with the body bug, and they tapped the officials'
phones.

   On the strength of the recorded evidence, a federal grand jury
was convened to take testimony about the murder plot in May
1972. At this point Brown pulled his second switch. When his turn
came to testify, he said that it had all been a mistake. There had
never been a plot to kill Westberry — the only plotting had been
done by Westberry and his friends, who had offered him $10,000
to try to frame the three officials. After his testimony was over,
Brown returned to his original story. Actually, there *had* been a
plot, he said, and the only reason he had denied it before the grand
jury was that the same men who hired him to do the killing threatened to kill him if he talked.

   Federal and state investigators wrestled with the case through
the summer of 1972 but took no decisive action. Westberry filed a
civil suit for damages arising from the conspiracy. The federal
district court judge in Savannah threw out the case, contending
that federal courts did not have jurisdiction. Westberry's young
lawyer, Fletcher Farrington, appealed. In January 1975, the Fifth
Circuit Court of Appeals reversed that decision and ordered the
suit to proceed. Within a week, the Big Man and the lawyer resigned, and the defendants settled Westberry's suit for an amount
all parties agreed not to disclose.

   In October 1975 a federal grand jury indicted the three for the
conspiracy. The trial was held in Savannah early in 1976. After a
few hours' deliberation, the jury found them guilty on all counts.
They appealed, and in October 1977 the Fifth Circuit Court of
Appeals reversed the conviction. The main problem, it held, was
the shakiness of Lawrence Brown's testimony.

98   Westberry was fully cleared of the acid-pouring charge: The *Con-*

stitution story, by Jeff Nesmith, appeared on September 19, 1972. One week later Westberry got a letter from the company saying it had found "new evidence" proving that he was the culprit. The new evidence consisted of letters from three people who, on the day after the *Constitution* story, supposedly remembered that Westberry had thrown the acid.

With his union's support, Westberry took his dismissal to arbitration. When the federal arbitrator got a look at the case, he came down resoundingly on Westberry's side, ordering the company to give him his job, back pay, and full seniority rights.

99 Turner frontier thesis: Turner later wrote: "Since the days when the fleet of Columbus sailed into the water of the New World, America has been another name for opportunity. Now, four centuries from the discovery of America, at the end of a hundred years under the Constitution, the frontier has gone, and with its going has closed the first period in American history." Quoted in Potter, *People of Plenty,* p. 156.

109 "The data . . . show": Peter M. Blau and Otis Dudley Duncan, *The American Occupational Structure* (New York: Wiley, 1967), p. 251.

Self-employment among Korean immigrants: Ivan Light, chapter on Korean immigrants in Nathan Glazer, ed., *Clamor at the Gates: The New American Immigration* (San Francisco: Institute for Contemporary Studies, 1985), pp. 168–170.

Children of immigrants earn more: Barry R. Chiswick, "An Analysis of the Economic Progress and Impact of Immigrants," report prepared for the Employment and Training Administration, U.S. Department of Labor, under Research and Development Grant No. 21–06–78–20, pp. 5–9.

This is a slightly skewed comparison. Since most Latin American immigrants have less schooling than most native-born Americans, they are being matched against the Americans with the worst chance to move ahead. In addition, Chiswick's study was based on immigrants who had entered the country before 1970, when the increased flow of Latin American and Asian immigrants was only beginning. Still, in light of the linguistic and cultural handicaps most immigrants face, it is remarkable that they catch up at all. Chiswick's study showed that the "earnings crossover" occurs after fifteen years for Mexican immigrants and after eleven for black immigrants.

"As self-selected persons": *U.S. Immigration Policy and the National Interest,* final report of the Select Commission on Immigration and Refugee Policy, Committees on the Judiciary, U.S. House of Representatives and U.S. Senate, 97th Congress, 1st Session, August 1981, p. 100.

110 "Migration . . . is the oldest action against poverty": John Ken-

neth Galbraith, *The Nature of Mass Poverty* (Cambridge, Mass.: Harvard University Press, 1979), p. 136.

Chapter 6

page

113 Republic Steel martyrs: One excellent academic study of South Chicago is William Kornblum, *Blue Collar Community* (Chicago: University of Chicago Press, 1974). Charles Spencer's *Blue Collar* (Chicago: Vanguard Books, 1977) is an anecdotal collection about South Chicago, by a man who spent twenty-five years in the steel mills.

114 US Steel shut down the South Works: Since the late 1970s, steel companies had been either warning or threatening, depending on your perspective, that they would be closing plants unless they got certain concessions. In the case of the South Works, US Steel asked the state government for relief from pollution laws and sales taxes, and the union for more flexible work rules. Only if those conditions were met, the company said, could it bring new hope to the South Works by investing $225 million in a new rail mill.

The union and the state of Illinois complied with the original requests. Then the company asked the city government for additional tax breaks. The city, too, agreed. Then the company said that further changes in union work rules would be necessary for the renovated mill to succeed. At this point the union leadership balked, and US Steel said that instead of rebuilding a rail mill it would close the South Works.

Each side viewed the dispute as an illustration of the other's bull-headedness. The unions were convinced that US Steel had been misleading them and never planned to build the mill at all. The company replied that it had been dealing in good faith but was hampered by a union whose selfishness and rigidity blinded it to the realities of world competition.

116 Lumpkin was "close to a saint": The article about Lumpkin was by R. C. Longworth, "System Founded on Lies, Selfishness," *Chicago Tribune,* February 17, 1988.

Very few of the workers ever came up with jobs: Researchers at the Center for Urban Economic Development, of the Chicago Circle campus of the University of Illinois, made a systematic study of what had happened to the laid-off Wisconsin Steel workers and found that most had not recovered. Of the dozen former steelworkers the researchers interviewed, only two had found new jobs. The results were in an unpublished research paper by David C. Ranney, research associate professor, Center for Urban Economic Development, University of Illinois at Chicago.

126 I wrote about this episode: "What Did You Do in the Class War, Daddy?" *The Washington Monthly,* October 1975.

130 Only 3 percent were left to be drafted: Michael Useem, "Conscription and Class," *Transaction/Society,* March–April 1981, p. 29.

Chapter 7

page

132 "An age never lent itself": Robert H. Wiebe, *The Search for Order* (New York: Hill & Wang, 1967), pp. 12, 45.

133 slap down the nouveaux riches: "To a number of gentlemen, each portion of this general ferment merely supplied new evidence that a decent world where their word mattered, where their standards were honored and their families secure, was either rapidly passing or had already disappeared," Wiebe wrote. "[They and others] considered the true and simple America in jeopardy from foes of extraordinary raw strength — huge, devouring monopolies, swarms of sexually potent immigrants, and the like." Ibid., pp. 51–52.

"The so-called professions meant little": The historian Burton Bledstein wrote, in *The Culture of Professionalism,* "Between 1865 and 1875 . . . the irrationality of life seemed to be deep indeed to many active middle-class Americans . . . The cosmic mutability of nature, the constant presence of bloodshed in America, the dread of imminent social-class warfare and labor rioting, agrarian unrest, the scandals of the Grant administration, the corruption of city bosses like Tweed, the ruthless practices of entrepreneurs like Vanderbilt and Gould: all seemed to mock authority and permanent standards in American civilization. Would any power prevail in America other than the mob or the man on horseback?" Burton Bledstein, *The Culture of Professionalism: The Middle Class and the Development of Higher Education in America* (New York: Norton, 1976), p. 322.

influential volume on economics: Mancur Olson, *The Rise and Decline of Nations.*

134 Prejudice against minority groups: Olson's theory of decline was more sweeping than the later arguments by Paul Kennedy and others, and it was less specifically tied to the burdens of managing a military empire. The real source of decline, Olson argued, was that as time went on societies naturally protected more and more of their groups from competition, which gradually slowed down the whole society. Olson said that stable societies, insulated from war or social upheaval, will naturally break up into "distributional coalitions," better known as special-interest groups, whose members try to protect themselves against adjustments to economic

change. Their common trait is the desire to shield their members from economic competition, even though that makes the whole society less efficient.

Practitioners . . . organized themselves: Details are in Magali Sarfati Larson, *The Rise of Professionalism: A Sociological Analysis* (Berkeley: University of California Press, 1977), and Harold L. Wilensky, "The Professionalization of Everyone," *American Journal of Sociology*, 70 (1964), pp. 137–158; also Institute for Electrical and Electronic Engineers (IEEE), "Engineers and Electrons," official history, published for its 1984 centennial, and Bledstein, *The Culture of Professionalism*, pp. 85–86.

"guilded age": Bledstein, *The Culture of Professionalism*, pp. 44–45.

135 Educational requirements for lawyers: See Larson, *The Rise of Professionalism*, pp. 172–173, 281, note 11; and Randall Collins, *The Credential Society: An Historical Sociology of Education and Stratification* (New York: Academic Press, 1979), pp. 145, 152–153.

136 Changes in medical education: What happened in American medicine has been chronicled more carefully than the growth of any other American profession, since the story turns on the fascinating interaction of real scientific advances and dramatically soaring incomes. Some of the most interesting accounts are in chapter 6 of Collins's *The Credential Society*, chapter 10 of Larson's *The Rise of Professionalism*, and all chapters of Paul Starr's *The Social Transformation of American Medicine* (New York: Basic Books, 1982).

Flexner report: Abraham Flexner, *Medical Education in the United States and Canada: A Report to the Carnegie Foundation for the Advancement of Teaching* (New York: The Carnegie Foundation for the Advancement of Teaching, 1910).

Prestige of doctors: See Larson, *The Rise of Professionalism*, pp. 159–160, and Collins, *The Credential Society*, p. 145.

Few foreign doctors licensed: Cited by S. David Young in *The Rule of Experts: Occupational Licensing in America* (Washington, D.C.: Cato Institute, 1987), p. 34. He refers in turn to Milton Friedman's *Capitalism and Freedom* (Chicago: University of Chicago Press, 1962), p. 154. Young's book is a valuable, short argument about the ill effects of licensing.

Business apprenticeships: See Collins, *The Credential Society*, p. 200.

Increasing degree requirements for managers: Ibid., pp. 6–7.

137 "Few Americans would guess": Young, *The Rule of Experts*, p. 4.

Excesses of spoils system: Paul Van Riper, *History of the*

United States Civil Service (Evanston: Row, Peterson & Company, 1958), p. 60.

Reagan could not legally fire: There were 2199 civilian federal employees in Washington at the beginning of Lincoln's term, of whom he fired about 1500. Van Riper, *History of the U.S. Civil Service*, p. 43, and *Historical Statistics of the United States*, p. 1103.

138 Eyeglass prices and contact lenses: Young, *The Rule of Experts*, pp. 66, 54.

139 Frank Lloyd Wright and Ludwig Mies van der Rohe: Ibid., p. 74.

140 When a bridge falls down: Randall Collins gave that example. He said that the layman's ability to assess professional skill made a big difference in the profession's status and earnings. "A strong profession requires a real technical skill that produces demonstrable results and can be taught," he wrote. "The skill must be difficult enough to require training and reliable enough to produce results. But it cannot be too reliable, for then outsiders can judge work by its results." Collins, *The Credential Society*, pp. 132–133.

141 "as a people": Quoted in Bledstein, *The Culture of Professionalism*, p. 323.

IQ testing: Two of the best popular accounts of how this science was born are Stephen Jay Gould, *The Mismeasure of Man* (New York: Norton, 1981), and Daniel Kevles, *In the Name of Eugenics* (New York: Knopf, 1985).

143 immigration specialists: Susan S. Forbes and Peter Lemos, "A History of American Language Policy," research paper prepared for the Select Commission on Immigration and Refugee Policy, 1981, p. 116.

human-classifying devices: Arguments over intelligence tests have spawned a voluminous literature. A few of the more valuable books, in addition to Gould's, are R. J. Herrnstein, *I.Q. in the Meritocracy* (Boston: Atlantic Monthly Press, 1971); Kevles, *In the Name of Eugenics*; R. C. Lewontin, Steven Rose, and Leon J. Kamin, *Not in Our Genes: Biology, Ideology, and Human Nature* (New York: Pantheon, 1984); David Owen, *None of the Above: Behind the Myth of Scholastic Aptitude* (Boston: Houghton Mifflin, 1985); N. J. Block and Gerald Dworkin, eds., *The IQ Controversy* (New York: Pantheon, 1976); Paul L. Houts, ed., *The Myth of Measurability* (New York: Hart Publishing Co., 1977); Leon Kamin, *The Science and Politics of IQ* (Potomac, Md.: Erlbaum, 1974); Arthur Jensen, *Bias in Mental Testing* (New York: Free Press, 1979). Jensen's seminal and controversial article on racial differences in intelligence was "How Much Can We Boost IQ and Scholastic Achievement?" *Harvard Educational Review*, 39 (1969). A long series of rebuttals appeared in the journal.

Original Binet tests: His first examination included these questions for children of various ages:

Age 3: Point to your nose, your eyes, your mouth.
Age 4: Are you a boy or a girl?
Age 5: Copy this square.
Age 6: What is a fork, a table, a house, a mama?
Age 7: What is missing from this picture (face with no mouth)?
Age 8: What is the difference between wood and glass?
Age 9: Same as for age 6, but more complete answers needed.

From Daniel Cohen, *Intelligence — What Is It?* (New York: M. Evans & Co., 1974), pp. 84–85.

145   Yerkes paper: "Psychological Examining in the United States Army," *Memoirs of the National Academy of Sciences,* vol. 15 (1921).

Low IQ scores among recent immigrants: H. H. Goddard, "The Binet Tests in Relation to Immigration," *Journal of Psycho-Asthenics,* 1913, pp. 105–107, discussed in Leon J. Kamin, "Politics of IQ," in Houts, *The Myth of Measurability,* p. 55.

"Thus it appears that feeble-mindedness": Gould, *Mismeasure of Man,* p. 223.

"vastly better off": Henry Goddard, *Psychology of the Normal and Subnormal* (New York: Dodd, Mead, 1919), p. 236; also see chapter 5 of Gould, *The Mismeasure of Man.*

147   compulsory-attendance laws: Sheldon H. White, "Social Implications of IQ," in Houts, *The Myth of Measurability,* p. 28; also Collins, *The Credential Society,* p. 4.

"bring as many 'plain people' ": David Nasaw, *Schooled to Order: A Social History of Public Schooling in the United States* (New York: Oxford University Press, 1979), p. 126.

148   fully half of the nation's children: Ibid., pp. 126–127.

The registration bill: George Q. Flynn, *Lewis B. Hershey: Mr. Selective Service* (Chapel Hill: University of North Carolina Press, 1985), p. 85.

149   Draft calls for Korea: Ibid., p. 179.

"I don't know exactly": According to Hershey's biographer, these words were used by one of Hershey's assistants, explaining the system to him. Ibid., p. 186.

150   "It is difficult to overestimate": E. W. Burgess, Leonard S. Cottrell, Paul E. Horst, E. Lowell Kelly, M. W. Richardson, and Samuel A. Stouffer, "Memorandum on Prediction and National Defense," in Paul Horst et al., *The Prediction of Personal Adjustment: A Survey of Logical Problems and Research Techniques, with Illustrative Applications to Problems of Vocational Selection, School Success, Marriage, and Crime* (New York: Social Science Research Council, 1941), pp. 160, 162. This report is discussed in Peter Buck's "Adjusting to Military Life: The Social Sciences Go

to War, 1941–1950," in Merritt Roe Smith, ed., *Military Enterprise and Technological Change: Perspectives on the American Experience* (Cambridge, Mass.: MIT Press, 1985), pp. 203–252.

"We are short of people": Joel Spring, *The Sorting Machine: National Educational Policy Since 1945* (New York: David McKay Co., 1976), p. 54.

"Korea has taught us": Flynn, *Lewis B. Hershey*, p. 182.

"whose educational aptitude": Ibid., p. 196.

Qualifying by IQ test: During World War II, Hershey had offered Vannevar Bush, then in charge of scientific mobilization, ten thousand deferments for "potential scientists" who were still in college. Bush declined. He said it was impossible to predict whose work would eventually prove most valuable. Bush remained opposed to predictive channeling. After the war, he advocated universal military training. In his view, all able-bodied males should be exposed to a brief period of training; only afterward should those interested in specialized scientific education be selected and nurtured. Ibid., p. 197.

Number of 4-F deferments: Ibid., p. 201.

70 percent had served: Ibid., p. 212.

Chapter 8

page
152 Michael Young satire: Michael Young, *The Rise of the Meritocracy, 1870–2033: An Essay on Education and Equality* (London: Thames & Hudson, 1958).

"The ties among": Herrnstein, *I.Q. in the Meritocracy*, pp. 124, 217.

154 Morrison essay: Philip Morrison, "The Bell Shaped Pitfall," in *The Myth of Measurability*, pp. 85–86.

155 The racial distinctions: Brazil was a Portuguese, not a Spanish, colony, but the point is the same. An outside researcher observed that because of the "obsession with whiteness and blackness and the shades in between, with a concomitant emphasis on features such as people's hair texture, nose shape, and size of lip, there exist further race and colour break-downs to the point where Brazilians have more than twenty different expressions to distinguish colour variations between the two extremes of black and white." Anani Dzidzienyo, *The Position of Blacks in Brazilian and Cuban Society* (London: Minority Rights Group, 1981), p. 4, cited by Klitgaard in private communication.

156 variety at the bottom: Herrnstein, *I.Q. in the Meritocracy*, pp. 118–124.

157 Kalamazoo brothers: Michael Olneck and James Crouse, *Myths of*

the Meritocracy: Cognitive Skills and Adult Success in the United States (Madison: University of Wisconsin, Institute for Research on Poverty Discussion Papers, #485–78, 1978), pp. 6–10.

first jobs: "Less desirable first jobs tended to draw men from a wider range of test scores . . . Some low scorers were to be found in desirable jobs. Fifteen to thirty-five years later, men with very high scores had moved out of low status occupations, consequently widening the range of ability in high status occupations and narrowing it in low status occupations." Ibid., p. 27.

Olneck and Crouse findings: Ibid., pp. 26, 48–50.

158   "colleges and universities": "The Threat to American Education," *Collier's,* December 1944, quoted in Keith W. Olson, *The G.I. Bill, the Veterans, and the Colleges* (Lexington: University Press of Kentucky, 1974), p. 25.

"we may find": Keith W. Olson, *The G.I. Bill,* p. 33.

159   most successful students: Ibid., pp. 45, 49, 51; also Nasaw, *Schooled to Order,* pp. 180–181.

G.I.s who would not otherwise have gone to college: Norman Frederiksen and William B. Shrader, *Adjustment to College* (Princeton: Educational Testing Service, 1951), p. 326, discussed in Keith W. Olson, *The G.I. Bill,* p. 55.

160   Intellectually demanding jobs: For figures from 1900, see *Historical Statistics of the United States,* p. 139; for 1980, see *Statistical Abstract of U.S., 1982–83,* p. 386.

161   McClelland article: David C. McClelland, "Testing for Competence Rather Than 'Intelligence,' " *American Psychologist* 28 (January 1973), pp. 1–14. The article was reprinted in Block and Dworkin, *The I.Q. Controversy.*

"It seems so self-evident": Ibid.

not necessarily proven more successful: Ibid.

163   Income-score correlation: For instance, in 1980 the Educational Testing Service released this chart, showing the relationship between income and test scores:

Reported Family Income

SAT AVERAGE	$0–5,999	$6,000–11,999	$12,000–17,999	$18,000 +	AVERAGE INCOME
750–800	17	117	169	415	$24,124
700–749	239	1,172	1,752	3,252	21,980
650–699	686	3,994	5,683	9,284	21,292
600–649	1,626	9,352	12,187	17,992	20,330
550–599	3,119	17,042	20,882	28,151	19,481
500–549	4,983	26,132	29,751	37,400	18,824
450–499	6,663	33,209	35,193	41,412	18,122
400–449	8,054	34,302	33,574	37,213	17,387

SAT AVERAGE	$0–5,999	$6,000–11,999	$12,000–17,999	$18,000+	AVERAGE INCOME
350–399	8,973	29,762	25,724	26,175	16,182
300–349	9,622	21,342	14,867	13,896	14,355
250–299	7,980	10,286	5,240	4,212	11,428
200–249	1,638	1,436	521	325	8,639
Total Number	53,600	188,146	185,483	219,727	
Average Score	403	447	469	485	

This table is a useful illustration of what "statistical correlation" means. If all you knew about two students was how much money their respective families had, you would be able to predict that the student from the richer family would probably get the higher score. In any specific case, however, you could not say for certain; after all, seventeen students from the lowest income group got higher scores than did 99 percent of the students from the highest income group.

The table is from *Test Scores and Family Income: A Response to Charges in the Nader/Nairn Report on ETS* (Princeton: Educational Testing Service, 1980), p. 7. The "Nader/Nairn report" referred to is Alan Nairn and Associates, *The Reign of ETS: The Corporation That Makes Up Minds* (Washington, D.C.: The Ralph Nader Report on the Educational Testing Service, 1980).

164   Ethnic groups' scores on tests: Statement by Harry Laughlin, "expert eugenics witness," to Committee on Immigration and Naturalization, March 8, 1924. Quoted in Allan Chase, *Legacy of Malthus* (Champaign: University of Illinois Press, 1980), pp. 298–299.

exactly the argument that R. J. Herrnstein made: Herrnstein used this chain of reasoning: Mental abilities, as measured by IQ tests, are more or less inherited. Those abilities are very important in determining occupational success. Therefore, social standing (including income and power) is based to some extent on inherited abilities — and the fairer America's social competition becomes, the less equal the resulting American society will be. Social standing really will be inherited, and this dismaying, undemocratic result will nonetheless be perfectly "fair."

165   taught people how to pass the test: S. David Young pointed out, "There were no such [cram] schools in 1964; by 1975 there were 57. Very simply, exam schools were making it possible for low-quality practitioners to circumvent the minimum-quality standards by teaching them to pass the exam without learning the skills of a contractor." Young, *The Rule of Experts*, p. 56.

Architects' exam: Ibid., p. 38.

Medical and judicial licensing: Ibid., pp. 42–43.

167 Hogan's study: Daniel Hogan, *The Regulation of Psychotherapists, Vol. 1: A Study in the Philosophy and Practice of Professional Regulations* (Cambridge, Mass.: Ballinger Publishing Co., 1979).

"contrary to . . . professional opinion": Hogan, *The Regulation of Psychotherapists.*

168 semideceptive study: The original study was described in an article by D. L. Rosenhan called "On Being Sane in Insane Places," *Science* 179 (1973), pp. 250–258.

169 Harold Howe speech: "Changing the Pecking Order," address by Harold Howe II, U.S. Commissioner of Education, before the College Entrance Examination Board, Chicago, October 24, 1967.

Football player not "certified": *The Washington Monthly,* October 1988.

170 hired an honors history graduate: During each new teacher's first year, the district provides some formal teacher-training courses and closely monitors the teacher's performance in the class. "Teachers Who Know Their Subjects," *Insight* magazine, September 29, 1986, p. 63.

"Occupational regulation": Young, *The Rule of Experts,* p. 1.

171 FAA study: Ivar Berg with Sherry Gorelick, *Education and Jobs: The Great Training Robbery* (Washington, D.C.: Praeger, 1970).

Chapter 9

page

174 Susan Gutfreund: From Kurt Anderson's review of Aldrich, *Old Money,* in *The Atlantic,* June 1988.

176 "no American institution": Joseph Epstein, "They Said You Was High Class," *The American Scholar,* reprinted in *Best American Essays: 1987,* Gay Talese, ed. (New York: Ticknor & Fields, 1987), pp. 90–91.

177 "The distinctive quality of the enlisted ranks": Charles C. Moskos, "The Enlisted Ranks in the All-Volunteer Army," in *The All-Volunteer Force and American Society,* John B. Keeley, ed. (Charlottesville: University of Virginia Press, 1978), pp. 73–74.

178 Russell Sage Foundation findings: O. G. Brim, J. Neulinger, and D. C. Glass, *Experiences and Attitudes of American Adults Concerning Standardized Intelligence Tests* (New York: Russell Sage Foundation, 1965), p. 89. I learned of this report through a citation in Clarence J. Karier, "Testing for Order and Control in the Corporate Liberal State," in Block and Dworkin, *The I.Q. Controversy,* pp. 339–369.

"upper class respondent": "New Intelligence Tests Emphasize Abilities Overlooked by IQ," David Stipp, *Wall Street Journal,* March 12, 1987, p. 35.

179 Psychological effects of test scores: The wounding effect of the Scholastic Aptitude Tests is compounded by a statistical quirk of scoring. Common sense would lead many people to think that if the test scale runs from 200 to 800, 500 would be an "average" score. Indeed it was, forty years ago, when the statistical norms for the SAT were established and 500 was set as the median score. But as times have changed and the sample of students taking the test has grown less select, the median has dropped nearly 100 points. These days, only a quarter of the students who take the test score above 500. The other three-quarters think they are "below average." At any given moment, three quarters of all teenagers probably also think they are below average in popularity, resistance to acne, or development of secondary sex traits. Those things pass, or most of them; the verdict on intelligence remains.

180 Disaster at the Somme: Paul Fussell, *The Great War and Modern Memory* (New York: Oxford University Press, 1975), p. 13.

Fussell quoted from the memoirs of Major General Herbert Essame, who one night observed five overcrowded troop trains at Victoria Station, jammed with soldiers trying to find a place to sleep amid the bulging packs. There was a sixth train, made exclusively of first-class cars and reserved for red-tabbed staff officers, with obsequious waiters taking orders for drinks. After watching the trains leave for the front, Essame wrote, "The irony of this nightly demonstration at Victoria Station of the great gap between the leaders and the led, this blatant display of privilege was to rankle in the minds of soldiers in the front lines and to survive in the national memory for the next half century." Fussell, *Great War,* pp. 83–84.

183 Rhodes scholars and Phi Beta Kappa members: Howard R. Bowen and Jack H. Schuster, "The Changing Career Interests of the Nation's Intellectual Elite," *Key Reporter,* Autumn 1985, pp. 1–3.

184 "Somebody who gets": *Washington Post,* August 10, 1982.

Chapter 10

page
188 Department of Defense budget: Military spending was 6 to 7 percent of the GNP during the 1980s, versus 8 to 9 percent in the 1950s and early 1960s, when the government had very small deficits and occasional surpluses.

Social Security and Medicare: These "entitlement" programs,

also known as "payment to individuals," now make up about half the federal budget, as opposed to about a fourth in the 1950s. Of that half, more than two-thirds are "not means tested" — that is, not directed at poor people.

189   Windfall benefits from Social Security: This is based on extrapolations and calculations from various sources, including "Social Security, Young vs. Old," *The Socioeconomic Newsletter* (White Plains, N.Y.: Institute of Socioeconomic Studies), June–July 1982, p. 1; and Michael J. Boskin, *Too Many Promises: The Uncertain Future of Social Security* (Homewood, Ill.: Dow Jones–Irwin, 1986). Also see "Non-Means-Tested Entitlement Reform Programs," Task Force on Entitlements, Uncontrollables, and Indexing, Committee on the Budget, U.S. House of Representatives, 98th Congress, 1st session, March 1, 1983, serial no. TF8–2.

190   half of all single women: Thomas C. Borzilleri, "The Distribution of Income and Social Security Benefits Within the Aged Social Security Population in 1980," Tables 4 and 5. Borzilleri's study is based on single women receiving Social Security. There were 2,037,452 of these women between the ages of sixty-five and seventy-one, and 3,750,304 aged seventy-two or older. Of them, 2,917,446, or slightly over 50 percent, had annual incomes of less than $5000.

190   Taxing Social Security benefits: There are three main objections to this proposal. First, people have already paid taxes on the money Social Security is paying back to them. That is true only of the employee's contribution, which is a small share of what today's retirees receive. The employer's contribution and the imputed interest are tax-free. Second, any kind of means testing will erode the political support for Social Security, making it just another unpopular welfare program. But making benefits taxable is the least objectionable sort of means testing and carries an implication of success, not failure. (You are making enough money to have your benefits taxed.) Third, any sort of means testing for Social Security will lessen people's incentive to save for retirement. Doubtless this is true to some degree, but the same objection applies to almost any insurance or benefit program — for instance, college scholarships based on need. On balance, the harm done by today's benefit structure seems worse.

191   "peasantry from other countries": Robert Hunter, *Poverty* (New York: Macmillan, 1965), Torchbook edition, p. 314.

192   Kaus essay: In "The Work Ethic State," a long essay published in *The New Republic* on July 7, 1986, Mickey Kaus examined the financial, legal, ethical, and political implications of guaranteeing all able-bodied people a subminimum-wage job but providing no other cash benefits, not even maternity benefits. Kaus recom-

mended providing day care for small children but requiring the parents to work to earn benefits. The main objections to the program, he said, were that public employees' unions would oppose cut-rate competition for work they might otherwise do, and that it would be expensive to create new jobs. But, he concluded, it was hard to see any other way to break a pathological cultural pattern.

193 Voucher program: As with retirement benefits and other forms of social insurance, the vouchers should reflect the "insurance" rather than the "guarantee" principle. They could be offered to very poor families, and to any family living in a district whose public school failed to meet certain performance standards.

195 Competence tests for nurses: Similar tests already exist for "emergency medical care technicians," such as ambulance attendants. A program called the National Registry for Emergency Medical Technicians assesses trainees on the skills most important to their success. *Pro-Forum*, a magazine that surveyed licensing requirements, said this program "has developed one of the most detailed, thorough, and job-related skill examinations of all certifying agencies."

"All medical careers would begin": Collins, *The Credential Society*, p. 201.

199 Pete Axthelm on John Elway: *Newsweek*, January 26, 1987, p. 80.

200 John Higham on immigration: Statement to the House Subcommittee on Immigration, Refugees, and International Law, July 30, 1986.

200 "Out of 5000 impoverished people": This was Roger Conner, a lawyer representing the anti-immigration group FAIR (Federation for American Immigration Reform) in 1981.

201 "if two million immigrants": *The Data*, The Environmental Fund, November 1983, p. 2.

202 "The unchanging pie": *New York Times*, November 28, 1982. In the same magnanimous vein, Lamm said in 1983, "Our immigration policy is making us poorer, not richer . . . To me, it's a matter of common sense: The unemployed in this state, and across the nation, will never get jobs as long as we continue to take in twice as many immigrants as the rest of the world combined." *New York Times*, August 1, 1983.

a major economic study: The study was called "The Fourth Wave," which was a way of emphasizing the similarities between today's immigration and the previous waves of mass migration that have affected America. (The first wave was the Anglo-Irish-German immigration of the mid nineteenth century; the second, from Southern and Eastern Europe at the turn of the century; and the third, the movement of American blacks from the rural South to the northern manufacturing cities during and after World War II.

It said, "Although Hispanic workers filled a large proportion of the jobs added during the decade, particularly in manufacturing, there is no indication that work opportunities for nonimmigrants lessened." Also, despite mass immigration to Southern California, "per capita income from all private sources . . . rose more rapidly in Los Angeles than in the nation as a whole," while per capita income from welfare programs and other government benefits was lower than in most other big cities. Thomas Muller, *The Fourth Wave: California's Newest Immigrants, A Summary* (Washington, D.C.: The Urban Institute, 1984), pp. 13–16.

Richard Freeman comments: *Washington Post,* January 25, 1988.

203   job prospects for black teenagers: Muller, *The Fourth Wave,* pp. 13–14.

Koreans were not "soaking up opportunities": Quoted in Glenn Simpson, "Asian Dreams, Black Hopes Clash," *Insight* magazine, February 9, 1987, p. 24.

204   Language patterns of earlier immigrants: For extensive discussion of how previous immigrants adjusted, often slowly, to English, see Forbes and Lemos, "History of American Language Policy"; François Grosjean, *Life with Two Languages: An Introduction to Bilingualism* (Cambridge: Harvard University Press, 1982); and Kenji Hakuta, *Mirror of Language* (New York: Basic Books, 1986). For evidence about language patterns among today's Spanish-speaking immigrants, see Rodolfo de la Garza and Robert Brischetto, *The Mexican American Electorate: A Demographic Profile* (San Antonio: Southwest Voter Registration Education Project, 1982). A study conducted by the RAND corporation, which reached similar conclusions, was reported in the *New York Times,* November 10, 1986.

208   Paul Simon statement: Charles Peters highlighted this quote in *The Washington Monthly,* June 1988, p. 8.

ACKNOWLEDGMENTS

I owe many thanks to many people for their generosity, patience, and help.

My greatest obligation is to my wife, Deborah Zerad Fallows, who has held our family together and provided advice and love while I've worked on this book. Our sons, Tommy and Tad Fallows, always did their part, especially as we traveled together through Asia. My parents have acted good-humored about having the family's foibles discussed in public, and my wife's parents have supported us in many ways.

My friend Nicholas Lemann has been on constant call as an adviser and confidant for many years. I am deeply indebted to him. He and Charles Peters, my first employer, read the manuscript and made invaluable suggestions.

William Whitworth, the editor of *The Atlantic*, gave me the freedom to look into many of the subjects I've written about, both in America and overseas. Michael Janeway, at Houghton Mifflin, gave me crucial advice in finding a tone for the book. I am also grateful to Frances Apt, a deft copy editor, and to Chris Coffin and Rebecca Saikia-Wilson, of Houghton Mifflin. Wendy Weil, my agent, has loyally and skillfully defended my interests. Jason Epstein, of Random House, read and advised me about previous versions of this book.

The Atlantic's business staff in New York graciously gave me a home during several trips back to the United States, and its editorial staff in Boston has not only made the magazine wonderful to read but has made *The Atlantic* a perfect place to work. For this I thank everyone associated with the magazine, and its owner, Mortimer Zuckerman.

In the United States, I owe additional thanks to Stephen Banker, Jack Beatty, Ray Bonner, Martin Bounds, Maureen Brown, Dominique

Browning, Connie Carpenter, Anne Convery, Avril Cornel, Peter Davison, William Douglass, Gregg Easterbrook, Carey English, Garrett Epps, Kassie Evashevski, Lawrence Fuchs, Judy Garlan, Thomas Geoghegan, Frank Gibney, Meryl Gordon, Ellen Grimm, Eric Haas, Irving Hamer, John Herrington, Donald Hicks, David Ignatius, Robin Johnson, Ed Jones, Mickey Kaus, Kim Killinger, Robert Klitgaard, Corby Kummer, Robert Lawrence, Art Levine, Diana Licht, Frank Lumpkin, Robert Manning, Lou Marano, Charles McCarry, Peggy Miller, Lisa Mirabile, Martin Moleski, Cullen Murphy, Ralph Nader, Joseph Nocera, Rita O'Connor and Ted Schell, Sue Parilla, Elizabeth Peters, Paul Pottinger, Amy Quarters, Vanessa Reed, Mark Reutter, Linda Richards, Sarah Rockwell, David Rothman, Edward Sadlowski, Kate and Todd Sedgwick, Walter Shapiro, Julian Simon, Martha Spaulding, Patricia Stacey, Jared Taylor, Sarah Timberman, Richard Todd, Anne Wallace, Barbara Wallraff, Robert Ward, James Webb, Karen Weslowski, Wyman Westberry, and Grace Yee.

The Japan Society of New York was responsible for my going to Japan in the first place. When we planned to move to Asia, my family intended to go directly to Southeast Asia, but a grant from the Japan Society made an initial stay in Tokyo possible. David Halberstam, who has generously given time and advice, suggested that I go to Japan and that the Japan Society could help me do so. Ruri Kawashima kept constant check on my family's welfare, and John Wheeler, Peter Grilli, and David MacEachron, all of the Japan Society, helped in various ways.

In Japan I owe deepest thanks to my friends Shigeki Hijino, editor of *Japan Newsweek,* and his family, and Hiroshi Ishikawa and Lona Sato, of the Foreign Press Center, all of whom have made my stay here much more enjoyable and informative than it otherwise would have been. The staff of Utsukushigaoka Shogakko, the Japanese public elementary school that my children attended, did everything possible to make us feel welcome. We will always be grateful to teachers Nobuyuki Sassa, Hitoshi Nakagawa, and Etsuko Iwata, and the school's principal, Masakazu Tomita. Yoko Asakawa and Itsuko Sakai, the two interpreters I have worked with most often, have also been generous friends.

In addition, I am grateful to Tasuku Asano, Bruce Carter, Chris and William Chapman, Susan Chira, Donald Cooke, Judy Forrest, Lydia and Stephen Gonersall, Mitsuya Goto, Ivan Hall, James Impoco, Shuichi Kato, Amy and Yuichi Katoh, Kinji Kawamura, Hidea Kimura, Takashi Kiuchi, Akira Kojima, Woody Landay, Mary Lord, Kazuyuki Mogi, the Nagahisa family, Kenichi Ohmae, the Ohtsuka family, Takashi Oka, the Kyohei Okugawa family, Yukio Satoh, Murray and Jenny Sayle, Wick Smith, Ritsu Suzuki, Tatsuya Tanami and his associates at the International House of Japan, Shunji Taoka, Michael Tharp, and Bernard Wysocki.

For help in the Philippines, I would like to thank Cesar Apostol, Tom

Green, Mary Carlin, Jason DeParle, F. Sionil Jose, Luisita Lopez, Katherine Manegold, Monica O'Keefe, and Joan Orendain. For their guidance in Korea, I am grateful to David and Jo Pierce. I would also like to thank Larry Heppinstall, Christopher Hill, Kenneth Kalliher, and Barbara Mintz. For his help in China, I thank William Palmer.

During the two years that we lived in Malaysia, my family was always grateful for the help of Sumimah Yusof. I also thank John Berthelson, Stephen Duthie, the Eisman family, Meg Gilroy, Tom and Joan Hubbard, Lee Boon Koo, Lewis Luchs, the McBride family, M. G. G. Pillai, Raphael Pura, the Shohtoku family, the Stromme family, Henry Tung, and Pari Vathi.

December 1988
Tokyo

INDEX

Ability, 141–47, 162–65, 172–73, 197–99. *See also* Competence
Accents, 82–83
Achieving Society, The (McClelland), 65–66, 161
Adaptability. *See* Capitalism; Possibility; Social change
Admission tests: to Japanese schools, 45, 142, 172. *See also* College entrance exams
Advertising, 177
Air Line Pilots Association, 197
Air-traffic controllers, 171
Aldrich, Nelson, Jr., 64
Amerasians (in Vietnam), 107–9
American Bar Association, 135
American Graffiti (movie), 75
American High (O'Neill), 60
American literature: self-made people in, 60, 75; of migration, 80–81
American Occupational Structure, The (Blau and Duncan), 109
American Psychologist (journal), 161
America Versus Japan (McCraw and O'Brien), 39
Amish, 51
Anderson, Hilding, 115
Anywhere But Here (Simpson), 51
Army Alpha tests, 144–45, 164
Asahi Glass, 40

Asahi Shimbun (Japanese newspaper), 7
Asian Drama (Myrdal), 23–24
Astor, John Jacob, 62
AT&T, 194
Atlanta Constitution (newspaper), 97
Australia, 2, 18
"Automation crisis," 54–55
Axthelm, Pete, 198

Bailyn, Bernard, 22
Ballmer, Stephen, 171
Banfield, Edward, 26
Baseball: in Japan, 45–46
Baskin, John, 64–65
Bell curve: and IQ testing, 153–55
Berg, Ivar, 171
Beyond National Borders (Ohmae), 32n
Bilingualism, 203–4
Binet, Alfred, 143–44, 154
Black immigrants, 119–20
"Black-platers," 87
Blacks (American): Japanese comments about, 6, 185; white racism toward, 33, 51; as underclass, 119–22, 186, 191–93; opportunities for, 185. *See also* Prejudice
Blau, Peter M., 109